EVERYDAY PHYSICAL SCIENCE MYSTERIES

STORIES FOR INQUIRY-BASED SCIENCE TEACHING

Richard Konicek-Moran, EdD
Professor Emeritus
University of Massachusetts
Amherst

NSTA press
National Science Teachers Association

National Science Teachers Association

Claire Reinburg, Director
Jennifer Horak, Managing Editor
Andrew Cooke, Senior Editor
Wendy Rubin, Associate Editor
Agnes Bannigan, Associate Editor
Amy America, Book Acquisitions Coordinator

ART AND DESIGN
Will Thomas Jr., Art Director
Rashad Muhammad, Designer, cover and interior design
Additional illustrations by D. W. Miller

PRINTING AND PRODUCTION
Catherine Lorrain, Director

NATIONAL SCIENCE TEACHERS ASSOCIATION
David L. Evans, Executive Director
David Beacom, Publisher

1840 Wilson Blvd., Arlington, VA 22201
www.nsta.org/store
For customer service inquiries, please call 800-277-5300.

NSTA is committed to publishing material that promotes the best in inquiry-based science education. However, conditions of actual use may vary, and the safety procedures and practices described in this book are intended to serve only as a guide. Additional precautionary measures may be required. NSTA and the authors do not warrant or represent that the procedures and practices in this book meet any safety code or standard of federal, state, or local regulations. NSTA and the authors disclaim any liability for personal injury or damage to property arising out of or relating to the use of this book, including any of the recommendations, instructions, or materials contained therein.

Cataloging-in-Publication Data is available from the Library of Congress.

CONTENTS

THE STORIES AND BACKGROUND MATERIALS FOR TEACHERS

acknowledgments

I would also like to dedicate these stories and materials to the dedicated and talented teachers in the Springfield Public Schools in Springfield, Massachusetts. They have been my inspiration to produce materials that work with city as well as rural children.

I would like to thank the following teachers, educators, and administrators who have helped me by field-testing the stories and ideas contained in this book over many years. These dedicated educators have helped me with their encouragement and constructive criticism:

Richard Haller
Jo Ann Hurley
Lore Knaus
Ron St. Amand
Renee Lodi
Deanna Suomala
Louise Breton
Ruth Chappel
Theresa Williamson
Third-grade team at Burgess Elementary in Sturbridge, Massachusetts
Second-grade team Burgess Elementary in Sturbridge, Massachusetts
Fifth-grade team at Burgess Elementary in Sturbridge, Massachusetts
Teachers at Millbury, Massachusetts, Elementary Schools
Teachers and children at Pottinger Elementary School, Springfield, Massachusetts
All the administrators and science specialists in the Springfield, Massachusetts, public schools, who are too numerous to mention individually

My thanks also go out to all of the teachers and students in my graduate and undergraduate classes who wrote stories and tried them in their classes as well as using my stories in their classes.

I will always be in the debt of my advisor at Columbia University, the late Professor Willard Jacobson who made it possible for me to find my place in teacher education at the university level.

I also wish to thank Skip Snow, Jeff Kline, Jean and Rick Seavey, and all of the biologists in the Everglades National Park with whom I have had the pleasure of working for the past ten years for helping me to remember how to be a scientist again. And to the members of the interpretation groups in the Everglades National Park, at Shark Valley and Pine Island, who helped me to realize again that it possible to help someone to look without telling them what to see and to help me to realize how important it is to guide people toward making emotional connections with our world.

My sincere thanks goes to Claire Reinburg of NSTA, who had the faith in my work to publish the original book and the second and third volumes and is now taking a chance on a fourth; and to Andrew Cooke, my editor, who helps me through the crucial steps. In addition I thank my lovely, brilliant and talented wife, Kathleen, for her support, criticisms, illustrations, and draft editing.

Finally, I would like to dedicate these words to all of the children out there who love the world they live in and to the teachers and parents who help them to make sense of that world through the study of science.

Preface

Ask elementary or middle school teachers which of the disciplines they are most afraid to teach and they will likely answer, "The physical sciences." Now with the new Standards, we get to add engineering and math to the list of possible responses. These too probably seem scary, but this need not be the case. When these subjects are taught conceptually and in everyday settings, teachers soon see that they, and their students, can tackle the topics without trepidation.

The positive thing about physical science and engineering activities is that they offer immediate feedback to the people doing the activity. In biology and Earth sciences, one might have to wait weeks or months for an activity to provide a result. In most physical science activities or investigations, the result takes only a minute or two, and students can either formulate a conclusion or do the activity over again.

As for math, the activities generated by these stories provide data that has meaning for the experimenter. Unlike the young student who told me "Math is pages and pages of other people's problems," the math involved in *Everyday Science Mysteries* provides immediate and relevant data. Students are doing calculations on numbers that have personal meaning to them, data they have collected. It is less a chore and more a means to answers that lie within the scope of their interest.

Your students will be asked to engage in engineering tasks that come about as a natural response to the stories—for instance to apply their knowledge about sound to improve a tin can telephone. Through helping to solve the mysteries the children in the stories encounter, your students get to invent a way to mark or keep time or apply their knowledge of pendulums to solve a crooked swing problem, just to name a few.

In this book, you will find enough background material and resources to give you the strength and courage to engage your students in inquiry into physical science concepts. And for additional comfort, there are now available many resources to help those who feel lacking in physics, math, or engineering.

These stories are packaged in separate subject matter volumes so those who teach only one of the three areas covered in these books can use them more economically. However, it bears repeating that the crosscutting concepts meld together the various principles of science across all disciplines. It is difficult, if not impossible, to teach about any scientific concept in isolation. Science is an equal opportunity field of endeavor, incorporating not only the frameworks and theories of its various specialties, but also its own structure and history.

We hope that you will find these stories without endings a stimulating and provocative opening into the use of inquiry in your classrooms. Be sure to become acquainted with the stories in the other disciplinary volumes and endeavor to integrate all the scientific practices, crosscutting concepts, and core ideas that inquiry demands.

INTRODUCTION

Case Studies on How to Use the Stories in the Classroom

I would like to introduce you to one of the stories from the first volume of *Everyday Science Mysteries* (Konicek-Moran 2008) and then show how the story was used by two teachers, Teresa, a second-grade teacher, and Lore, a fifth-grade teacher. Then in the following chapters I will explain the philosophy and organization of the book before going to the stories and background material. Here is the story, "Where Are the Acorns?"

Where are the acorns?

Cheeks looked out from her nest of leaves, high in the oak tree above the Anderson family's backyard. It was early morning and the fog lay like a cotton quilt on the valley. Cheeks stretched her beautiful gray, furry body and looked about the nest. She felt the warm August morning air, fluffed up her big gray bushy tail and shook it. Cheeks was named by the Andersons since she always seemed to have her cheeks full of acorns as she wandered and scurried about the yard.

"I have work to do today!" she thought and imagined the fat acorns to be gathered and stored for the coming of the cold times.

Now the tough part for Cheeks was not gathering the fruits of the oak trees. There were plenty of trees and more than enough acorns for all of the gray squirrels who lived around the yard. No, the problem was finding them later on when the air was cold and the white stuff might be covering the lawn. Cheeks had a very good smeller and could sometimes smell the acorns she had buried earlier. But not always. She needed a way to remember where she had dug the holes and buried the acorns. Cheeks also had a very small memory and the yard

was very big. Remembering all of these holes she had dug was too much for her little brain.

The Sun had by now risen in the East and Cheeks scurried down the tree to begin gathering and eating. She also had to make herself fat so that she would be warm and not hungry on long cold days and nights when there might be little to eat.

"What to do ... what to do?" she thought as she wiggled and waved her tail. Then she saw it! A dark patch on the lawn. It was where the Sun did not shine. It had a shape and two ends. One end started where the tree trunk met the ground. The other end was lying on the ground a little ways from the trunk. "I know," she thought. "I'll bury my acorn out here in the yard, at the end of the dark shape and in the cold times, I'll just come back here and dig it up! Brilliant Cheeks," she thought to herself and began to gather and dig.

On the next day she tried another dark shape and did the same thing. Then she ran around for weeks and gathered acorns to put in the ground. She was set for the cold times for sure!

Months passed and the white stuff covered the ground and trees. Cheeks spent more time curled up in her home in the tree. Then one bright crisp morning, just as the Sun was lighting the sky, she looked down and saw the dark spots, brightly dark against the white ground. Suddenly she had a great appetite for a nice juicy acorn. "Oh yes," she thought. "It is time to get some of those acorns I buried at the tip of the dark shapes."

She scampered down the tree and raced across the yard to the tip of the dark shape. As she ran, she tossed little clumps of white stuff into the air, and they floated back onto the ground. "I'm so smart," she thought to herself. "I know just where the acorns are." She did seem to feel that she was a bit closer to the edge of the woods than she remembered, but her memory was small and she ignored the feelings. Then she reached the end of the dark shape and began to dig and dig and dig!

And she dug and she dug and she dug! Nothing! "Maybe I buried them a bit deeper," she thought, a bit out of breath. So she dug deeper and deeper and still, nothing. She tried digging at the tip of another of the dark shapes and again found nothing. "But I know I put them here," she cried. "Where could they be?" She was angry and confused. Did other squirrels dig them up? That was not fair. Did they just disappear? What about the dark shapes?

HOW TWO TEACHERS USED "WHERE ARE THE ACORNS?"

Teresa, a veteran second-grade teacher

Teresa usually begins the school year with a unit on fall and change. This year she looked at the National Science Education Standards (NSES) and decided that a unit on the sky and cyclic changes would be in order. Since shadows were something that the children often noticed and included in playground games (shadow tag), Teresa thought using the story of Cheeks the squirrel would be appropriate.

To begin, she felt that it was extremely important to know what the children already knew about the Sun and the shadows cast from objects. She wanted to know what kind of knowledge they shared with Cheeks and what kind of knowledge they had that the story's hero did not have. She arranged the children in a circle so that they could see one another and hear one another's comments. Teresa read the story to them, stopping along the way to see that they knew that Cheeks had made the decision on where to bury the acorns during the late summer and that the squirrel was looking for her buried food during the winter. She asked them to tell her what they thought they knew about the shadows that Cheeks had seen. She labeled a piece of chart paper, "Our best ideas

so far." As they told her what they "knew," she recorded their statements in their own words:

"Shadows change every day."
"Shadows are longer in winter."
"Shadows are shorter in winter."
"Shadows get longer every day."
"Shadows get shorter every day."
"Shadows don't change at all."
"Shadows aren't out every day."
"Shadows move when you move."

She asked the students if it was okay to add a word or two to each of their statements so they could test them out. She turned their statements into questions and the list then looked like this:

"Do shadows change every day?"
"Are shadows longer in winter?"
"Are shadows shorter in winter?"
"Do shadows get longer every day?"
"Do shadows get shorter every day?"
"Do shadows change at all?"
"Are shadows out every day?"
"Do shadows move when you move?"

Teresa focused the class on the questions that could help solve Cheeks's dilemma. The children picked "Are shadows longer or shorter in the winter?" and "Do shadows change at all?" The children were asked to make predictions based on their experiences. Some said that the shadows would get longer as we moved toward winter and some predicted the opposite. Even though there was a question as to whether they would change at all, they agreed unanimously that there would probably be some change over time. If they could get data to support that there was change, that question would be removed from the chart.

Now the class had to find a way to answer their questions and test predictions. Teresa helped them talk about fair tests and asked them how they might go about answering the questions. They agreed almost at once that they should measure the shadow of a tree each day and write it down and should use the same tree and measure the shadow every day at the same time. They weren't sure why time was important except that they said they wanted to make sure everything was fair. Even though data about all of the questions would be useful, Teresa thought that at this stage, looking for more than one type of data might be overwhelming for her children.

Teresa checked the terrain outside and realized that the shadows of most trees might get so long during the winter months that they would touch one of the buildings and become difficult to measure. That could be a learning experience but at the same time it would frustrate the children to have their investigation ruined after months of work. She decided to try to convince the children to use an artificial "tree" that was small enough to avoid our concern. To her surprise, there was no objection to substituting an artificial tree since, "If we measured that same tree every day, it would still be fair." She made a tree out of a dowel that was about 15 cm tall and the children insisted that they glue a triangle on the top to make it look more like a tree.

The class went outside as a group and chose a spot where the Sun shone without obstruction and took a measurement. Teresa was concerned that her students were not yet adept at using rulers and tape measures so she had the children measure the length of the shadow from the base of the tree to its tip with a piece of yarn and then glued that yarn onto a wall chart above the date when the measurement was taken. The children were delighted with this.

For the first week, teams of three went out and took daily measurements. By the end of the week, Teresa noted that the day-to-day differences were so small that perhaps they should consider taking a measurement once a week. This worked much better, as the chart was less "busy" but still showed any important changes that might happen.

As the weeks progressed, it became evident that the shadow was indeed getting longer each week. Teresa talked with the students about what would make a shadow get longer, and armed with flashlights, the children were able to make longer shadows of pencils by lowering the flashlight. The Sun must be getting lower too if this was the case, and this observation was added to the chart of questions. Later, Teresa wished that she had asked the children to keep individual science notebooks so that she could have been more aware of how each individual child was viewing the experiment.

The yarn chart showed the data clearly and the only question seemed to be, "How long will the shadow get?" Teresa revisited the Cheeks story and the children were able to point out that Cheeks's acorns were probably much closer to the tree than the winter shadows indicated. Teresa went on with another unit on fall changes and each week added another piece of yarn to the chart. She was relieved that she could carry on two science units at once and still capture the children's interest about the investigation each week after the measurement. After winter break, there was great excitement when the shadow began getting shorter. The shortening actually began at winter solstice around December 21 but the children were on break until after New Years Day. Now, the questions became "Will it keep getting shorter? For how long?" Winter passed and spring came and finally the end of the school year was approaching. Each week, the measurements were taken and each week a discussion was held on the meaning of the data. The chart was full of yarn strips and the pattern was obvious. The fall of last year had produced longer and longer shadow measurements until the New Year and then the shadows had begun to get shorter. "How short will they get?" and "Will they get down to nothing?" questions were added to the chart. During the last week of school, students talked about their conclusions and they were convinced that the Sun was lower and cast longer shadows during the fall to winter time and that after the new year, the Sun got higher in the sky and made the shadows shorter. They were also aware that the seasons were changing and that the higher Sun seemed to mean warmer weather and trees producing leaves.

The students were ready to think about seasonal changes in the sky and relating them to seasonal cycles. At least Teresa thought they were.

On the final meeting day in June, she asked her students what they thought the shadows would look like next September. After a great deal of thinking, they agreed that since the shadows were getting so short, that by next September, they would be gone or so short that they would be hard to measure. Oh my! The idea of a cycle had escaped them, and no wonder, since it hadn't really been discussed. The obvious extrapolation of the chart would indicate that the trend of shorter shadows would continue. Teresa knew that she would not have a chance to continue the investigation next September but she might talk to the third-grade team and see if they would at least carry it on for a few weeks so that the children could see the repeat of the previous September data. Then the students might be ready to think more about seasonal changes and certainly their experience would be useful in the upper grades where seasons and the reasons for seasons would become a curricular issue. Despite these shortcomings, it was a marvelous experience and the children were given a great opportunity to design an investigation and collect data to answer their questions about the squirrel story at a level appropriate to their development. Teresa felt that the children had an opportunity to carry out a long-term investigation, gather data, and come up with conclusions along the way about Cheek's dilemma. She felt also that the standard had been partially met or at least was in progress. She would talk with the third-grade team about that.

Lore (pronounced Laurie), a veteran fifth-grade teacher

In September while working in the school, I had gone to Lore's fifth-grade class for advice. I read students the Cheeks story and asked them at which grade they thought it would be most appropriate. They agreed that it would most likely fly best at second grade. It seemed, with their advice, that Teresa's decision to use it there was a good one.

However, about a week after Teresa began to use the story, I received a note from Lore, telling me that her students were asking her all sorts of questions about shadows, the Sun, and the seasons and asking if I could help. Despite their insistence that the story belonged in the second grade, the fifth graders were intrigued enough by the story to begin asking questions about shadows. We now had two classes interested in Cheeks's dilemma but at two different developmental levels. The fifth graders were asking questions about daily shadows, direction of shadows, and seasonal shadows, and they were asking, "Why is this happening?" Lore wanted to use an inquiry approach to help them find answers to their questions but needed help. Even though the Cheeks story had opened the door to their curiosity, we agreed that perhaps a story about a pirate burying treasure in the same way Cheeks had buried acorns might be better suited to the fifth-grade interests in the future.

Lore looked at the NSES for her grade level and saw that they called for observing and describing the Sun's location and movements and studying natural objects in the sky and their patterns of movement. But the students' questions, we felt, should lead the investigations. Lore was intrigued by the 5E approach to inquiry (*engage, elaborate, explore, explain,* and *evaluate*) and because the students were already "engaged," she added the "elaborate" phase to find out what her students already knew. (The five Es will be defined in context as this vignette evolves.) So, Lore started her next class asking the students what they "knew" about the shadows that Cheeks used and what caused them. The students stated:

"Shadows are long in the morning, short at midday, and longer again in the afternoon."

"There is no shadow at noon because the Sun is directly overhead."

"Shadows are in the same place every day so we can tell time by them."

"Shadows are shorter in the summer than in the winter."

"You can put a stick in the ground and tell time by its shadow."

Just as Teresa had done, Lore changed these statements to questions, and they entered the "exploration" phase of the 5E inquiry method.

Luckily, Lore's room opened out onto a grassy area that was always open to the Sun. The students made boards that were 30 cm² and drilled holes in the middle and put a toothpick in the hole. They attached paper to the boards and drew shadow lines every half hour on the paper. They brought them in each afternoon and discussed their results. There were many discussions about whether or not it made a difference where they placed their boards from day to day.

They were gathering so much data that it was becoming cumbersome. One student suggested that they use overhead transparencies to record shadow data and then overlay them to see what kind of changes occurred. Everyone agreed that it was a great idea.

Lore introduced the class to the *Old Farmer's Almanac* and the tables of sunsets, sunrises, and lengths of days. This led to an exciting activity one day that involved math. Lore asked them to look at the sunrise time and sunset time on one given day and to calculate the length of the daytime Sun hours. Calculations went on for a good 10 minutes and Lore asked each group to demonstrate how they had calculated the time to the class. There must have been at least six different methods used and most of them came up with a common answer. The students were amazed that so many different methods could produce the same answer. They also agreed that several of the methods were more efficient than others and finally agreed that using a 24-hour clock method was the easiest. Lore was ecstatic that they had created so many methods and was convinced that their understanding of time was enhanced by this revelation.

This also showed that children are capable of metacognition—thinking about their thinking.

Research (Metz 1995) tells us that elementary students are not astute at thinking about the way they reason but that they can learn to do so through practice and encouragement. Metacognition is important if students are to engage in inquiry. They need to understand how they process information and how they learn. In this particular instance, Lore had the children explain how they came to their solution for the length-of-day problem so that they could be more aware of how they went about solving the challenge. Students can also learn about their thinking processes from peers who are more likely to be at the same developmental level. Discussions in small groups or as an entire class can provide opportunities for the teacher to probe for more depth in student explanations. The teacher can ask the students who explain their technique to be more specific about how they used their thought processes: dead ends as well as successes. Students can also learn more about their metacognitive processes by writing in their notebooks about how they thought through their problem and found a solution. Talking about their thinking or explaining their methods of problem solving in writing can lead to a better understanding of how they can use reasoning skills better in future situations.

I should mention here that Lore went on to teach other units in science while the students continued to gather their data. She would come back to the unit periodically for a day or two so the children could process their findings. After a few months, the students were ready to get some help in finding a model that explained their data. Lore gave them globes and clay so that they could place their observers at their latitude on the globe. They used flashlights to replicate their findings. Since all globes are automatically tilted at a 23.5-degree angle, it raised the question as to why globes were made that way. It was time for the "explanation" part of the lesson and Lore helped them to see how the tilt of the Earth could help them make sense of their experiences with the shadows and the Sun's apparent motion in the sky.

The students made posters explaining how the seasons could be explained by the tilt of the Earth and the Earth's revolution around the Sun each year. They had "evaluated" their understanding and "extended" it beyond their experience. It was, Lore agreed, a very successful "6E" experience. It had included the engage, elaborate, explore, explain, and evaluate phases, and the added extend phase.

references

Konicek-Moran, R. 2008. *Everyday science mysteries*. Arlington, VA: NSTA Press.

CHAPTER 1

THEORY BEHIND THE BOOK

We have all heard people refer to any activity that takes place in a science lesson as an "experiment." Actually, as science is taught today, true experiments are practically nonexistent. Experiments by definition test hypotheses, which are themselves virtually nonexistent in school science. A hypothesis, a necessary ingredient in any experiment, is a human creation developed by a person who has been immersed in a problem for a sufficient amount of time to feel the need to come up with a theory to explain events over which he or she has been puzzled.

However, it is quite common and proper for us to investigate our questions without proper hypotheses. Investigations can be carried out as "fair tests," which are possibly more appropriate for elementary classrooms, where children often lack the experience of creating a hypothesis in the true scientific mode. I recently asked a fourth-grade girl what a "fair experiment" was and she replied, "It's an experiment where the answer is the one I expected." We cannot assume even at the fourth-grade level students are comfortable with controlling variables; it needs repeating.

A hypothesis is more than a guess. It will most often contain an "if… then…" statement, such as, "If I put a thermometer in a mitten and the temperature stays the same, **then** perhaps the mitten did not produce heat." In school science, predictions should also be more than mere guesses or hunches, but rather based on experience and thoughtful consideration. Consistently asking children to give reasons for their predictions is a good

way to help them see the difference between guessing and predicting.

Two elements are often missing in most school science curricula: sufficient *time* to puzzle over problems that have some *real-life applications*. It is much more likely that students will use a predetermined amount of time to "cover" an area of study—pond life, for example—with readings, demonstrations, and a field trip to a pond with an expert, topped off with individual or group reports on various pond animals and plants, complete with shoe box dioramas and giant posters. Or there may be a study of the solar system, with reports on facts about the planets and culminating with a class model of the solar system hung from the ceiling. These are naturally fun to do, but the issue is that there are seldom any real problems—nothing into which the students can sink their collective teeth into and use their minds to ponder, puzzle, hypothesize, and experiment.

You have certainly noticed that most science curricula have a series of "critical" activities in which students participate that supposedly lead to an understanding of a particular concept. In most cases, there is an assumption that students enter the study of a new unit with a common view or a common set of preconceptions about certain concepts and the activities will move the students closer to the accepted scientific view. This is a particularly dangerous assumption, since research shows that students enter into learning situations with a variety of preconceptions. These preconceptions are not only well ingrained in the students' minds but are exceptionally resistant to change. Going through the series of prescribed activities will have little meaning to students who have preconceptions that have little connection to the planned lessons, especially if the preconceptions are not recognized or addressed.

Bonnie Shapiro, in her book, *What Children Bring to Light* (1994), points out in indisputable detail how a well-meaning science teacher ran his students through a series of activities on the nature of light without knowing that the students in the class all shared the misconception that seeing any object originates in the eye of the viewer and not from the reflection of light from an object into the eye. The activities were, for all intents and purposes, wasted, although the students had "solved the teacher" to the extent that they were able to fill in the worksheets and pass the test at the end of the unit—all the while doubting the critical concept that light reflecting from object to eye was the paramount fact and meaning of the act of seeing. *Solving the teacher* means that the students have learned a teacher's mannerisms, techniques, speech patterns, and teaching methods to the point that they can predict exactly what the teacher wants, what pleases or annoys her, and how to perform so the teacher believes her students have learned and understood the concepts she attempted to teach.

In her monograph *Inventing Density* (1986), Eleanor Duckworth says, "The critical experiments themselves cannot impose their own meanings. One has to have done a major part of the work already. One has to have developed a network of ideas in which to imbed the experiments." This may be the most important quote in this book!

How does a teacher make sure students develop a network of ideas in which to imbed the class activities? How does the teacher uncover student misconceptions about the topic to be studied? I believe that this book can offer some answers to these questions and offer some suggestions for remedying the problems mentioned above.

WHAT IS INQUIRY, ANYWAY?

There is probably no one definition of "teaching for inquiry," but at this time the acknowledged authorities on this topic have to be the National Research Council (NRC) and the American Association for the Advancement of Science (AAAS). After all, they are respectively the authors of the *National Science Education Standards* (1996) and the *Benchmarks for Science Literacy* (1993), upon which most states have based their curriculum standards. For this reason, I will use their definition, which I will follow throughout the book. The NRC, in *Inquiry and the National Science Education Standards: A Guide for Teaching and Learning* (2000), says that for real inquiry to take place in the classroom, the following five essentials must occur:

- Learner engages in scientifically oriented questions.
- Learner gives priority to evidence in responding to questions.
- Learner formulates explanations from evidence.
- Learner connects explanations to scientific knowledge.
- Learner communicates and justifies explanations. (p. 29)

In essence the NRC strives to encourage more learner self-direction and less direction from the teacher as time goes on during the school years. The NRC also make it very clear that all science cannot be taught in this fashion. Science teaching that uses a variety of strategies is less apt to bore students and be more effective. Giving demonstrations, leading discussions, solving presented problems, and entering into a productive discourse about science are all viable alternatives. However, the NRC does suggest that certain common components should be shared by whichever instructional model is used:

- Students are involved with a scientific question, event, or phenomenon that connects with what they already know and creates a dissonance with their own ideas. In other words, they confront their preconceptions through an involvement with phenomena.
- Students have direct contact with materials, formulate hypotheses, test them, and create explanations for what they have found.
- Students analyze and interpret data, and come up with models and explanations from these data.
- Students apply their new knowledge to new situations.
- Students engage in metacognition, thinking about their thinking, and review what they have learned and how they have learned it.

You will find opportunities to do all of the above by using these stories as motivators for your students to engage in inquiry-based science learning.

The Reasons for This Book

According to a summary of current thinking in science education in the journal *Science Education,* "one result seems to be consistently demonstrated: students leave science classes with more positive attitudes about science (and their concepts of themselves as science participants) when they learn science through inductive, hands-on techniques in classrooms where they're encouraged by a caring adult and allowed to process the information they have learned with their peers" (1993).

This book, and particularly the stories that lie within, provide an opportunity for students to take ownership of their learning and as stated in the quotation above, learn science in a way that will give them a more positive attitude about science and to process their learning with their classmates and teachers. Used as intended, the stories will require group discussions, hands-on and minds-on techniques, and a caring adult.

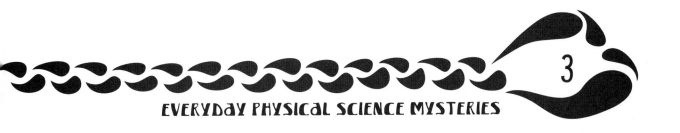

The Stories

These stories are similar to mystery tales but purposely lack the final chapter where the clever sleuth finally solves the mystery and tells the readers not only "whodunit," but how she knew. Because of the design of the tales in this book, the students are challenged to become the sleuths and come up with likely "suspects" (the hypotheses or predictions) and carry out investigations (the experiments or investigations) to find out "whodunit" (the results). In other words, they write the final ending or perhaps endings. They are placed in a situation where they develop, from the beginning, "the network of ideas in which to imbed activities," as Duckworth suggests (1986, p. 39). The students are also the designers of the activities and therefore have invested themselves in finding the outcomes that make sense to them. I want them to have solved the problem rather than having solved the teacher. I do want to reemphasize, however, that we should all be aware that successful students do spend energy in solving their teachers.

In one story ("Pasta in a Hurry"), a brother and sister debate the fastest way to boil water and whether water continues to get hotter after it starts boiling. Truly this is science as process and product. It also means that the students "own" the problem. This is what we mean by "hands-on, minds-on" science instruction. The teachers' belief in the ability of their students to own the questions and to carry out the experiments to reach conclusions, is paramount to the process. Each story has suggestions as to how the teachers can move from the story reading to the development of the problems, the development of the hypotheses, and eventually the investigations that will help their students come to conclusions.

Learning science through inquiry is a primary principle in education today. You might well ask, "instead of what?" Well, instead of learning science as a static or unchanging set of facts, ideas, and principles without any attention being paid to how these ideas and principles were developed. Obviously, we cannot expect our students to discover all of the current scientific models and concepts. We do however, expect them to appreciate the processes through which the principles are attained and verified. We also want them to see that science includes more than just what occurs in a classroom; that the everyday happenings of their lives are connected to science. Exploring the implications of heat transfer, exploring magnet strength, and observing condensation are only some of the examples of everyday life connected to science as a way of thinking and as a way of constructing new understandings about our world.

There are 21 stories in this book, each one focused on a particular conceptual area, such as thermodynamics, heat energy, melting or dissolving, the chemistry of cooking, and rusting as a chemical reaction. Each story can be photocopied and distributed to students to read and discuss or they can be read aloud to students and discussed by the entire class. During the discussion, it is ultimately the role of the teacher to help the students to find the problem or problems and then design ways to find out answers to the questions they have raised.

National Science Teachers Association

Most stories also include a few "distractors," also known as common misconceptions or alternative conceptions. The distractors are usually placed in the stories as opinions voiced by the characters who discuss the problematic situation. For example, in "Party Meltdown," Kelsey and her friends wonder why ice left in a plastic bowl did not melt while ice left in a metal bowl did. Each friend has her own preconception or misconception. The identification of these misconceptions is the product of years of research, and the literature documents the most common, often shared by both children and adults. Where do these common misconceptions come from and how do they arise?

Development of Mental Models

Until recently, educational practice has operated under the impression that children and adults come to any new learning situation without the benefit of prior ideas connected to the new situation. Research has shown that in almost every circumstance, learners have developed models in their mind to explain many of the everyday experiences they have encountered (Bransford, Brown, and Cocking 1999; Watson and Konicek 1990; Osborne and Fryberg 1985). Everyone has had experience with differences in temperature as they place their hands on various objects. Everyone has seen objects in motion and certainly has been in motion, either in a car, plane, or bicycle. Everyone has experienced forces in action, upon objects or upon themselves. Finally, each of us has been seduced into developing a satisfactory way to explain these experiences and to have developed a mental model, which explains these happenings to our personal satisfaction. Probably, most individuals have read books, watched programs on TV or in movie theaters, and used these presented images and ideas to embellish their personal models. It is even more likely that they have been in classrooms where these ideas have been discussed by a teacher or by other students. The film *A Private Universe* (Schneps 1987), documents that almost all of the interviewed graduates and faculty of Harvard University showed some misunderstanding for either the reasons for the seasons, or for the reasons for the phases of the Moon. Many had taken high-level science courses either in high school or at the university.

According to the dominant and current learning theory called *constructivism*, all of life's experiences are integrated into the person's mind; they are accepted or rejected or even modified to fit existing models residing in that person's mind. Then, these models are used and tested for their usefulness in predicting outcomes experienced in the environment. If a model works, it is accepted as a plausible explanation; if not, it is modified until it does fit the situations one experiences. Regardless, these models are present in everyone's minds and brought to consciousness when new ideas are encountered. They may be in tune with current scientific thinking but more often they are "common sense science" and not clearly consistent with current scientific beliefs.

One of the reasons for this is that scientific ideas are often counterintuitive to everyday thinking. For example, when you place your hand on a piece of metal in a room, it feels cool to your touch. When you place your hand on a piece of wood in the same room it feels warmer to the touch. Many people will deduce that the temperature of the metal is cooler than that of the wood. Yet, if the objects have been in the same room for any length of time, their temperatures will be equal. It turns out that when you place your hand on the metal, it conducts heat out of your hand quickly, thus giving the impression that it is cold. The wood does not conduct heat as rapidly as the metal and therefore feels warmer than the metal. In other words, our senses have fooled us into thinking that instead of everything in the room being at room temperature, the metal is cooler than anything else. Therefore our erroneous conclusion is that metal objects are always cooler than other objects in a room. Indeed, if you go from room to room and touch many objects, your idea is reinforced and becomes more and more resistant to change.

These ideas are called by many names: *misconceptions, prior conceptions, children's thinking,* or *common sense ideas.* They all have two things in common. They are usually firmly embedded in the mind, and they are highly resistant to change. Finally, if allowed to remain unchallenged, these ideas will dominate a student's thinking, for example, about heat transfer, to the point that the scientific explanation will be rejected completely regardless of the method by which it is presented.

Our first impression is that these preconceptions are useless and must be quashed as quickly as possible. However, they are useful since they are the precursors of new thoughts and should be modified slowly toward the accepted scientific thinking. New ideas will replace old ideas only when the learner becomes dissatisfied with the old idea and realizes that a new idea works better than the old. It is our role to challenge these preconceptions and move learners to consider new ways of looking at their explanations and to seek ideas that work in broader contexts with more reliable results.

WHY STORIES?

Why stories? Primarily, stories are a very effective way to get someone's attention. Stories have been used since the beginning of recorded history and probably long before that. Myths, epics, oral histories, ballads, dances, and such have enabled humankind to pass on the culture of one generation to the next, and the next, *ad infinitum*. Anyone who has witnessed story time in classrooms, libraries, or at bedtime knows the magic held in a well-written, well-told tale. They have beginnings, middles, and ends.

These stories begin like many familiar tales do: in homes or classrooms; with children interacting with siblings, classmates, or friends; with parents or other adults in family situations. But here the resemblance ends between our stories and traditional ones.

NATIONAL SCIENCE TEACHERS ASSOCIATION

Science stories normally have a theme or a scientific topic that unfolds giving a myriad of facts, principles, and perhaps a set of illustrations or photographs, which try to explain to a child the current understanding about the given topic. For years science books have been written as reviews of what science has constructed to the present. These books have their place in education, even though children often get the impression from these books that the information they have just read about appeared magically as scientists went about their work and "discovered" truths and facts depicted in those pages. But as Martin and Miller (1990) put it: "The scientist seeks more than isolated facts from nature. The scientist seeks a *story* [emphasis mine]. Inevitably the story is characterized by a *mystery* [emphasis mine]. Since the world does not yield its secrets easily, the scientist must be a careful and persistent observer."

As our tales unfold, discrepant events and unexpected results tickle the characters in the stories and stimulate their wonder centers making them ask, "What's going on here?" Most important of all, our stories have endings that are different than most. They are the mysteries that Martin and Miller talk about. They end with an invitation to explore and extend the story and to engage in inquiry.

These stories do not come with built-in experts who eventually solve the problem and expound on the solution. There is no Doctor Science who sets everybody straight in short order. Moms, dads, big sisters, brothers, and friends may offer opinionated suggestions ripe for consideration, or tests to be designed and carried out. It is the readers who are invited to become the scientists and solve the problem.

references

American Association for the Advancement of Science (AAAS). 1993. *Benchmarks for science literacy.* New York: Oxford University Press.

Bransford, J. D., A. L. Brown, and R. R. Cocking, eds. 1999. *How people learn.* Washington, DC: National Academies Press.

Duckworth, E. 1986. *Inventing density.* Grand Forks, ND: Center for Teaching and Learning, University of North Dakota.

Martin, K., and E. Miller. 1990. Storytelling and science. In *Toward a whole language classroom: Articles from language arts, 1986–1989,* ed. B. Kiefer. Urbana, IL: National Council of Teachers of English.

National Research Council (NRC). 2000. *Inquiry and the national science education standards: A guide for teaching and learning.* Washington, DC: National Academies Press.

Osborne, R., and P. Fryberg. 1985. *Learning in science: The implications of children's science.* Auckland, New Zealand: Heinemann.

Schneps, M. 1996. *A private universe project.* Harvard Smithsonian Center for Astrophysics.

Shapiro, B. 1994. *What children bring to light.* New York: Teachers College Press.

Watson, B., and R. Konicek. 1990. Teaching for conceptual change: Confronting children's experience. *Phi Delta Kappan* 71 (9): 680–684.

CHAPTER 2

USING THE BOOK AND THE STORIES

It is often difficult for overburdened teachers to develop lessons or activities that are compatible with the everyday life experiences of their students. A major premise of this book is that if students can see the real-life implications of science content, they will be motivated to carry out hands-on, minds-on science investigations and personally care about the results. Science educators have, for decades, emphasized the importance of science experiences for students that emphasize personal involvement in the learning process. I firmly believe that the use of open-ended stories that challenge students to engage in real experimentation about real science content can be a step toward this goal. Furthermore, I believe that students who see a purpose to their learning and experimentation are more likely to understand the concepts they are studying. I sincerely hope that the contents of this book will relieve the overburdened teacher from the exhausting work of designing inquiry lessons from scratch.

These stories feature children in natural situations at home, on the playground, at parties, in school, or in the outdoors. Students should identify with the story characters, to share their frustrations, concerns, and questions. The most important role for the adult is to help guide and facilitate investigations and to debrief activities with them and to think about their analyses of results and conclusions. The children often need help to go to the next level and to develop new questions and find ways of following these questions to a conclusion. Our philosophy of science education is based on the belief that children can and want to care enough about problems to make them their own. This should enhance and invigorate any curriculum. In short, students can begin to lead the curriculum and because of their personal interest in the questions that evolve from their activities, they will maintain interest for much longer than they would if they were following someone else's lead.

A teacher told me that one of her biggest problems is to get her students to "care" about the topics they are studying. She says they go through the motions but without affect. Perhaps this same problem is familiar to you. I hope that this book can help you to take a step toward solving that problem. It is difficult if not impossible to make each lesson personally relevant to every student. However, by focusing on everyday situations and highlighting kids looking at everyday phenomena, I believe that we can come closer to reaching student interests.

I strongly suggest the use of complementary books as you go about planning for inquiry teaching. Five special books are *Uncovering Student Ideas* (volumes 1, 2, 3, and 4) by Page Keeley et al., published by the NSTA Press and *Science Curriculum Topic Study* by Page Keeley, published by Corwin Press and NSTA. The multivolume *Uncovering Student Ideas* helps you to find out what kinds of preconceptions your students bring to your class. *Science Curriculum Topic Study* focuses on finding the background necessary to plan a successful standards-based unit. I would also strongly recommend that you find a copy of *Science Matters: Achieving Scientific Literacy*, by Robert Hazen and James Trefil. This book will become your reference for many scientific matters. It is written in a simple, direct and accurate manner and will give you the necessary background in the sciences when you need it. Finally please acquaint yourself with *Making Sense of Secondary Science: Research Into Children's Ideas* (Driver et al. 1994). The title of this book can be misleading to American teachers, because in Great Britain, anything above primary level is referred to as secondary. It is a compilation of the research done on children's thinking about science and is a must-have for teachers. Use it as a reference in looking for the preconceptions your students probably bring to your classroom.

In 1978, David Ausubel made one of the most simple but telling comments about teaching: "The most important single factor influencing learning is what the learner already knows; ascertain this, and teach him accordingly." The background material that accompanies each story is designed to help you to find out what your learners already know about your chosen topic and what to do with that knowledge as you plan. The above-mentioned books will supplement the materials in this book and deepen your understanding of teaching for inquiry.

How then, is this book set up to help you to plan and teach inquiry-based science lessons?

HOW THIS BOOK IS ORGANIZED

There is a concept matrix (p. 41) that can be used to select a story most related to your content need. Following this matrix you will find the stories and the background material in separate chapters. Each chapter, starting with Chapter 5, will have the same organizational format. First you will find the story, followed by background material for using the story. The background material will contain the following sections:

Purpose

This section describes the concepts and/or general topic that the story attempts to address. In short, it tells you where this story fits into the general scheme of science concepts. It may also place the concepts within a conceptual scheme of a larger idea.

Related Concepts

A concept is a word or combination of words that form a mental construct of an idea. Examples are *motion, reflection, rotation, heat transfer, acceleration*. Each story is designed to address a single concept but often the stories open the door to several

NATIONAL SCIENCE TEACHERS ASSOCIATION

concepts. You will find a list of possible related concepts in the teacher background material. You should also check the matrices of stories and related concepts.

Don't Be Surprised

In most cases, this section will include projections of what your students will most likely do and how they may respond to the story. The projections relate to the content but focus more on the development of their current understanding of the concept. The explanation will be related to the content but will focus more on the development of the understanding of the concept. There will be references made to the current alternative conceptions your students might be expected to bring to class. It may even challenge you to prepare for teaching by doing some of the projected activities yourself, so that you are prepared for what your students will bring to class.

Content Background

This material will be a very succinct "short course" on the conceptual material that the story targets. It will not, of course, be a complete coverage but should give you enough information to feel comfortable in using the story and planning and carrying out the lessons. In most instances, references to books, articles and internet connections will also help you in preparing yourself to teach the topic. It is important that you have a reasonable knowledge of the topic in order for you to lead the students through their inquiry. It is not necessary, however, for you to be an expert on the topic. Learning along with your students can help you to understand how their learning takes place and make you a member of the class team striving for understanding of natural phenomena.

Table 2.1.
Thematic Crossover Between Stories in This Book and *Uncovering Student Ideas in Science*, **Volumes 1–4**

Story in this book	*Uncovering Student Ideas in Science*			
	Volume 1	**Volume 2**	**Volume 3**	**Volume 4**
Grandfather's Clock	n/a	n/a	The Scientific Method	Is It a System?
The Crooked Swing	n/a	n/a	Doing Science; What Is a Hypothesis?	Is It a System? Is It a Model?

(continued to next page)

(continued from previous page)

Story in this book	Uncovering Student Ideas in Science			
	Volume 1	**Volume 2**	**Volume 3**	**Volume 4**
The Magic Balloon	Is It Matter?	Floating High and Low	Why Is It Warmer? Hot Air Balloon	Is It a Model?
Bocce, Anyone?	n/a	n/a	Falling Objects; Slippery Slope; Does It Need a Force?	Is It a Model?
Cooling Off	The Mitten Problem; Objects and Temperature	Ice Cold Lemonade; Mixing Water	Thermometer; What Is a Hypothesis?	Warming Water; Is It a System? Ice Water
Warm Clothes?	The Mitten Problem	n/a	Thermometer; What Is a Hypothesis?	Warming Water; Is It a System?
Party Meltdown	Ice Cubes in a Bag	Ice Cold Lemonade; Freezing Ice	Is It a Theory? Thermometer	n/a
How Cold Is Cold?	n/a	Ice Cold Lemonade; Mixing Water	Ice Cubes in a Glass	Ice Water; Warming Water
Dancing Popcorn	n/a	Comparing Cubes; Floating Logs; Floating High and Low	Floating Balloon	n/a
Color Thieves	Can It Reflect Light? Apple in the Dark	n/a	n/a	n/a
A Mirror Big Enough	Can It Reflect Light	n/a	Mirror on the Wall	n/a
Stuck!	n/a	n/a	Apple on a Desk	Is It a System?
St. Bernard Puppy	n/a	n/a	Doing Science; What Is a Hypothesis? Sam's Puppy	Standing on One Foot

Story in this book	Uncovering Student Ideas in Science			
	Volume 1	**Volume 2**	**Volume 3**	**Volume 4**
Iced Tea	Is It Melting?	Ice Cold Lemonade	Thermometer	Ice Water; Sugar Water
Pasta In a Hurry	Going Through a Phase	Boiling Time and Temperature; What's in the Bubbles?	Thermometer	Warming Water
The Magnet Derby	Is It Matter?	n/a	n/a	Magnets in Water
The Cookie Dilemma	n/a	n/a	Doing Science; What Is a Hypothesis?	Salt Crystals
Sweet Talk	Is It Melting?	n/a	Doing Science; What Is a Hypothesis? Thermometer	Sugar Water
The Slippery Glass	Is It Made of Molecules? Wet Glass	Ice Cold Lemonade	Where Did the Water Come From?	n/a
Florida Cars	The Rusty Nails	n/a	Doing Science; What Is a Hypothesis?	n/a
The Neighborhood Telephone System	Making Sound	n/a	Is It Scientific Inquiry?	Is It a System?

Related Ideas from the National Science Education Standards *(NRC 1996) and* Benchmarks for Science Literacy *(AAAS 1993)*

These two documents are considered to be the National Standards upon which most of the local and state standards documents are based. For this reason, the concepts listed for the stories are almost certainly the ones listed to be taught in your local curriculum. It is possible that some of the concepts are not mentioned specifically in the Standards but are clearly related. I suggest that you obtain a copy of

Curriculum Topic Study (Keeley 2005), which will help you immensely with finding information about content, children's preconceptions, standards, and more resources. Even though it may not be mentioned specifically in each of the stories, you can assume that all of the stories will have connections to the Standards and Benchmarks in the area of Inquiry, Standard A.

Using the Story With Grades K–4 and 5–8

These stories have been tried with children of all ages. We have found that the concepts apply to all grade levels but at different levels of sophistication. Some of the characters in the stories have themes and characters that resonate better with one age group than another. However, the stories can be easily altered to appeal to an older or younger group by changing the characters to a more appropriate age or using slightly different age-appropriate dialog. The theme should be the same; just the characters and setting modified. Please read the suggestions for both grade levels.

As you may remember from the case study in the introduction, grade level is of little consequence in determining which stories are appropriate at which grade level. Both classes developed hypotheses and experiments appropriate to their developmental abilities. Second graders were satisfied to find out what happens to the length of a tree's shadow over a school year while the fifth-grade class developed more sophisticated experiments involving length of day, direction of shadows over time, and the daily length of shadows over an entire year. The main point here is that by necessity some stories are written with characters more appealing to certain age groups than others. Once again, I encourage you to read both the K–4 and 5–8 sections of Using the Story because ideas presented for either grade level may be suited to your particular students.

There is no highly technical apparatus required. Readily available materials found in the kitchen, bathroom, or garage will usually suffice. Each chapter includes background information about the principles and concepts involved and a list of materials you might want to have available. These suggestions of ideas and materials are based upon our experience while testing these stories with children. While we know that classrooms, schools, and children differ, we feel that most childhood experiences and development result in similar reactions to explaining and developing questions about the tales. The problems beg for solutions and most importantly, create new questions to be explored by your young scientists.

Here you will find suggestions to help you to teach the lessons that will allow your students to become active inquirers, develop their hypotheses, and finally finish the story that you may remember was left open for just this purpose. I have not listed a step-by-step approach or set of lesson plans to accomplish this end. Obviously, you know your students, their abilities, their developmental levels, and their learning abilities and disabilities better than anyone. You will find however, some suggestions and some techniques that we have found work well in teaching for inquiry. You may use them as written or modify them to fit your particular situation. The main point is that you try to involve your students as deeply as possible in trying to solve the mysteries posed by the stories.

Related Books and NSTA Journal Articles

Here, we will list specific books and articles from the constantly growing treasure trove of National Science Teacher Association (NSTA) resources for teachers. While our listings are not completely inclusive, you may access the entire scope of resources on the internet at *www.nsta.org/store*. Membership in NSTA will allow you to read all articles online.

References

References will be provided for the articles and research findings cited in the background section for each story.

Concept Matrix

At the beginning of the story section you will find a concept matrix listing the concepts most related to each story. It can be used to select a story that matches your instructional needs.

FINAL WORDS

I was pleased find that Michael Padilla, past president of NSTA, asked the same questions as I did when I decided to write a book that focused on inquiry. In the May 2006 edition of *NSTA Reports*, Mr. Padilla in his "President's Message" commented, "To be competitive in the future, students must be able to think creatively, solve problems, reason and learn new, complex ideas… [Inquiry] is the ability to think like a scientist, to identify critical questions to study; to carry out complicated procedures, to eliminate all possibilities except the one under study; to discuss, share and argue with colleagues; and to adjust what you know based on that social interaction." Further, he asks, "Who asks the question?…Who designs the procedures?…Who decides which data to collect?…Who formulates explanations based upon the data?…Who communicates and justifies the results?…What kind of classroom climate allows students to wrestle with the difficult questions posed during a good inquiry?"

I believe that this book speaks to these questions and that the techniques proposed here are one way to answer the above questions with, "The students do!" in the kind of science classroom this book envisions.

REFERENCES

Ausubel, D., J. Novak, and H. Hanensian. 1978. *Educational psychology: A cognitive view.* New York: Holt, Rinehart, and Winston.

Driver, R., A. Squires, P. Rushworth, and V. Wood-Robinson. 1994. *Making sense of secondary science: Research into children's ideas.* London and New York: Routledge Falmer.

Hazen, R., and J. Trefil. 1991. *Science matters: Achieving scientific literacy.* New York: Anchor Books.

Keeley, P. 2005. *Science curriculum topic study: Bridging the gap between standards and practice.* Thousand Oaks, CA: Corwin Press.

Keeley, P., F. Eberle, and C. Dorsey. 2008. *Uncovering student ideas in science, volume 3: Another 25 formative assessment probes.* Arlington, VA: NSTA Press.

Keeley, P., F. Eberle, and L. Farrin. 2005. *Uncovering student ideas in science, volume 1: 25 formative assessment probes.* Arlington, VA: NSTA Press.

Keeley, P., F. Eberle, and J. Tugel. 2007. *Uncovering student ideas in science, volume 2: 25 more formative assessment probes.* Arlington, VA: NSTA Press.

Keeley, P., and J. Tugel. 2009. *Uncovering student ideas in science, volume 4: 25 new formative assessment probes.* Arlington, VA: NSTA Press.

Konicek-Moran, R. 2008. *Everyday science mysteries: Stories for inquiry-based science teaching.* Arlington, VA: NSTA Press.

Konicek-Moran, R. 2009. *More everyday science mysteries: Stories for inquiry-based science teaching.* Arlington, VA: NSTA Press.

Padilla, M. 2006. President's message. *NSTA Reports* 18 (9): 3.

CHAPTER 3
USING THIS BOOK IN DIFFERENT WAYS

Although the book was originally designed for use with K–8 students by teachers or adults in informal settings, it became obvious that a book containing stories and content material for teachers intent on teaching in an inquiry mode had other potential uses. I list a few of them below to show that the book has several uses beyond the typical elementary and middle school population in formal settings.

USING THE BOOK AS A CONTENT CURRICULUM GUIDE

When asked by the University of Massachusetts to teach a content course for a special master's degree program in teacher education, I decided to use *Everyday Science Mysteries* as one of several texts to teach content material. A major premise in the book is that students, when engaged in answering their own questions will delve into a topic at a level commensurate with their intellectual development and learning skills. Therefore, even though the stories were designed for people younger than themselves, the students in the class were able to find questions to answer that were at a level of sophistication that challenged them.

During the fall 2007 semester this book was used as a text and curriculum guide for a class titled Exploring the Natural Sciences Through Inquiry at the University of Massachusetts in Amherst. The shortened version of the syllabus for the course follows on pages 18–22.

Exploring the Natural Sciences Through Inquiry
EDUC 692 O
Fall 2007

Instructor: Dr. Richard D. Konicek, Professor Emeritus

Course Description:

This course is designed for elementary and middle school teachers who need, not only to deepen their content knowledge in the natural sciences, but also to understand how inquiry can be used in the elementary and middle school classroom. Natural sciences mean the Biological Sciences, Earth and Space Sciences, and the Physical Sciences. Teachers will sample various topics from each of the above areas of science through inquiry techniques. The topics will be chosen from everyday phenomena such as Astronomy (Moon and Sun observations), Physics (motion, energy, thermodynamics, sound periodic motion), and Biology (botany, zoology, animal and plant behavior, evolution).

Course Objectives:

It is expected that each student will:

- Gain content background in each of the three areas of natural science.
- Be able to apply this content to their teaching methods.
- Develop questions concerning a particular phenomenon in nature.
- Design and carry out experiments to answer their questions.
- Analyze experimental data and draw conclusions.
- Consult various sources to verify the nature of their conclusions.
- Read scientific literature appropriate to their studies.
- Extend their knowledge to use with middle school children both in content and methodology.

Relationship to the Conceptual Framework of the School of Education:

Collaboration:	Teachers will work in collaborative teams during class meetings to acquire science content and pedagogical knowledge and skills.
Reflective Practice:	Teachers will develop and implement formative assessment probes with their students.
Multiple Ways of Knowing:	Teachers will share science questions and their methods of inquiry chosen to answer those questions.
Access, Equity, and Fairness:	Teachers reflect on student understandings based on students' stories.
Evidence-Based Practice:	Teachers will explore formative assessment through the use of probes.

Required Texts:

Hazen, R. M., and J. Trefil. 1991. *Science matters*. New York: Anchor Books.

Keeley, P., F. Eberle, and J. Tugel. 2007. *Uncovering student ideas in science: 25 more formative assessment probes, vol. 2.* Arlington, VA: NSTA Press. Konicek-

Moran, R. 2008. *Everyday science mysteries.* Arlington, VA: NSTA Press.

Resource Texts:

American Association for the Advancement of Science (AAAS). 2001. *Atlas of science literacy* (vol. 1). Washington, DC: Project 2061.

American Association for the Advancement of Science (AAAS). 2007. *Atlas of science literacy* (vol. 2). Washington, DC: Project 2061.

Driver, R., A. Squires, P. Rushworth, and V. Wood-Robinson. 1994. *Making sense of secondary science.* London: Routledge-Falmer.

Keeley, P., F. Eberle, and L. Farrin. 2005. *Uncovering student ideas in science, vol. 1.* Arlington, VA: NSTA Press.

Topics To Be Investigated in Volume 1:

Everyday Science Mysteries is organized around stories. The core concepts related to the National Science Education Standards developed by the National Research Council in 1996 are the basis for the concept selection. The story titles and related core concepts are shown in the matrices below.

Earth Systems Science

Core Concepts	Stories				
	Moon Tricks	Where Are the Acorns?	Master Gardener	Frosty Morning	The Little Tent That Cried
States of Matter			X	X	X
Change of State			X	X	X
Physical Change			X	X	X
Melting			X	X	
Systems	X	X	X	X	X
Light	X	X			
Reflection	X	X		X	
Heat Energy			X	X	X
Temperature				X	X
Energy			X	X	X
Water Cycle				X	X
Rock Cycle			X		
Evaporation				X	X
Condensation				X	X
Weathering			X		
Erosion			X		
Deposition			X		
Rotation/Revolution	X	X			
Moon Phases	X				
Time	X	X			

Physical Sciences

Core Concepts	Magic Balloon	Bocce Anyone?	Grandfather's Clock	Neighborhood Telephone Service	How Cold Is Cold?
Energy	X	X	X	X	X
Energy Transfer	X	X	X	X	X
Conservation of Energy		X			X
Forces	X	X	X		
Gravity	X	X	X		
Heat	X				X
Kinetic Energy		X	X		
Potential Energy		X	X		
Position and Motion		X	X		
Sound				X	
Periodic Motion			X	X	
Waves				X	
Temperature	X				X
Gas Laws	X				
Buoyancy	X				
Friction		X	X		
Experimental Design	X	X	X	X	X
Work		X	X		
Change of State					X
Time		X	X		

Biological Sciences

Core Concepts	About Me	Bugs	Dried Apples	Seed Bargains	Trees From Helicopters
Animals	X	X			
Classification		X	X	X	X
Life Processes	X	X	X	X	X
Living Things	X	X	X	X	X
Structure and Function		X	X		X
Plants			X	X	X
Adaptation		X			X

Genetics/Inheritance	X		X	X	X
Variation	X		X	X	X
Evaporation			X		
Energy		X	X	X	X
Systems	X	X	X		X
Cycles	X	X	X	X	X
Reproduction	X	X	X	X	X
Inheritance	X	X	X		X
Change		X	X		
Genes	X		X		X
Metamorphosis		X			
Life Cycles		X	X		X
Continuity of Life	X	X	X	X	X

Assignments:

<u>Astronomy (25%)</u>: Everyone will be expected to explore the daytime astronomy sequence, which will aim to develop models of the Earth, Moon, and Sun relationships. Students will keep a Moon journal and Sun shadow journal over the course of the semester, which they will turn in periodically.

<u>Topics (50%)</u>: In addition, students will pick at least two topics from each of the Earth, Physical and Biological areas for study during the semester. Students will come up with a topic question and do an investigation or experiment regarding the topic questions posed. (For example: Are there acorns that do not need a dormancy period before germinating?) These questions and experiments will be shared with the class as they progress so that all students will either be directly involved in learning about the content or indirectly involved by listening to reports and critiquing those reports. In addition to the experiments, students will (1) involve their students in their experiments/investigations and (2) design and give formative assessment probes to their students to find out what knowledge they already possess. Students will be graded on their experimental designs, their presentations of their data and upon their conclusions. I will develop a rubric with the students that will address the goals stated above and their values to be calculated for their grades.

<u>Attendance/Participation (25%)</u>: Attendance at all course meetings is required.

References for Course Development:

American Association for the Advancement of Science (AAAS).1993. *Benchmarks for science literacy.* New York: Oxford University Press.

Ausubel, D., J. Novak, and H. Hanensian. 1978. *Educational psychology: A cognitive view.* New York: Holt, Rinehart and Winston.

Bransford, J. D., A. L. Brown, and R. R. Cocking, eds. 1999. *How people learn.* Washington, DC: National Academy Press.

Duckworth, E. 1986. *Inventing density.* Grand Forks, ND: Center for Teaching and Learning, University of North Dakota.

Driver, R., A. Squires, P. Rushworth, and V. Wood-Robinson. 1994. *Making sense of secondary science: Research into children's ideas.* London and New York: Routledge Falmer.

Hazen, R., and J. Trefil. 1991. *Science matters: Achieving scientific literacy.* New York: Anchor Books.

Keeley, P. 2005. *Science curriculum topic study: Bridging the gap between standards and practice.* Thousand Oaks, CA: Corwin Press.

Keeley, P., F. Eberle, and L. Farrin. 2005. *Uncovering student ideas in science: 25 formative assessment probes, volume 1.* Arlington, VA: NSTA Press.

Keeley, P., F. Eberle, and J. Tugel. 2007. *Uncovering student ideas in science: 25 more formative assessment probes, volume 2.* Arlington, VA: NSTA Press.

Konicek-Moran, R. 2008. *Everyday science mysteries.* Arlington, VA: NSTA Press.

Martin, K., and E. Miller. 1990. Storytelling and science. In *Toward a whole language classroom: Articles from language arts,* ed. B. Kiefer, 1986–1989. Urbana, IL: National Council of Teachers of English.

National Research Council (NRC). 2000. *Inquiry and the national science education standards: A guide for teaching and learning.* Washington, DC: National Academies Press.

Osborne, R., and P. Fryberg. 1985. *Learning in science: The implications of children's science.* Auckland, New Zealand: Heinemann.

Schneps, M. 1996. *A private universe project.* Washington, DC: Harvard Smithsonian Center for Astrophysics.

Shapiro, B. 1994. *What children bring to light.* New York: Teachers College Press.

Watson, B., and R. Konicek. 1990. Teaching for conceptual change: Confronting children's experience. *Phi Delta Kappan* 71(9): 680–684.

The course was taught as a graduate course for teachers or prospective teachers of elementary or middle school students. The course could be classified as a content/pedagogy class for teachers who had minimal science backgrounds as well as minimal skills in teaching for inquiry. My premise was that if teachers would learn content through inquiry techniques, they would be convinced of their efficacy as learning techniques and would be likely to use them to teach content, in their own classes. As it turned out, those teacher-students who had classes of their own and were full time teachers did work on their projects with their students with very satisfactory results according to the teachers. As a result, both teachers and students were learning science content through inquiry techniques. Because the teachers in the class were completing an assignment, they were able to be honest

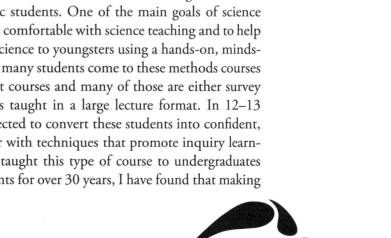

with their students about not knowing the outcome of their investigations. This is often a problem with teachers who are afraid to admit that they are learning along with the students. In this case the students were excited about learning along with their teachers and vice versa. Teachers with classrooms were also able to develop rubrics with their students for the grading of their explorations and therefore were involved with some metacognition as well.

As a result of this small foray into the use of the book in this manner, I am convinced that the book can be used as a content guide for undergraduate and graduate content-oriented courses for teachers. As noted in the syllabus, the use of other supplementary texts for content and pedagogy add to the strength of the course in preparing teachers to use inquiry techniques and to learn content themselves. With the use of the Internet, very little information is hidden from anyone with minimum computer skills. Unlike many survey courses chosen by teachers who are science-phobic, this course did not attempt to cover a great number of topics but to teach a few topics for understanding. The basic premise of this author is that when deciding between coverage and understanding science topics and concepts, understanding wins every time. It is well known that our current curriculum in the United States has been faulted for being a mile wide and an inch deep. High stakes testing seems to also add to the problem since almost all teachers whom I have interviewed over the last few years are reluctant to teach for understanding using inquiry methods because teaching for understanding takes more time and does not allow for coverage of the almost infinite amount of material that might appear on standardized tests. Thus, student misconceptions are seldom addressed and continue to persist even though students can do reasonably well on teacher made tests and assessment tools and still hold on to their misconceptions. See Bonnie Shapiro's book *What Children Bring to Light* (1994).

USING THIS BOOK AS A RESOURCE BOOK FOR SCIENCE METHODS COURSES IN TEACHING PREPARATION PROGRAMS

Traditionally, science methods courses in the United States are taught to classes mainly composed of science-phobic students. One of the main goals of science methods courses is to make students comfortable with science teaching and to help students develop skills in teaching science to youngsters using a hands-on, minds-on approach. Unfortunately, a great many students come to these methods courses with a minimum of science content courses and many of those are either survey (non-laboratory) courses or courses taught in a large lecture format. In 12–13 weeks, methods instructors are expected to convert these students into confident, motivated teachers who are familiar with techniques that promote inquiry learning among their students. Having taught this type of course to undergraduates and career-changing graduate students for over 30 years, I have found that making students comfortable with science is the first goal. This is often accomplished by assigning students science tasks that can be accomplished with a minimum of stress and with a maximum of success. Second, I try to instill the ideas commensurate with the nature of science as a discipline. Third, I find that it is often necessary to teach a little content for those who are rusty and need to clarify some of their own misconceptions. Lastly, but not least important, I try to acquaint them with resources in the field so that they know what is available to them as they enter their teaching careers. Obviously, here is an opportunity to acquaint them with current information about the learners themselves, how they learn, and how to teach for inquiry.

As a final assignment for my methods classes, I assign the students the task of writing an everyday science mystery and a paper to accompany it, which will describe how they will use the story to teach a concept using the inquiry approach. The results have far exceeded what I had been receiving from the typical lesson plan used by others and me through the years. This book would not only provide the text on teaching science found in the early chapters but would provide a model for producing everyday science mysteries for topics of the students' choices.

USING THE STORIES AS INTERACTIVE INQUIRY PLAYS

Due to the innovation of the teachers of Knox County, Tennessee, and the actions of instructional coaches Andrea Allen and Theresa Nixon, a new and exciting method of introducing the stories has been invented. These teachers have adapted the mystery stories into a theatrical mode called the "Everyday Science Mystery Readers Theater." They invite teachers to make an interactive play out of the mystery stories instead of reading them. This involves the students in acting out the stories and in doing so, puts them further into the mysteries. We thank them for this innovation and invite you all to try this with your students. See Chapter 4: Science and Literacy for more information on student reading and writing in science. One of the plays, "Florida Cars," is reproduced here with the teachers' kind permission (see Chapter 24 for the original story and discussion).

NATIONAL SCIENCE TEACHERS ASSOCIATION

SCIENCE MYSTERY THEATER PRESENTS:
FLORIDA CARS

Characters:
Narrator 1
Amber
Jake
Car salesperson

Scene 1: Riding in the car

Narrator 1: Amber was riding along with her brother, Jake, in their mother's car. They were going to see if Jake could find a used car he could afford. That meant visiting a lot of car dealers along the road. This is what Amber was thinking…..

Amber: I like to listen to my brother and the car salesmen talk about prices. It is like a big game, and I like to hear them go back and forth bartering for a deal.

Scene 2: At the car dealership

Car salesperson: This one is a little more expensive. First of all, it is red, and second, but most importantly …**IT…IS…A…Florida…Car!** It just came on the truck yesterday. Guaranteed Florida! Low mileage too, but most important… it is a Florida car!

Jake: Owned by a little old lady who only drove it to church on Sunday too, I'll bet.

Narrator: Amber wondered what was so important about Florida.

Amber: I wonder if they make better cars in Florida than they do in Detroit.

Car salesperson: Go ahead and look her over, and see if you can find one speck of rust on her! I'll even put the car on the lift for you so you can look underneath.

Jake: Can I see the transportation documents so that I can be sure it came up from Florida? Not that I don't trust you, but it will put my mind at ease to be sure it came from Florida.

Narrator: The car salesperson got the documents and sure enough the car had been picked up in Homestead, in south Florida.

Jake: (whispers to Amber) Even better than expected.

Jake: I'll have to think it over. I will be back in a day or two.

Car salesperson: Don't wait too long, young fella. It won't be here long!

Narrator: Jake and Amber leave the car salesperson and get in their mom's car and drive back home.

Amber: What is so special about a Florida car?

Jake: Well, for one thing we don't have to worry about a lot of rust on the car.

Amber: Why is that?

Jake: Think about it sis. Down there it almost never snows and they don't have to put salt on the roads so it doesn't rust.

Amber: Does rust always need salt to make it happen?

Jake: Sure it does; don't you know anything about rust?

Amber: Actually I do know some things about it, I think. It's something that seems to happen to everything I leave out in the weather.

Jake: Well, sure, it happens a lot to bicycles and metal stuff that we leave out, but salt makes it happen faster and better!

Amber: Always?

Jake: I don't believe in always. There are always exceptions to the rule.

Amber: Always?

Jake: OK, don't get smart with me little sister. You know what I mean.

Amber: Well, I think I'll just go ahead and test that idea about salt 'cause I'm not so sure salt is *always* needed for things to rust. Maybe other things cause rust to form faster and maybe other things stop it from happening.

Jake: Knock yourself out, sis, and then let me know if a Florida car is a sure bet.

USE FOR HOMESCHOOL PROGRAMS

Homeschooling parents have a great many resources at their disposal, as any internet search will show. Curricular suggestions and materials are available for those parents and children who choose to conduct their education at home. Science is one of those subjects that might be difficult for many parents whose science backgrounds are a bit weak or outdated. Parents and children working together to solve a story-driven mystery could use this book easily. The connections to the national Standards and the Benchmarks in science also help in making sure that the home schooling curriculum is uncovering the nationally approved scientific concepts. Parents would use the book just as any teacher would use it except there would be fewer opportunities for class discussions and the parents would have to do a bit more discussion with their children to solidify their understanding of their investigations.

reference

Shapiro, B. 1994. *What children bring to light*. New York: Teachers College Press.

CHAPTER 4

SCIENCE AND LITERACY

While heading into the final chapter before launching into the stories, I couldn't resist introducing you to a piece of literature that is seldom read except by English majors. The quotation that follows is from Irish novelist James Joyce in his classic book *Ulysses*, written in 1922:

> Where was the chap I saw in that picture somewhere? Ah yes, in the dead sea, floating on his back, reading a book with a parasol open. Couldn't sink if you tried: so thick with salt. Because the weight of the water, no, the weight of the body in the water is equal to the weight of the what? Or is it the volume is equal to the weight? It's a law something like that. Vance in High school cracking his finger-joints, teaching. The college curriculum. Cracking curriculum. What is weight really when you say the weight? Thirtytwo feet per second, per second. Law of falling bodies: per second, per second. They all fall to the ground. The earth. It's the force of gravity of the earth is the weight. (p. 73)

In the novel, Joyce's main character Bloom recalls a picture of someone floating in the Dead Sea, and tries to recall the science behind it. Have you or have you observed others who, while trying to recall something scientific, resorted to a mishmash of scientic knowledge, half-remembered and garbled? (For this foray into literature, I am indebted to Michael J. Reiss who called my attention to this passage in an article of his in *School Science Review*.)

In his school days, Bloom seems to have been fascinated both with the curriculum and the teacher in his physics class. However, Bloom's memory of the science behind buoyancy runs the gamut from unrelated science language pouring out of his memory bank to visions of his teacher cracking his finger joints. Unfortunately, even today, this might well be the norm rather than the exception. This phenomenon is exactly what we are trying to avoid in our modern pedagogy and now leads us to the main point of this chapter.

There are many ways of connecting literacy and science. We shall look briefly at the research literature and find some ideas that will make the combination of literacy and science not only worthwhile but also essential for learning.

LITERACY AND SCIENCE

In pedagogical terms there are differences between scientific literacy and the curricular combination of science and literacy, but perhaps they have more in common than one might expect. *Scientific literacy* is the ability to understand scientific concepts so that they have a personal meaning in everyday life. In other words, a scientifically literate population can use their knowledge of scientific principles in situations other than those in which they learned them. For example, I would consider people scientifically literate if they were able to use their understanding of ecosystems and ecology to make informed decisions about saving wetlands in their community. This is of course, what we would hope for in every aspect of our educational goals regardless of the subject matter. *Literacy* refers to the ability to read, write, speak, and make sense of text. Since most schools emphasize reading, writing, and mathematics, they often take priority over all other subjects in the school curriculum. How often have I heard teachers say that their major responsibility is reading and math, and that there is no time for science? But there is no need for competition for the school day. I believe that this misconception is caused by the lack of understanding of the synergy created by integration of subjects. In *synergy*, you get a combination of skills that surpasses the sum of the individual parts.

So what does all of this have to do with teaching science as inquiry? There is currently a strong effort to combine science and literacy. One reason is that there is a growing body of research that stresses the importance of language in learning science. "Hands-on" science is nothing without its "minds-on" counterpart. I am fond of reminding audiences that a food fight is a hands-on activity, but one does not learn much through mere participation, except perhaps the finer points of the aerodynamic properties of Jell-O. The understanding of scientific principles is not imbedded in the materials themselves or in the manipulation of these materials. Discussion, argumentation, discourse of all kinds, group consensus and social interaction—all forms of communication are necessary for students to make meaning out of the activities in which they have engaged. And these require *language* in the form of writing, reading, and particularly speaking. They require that students think about their thinking—that they hear their own and others' thoughts and ideas spoken out loud and perhaps eventually see them in writing to make sense of what they have been doing and the results they have been getting in their activities. This is the often forgotten "minds-on" part of the "hands-on, minds-on" couplet. Consider the following:

> In schools, talk is sometimes valued and sometimes avoided, but—and this is surprising—talk is rarely taught. It is rare to hear teachers discuss their efforts to teach students to talk well. Yet talk, like reading and writing, is a major motor—I could even say the major motor—of intellectual development. (Calkins 2000, p. 226)

For a detailed and very useful discussion of talk in the science classroom, I refer you to Jeffrey Winokur and Karen Worth's chapter, "Talk in the Science Classroom: Looking at What Students and Teachers Need to Know and Be Able to Do" in *Linking Science and Literacy in the K–8 Classroom* (2006). Also check out Chapter 8 in this book. There is also recent evidence that ELL learners gain a great deal from talking, in both their science learning and new language acquisition (Rosebery and Warren 2008).

Linking inquiry-based science and literacy has strong research support. First, the conceptual and theoretical work of Padilla and his colleagues suggest that inquiry science and reading share a set of intellectual processes (e.g., observing, classifying, inferring, predicting, and communicating) and that these processes are used whether the student is conducting scientific experiments or reading text (Padilla, Muth, and Padilla 1991). Helping children become aware of their thinking as they read and investigate with materials will help them understand and practice more *metacognition*.

You, the teacher, may have to model this for them by thinking out loud yourself as you view a phenomenon. Help them to understand why you spoke as you did and why it is important to think about your process of thinking. You may say something like, "I think that warm weather affects how fast seeds germinate. I think that I should design an experiment to see if I am right." Then later, "Did you notice how I made a prediction that I could test in an experiment?" Modeling your thinking can help your students see how and why the talk of science is used in certain situations.

Science is about words and their meanings. Postman made a very interesting statement about words and science. He said "Biology is not plants and animals. It is language about plants and animals.... Astronomy is not planets and stars. It is a way of talking about planets and stars" (1979, p.165). To emphasize this point even further, I might add that science is a language, a language that specializes in talking about the world and being in that world we call science. It has a special vocabulary and organization. Scientists use this vocabulary and organization when they talk about their work. Often, it is called "discourse" (Gee 2004). Children need to learn this discourse when they present their evidence, when they argue the fine points of their work, evaluate their own and others' work and refine their ideas for further study.

Students do not come to you with this language in full bloom; in fact the seeds may not even have germinated. They attain it by doing science and being helped by knowledgeable adults who teach them about controlling variables, conducting fair tests, having evidence to back up their statements, and using the processes of science in their attempts at what has been called "firsthand inquiry" (Palincsar and Magnusson 2001). This is inquiry that uses direct involvement with materials, or in other more familiar words, the hands-on part of scientific investigation. The term *secondhand investigations* refers to the use of textual matter, lectures, reading data, charts, graphs, or other types of instruction that do not feature direct contact with materials. Cervetti et al. (2006) put it so well:

[W]e view firsthand investigations as the glue that binds together all of the linguistic activity around inquiry. The mantra we have developed for ourselves in helping students acquire conceptual knowledge and the discourse in which that knowledge is expressed (including particular vocabulary) is "read it, write it, talk it, do it!"—and in no particular order, or better yet, in every possible order. (p. 238)

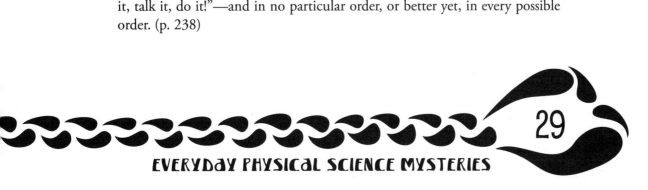

So you can see that it is also important that the students talk about their work; write about their work; read about what others have to say about the work they are doing, in books or via visual media; and take all possible opportunities to document their work in a way that is useful to them in looking back at what they have found out about their work.

THE LANGUAGE OF SCIENCE

Of course, writing, talking, and reading in the discipline of science is different than other disciplines. For example, science writing is simple and focuses on the evidence obtained to form a conclusion. But science includes things other than just verbal language. It includes tactile, graphic, and visual means of designing studies, carrying them out, and communicating the results to others. Also important is that science has many unfamiliar words; many common words such as *work, force, plant food, compound,* and *density* have different meanings in the real world of the student but have precise and often counterintuitive meanings in science. For example, if you push against a car for 30 minutes until perspiration runs off your face, you feel as though you have "worked" hard even though the car has not budged a centimeter. In physics, unless the car has moved, you have done no work at all. We tell students that plants make their own food and then show them a bag of "plant food." We tell children to "put on warm clothes," yet the clothes have nothing to do with producing warmth.

Students have to change their way of communicating when they study science. They must learn new terminology and clarify old terms in scientific ways. We as teachers can help in this process by realizing that we are not just science teachers but also language teachers. When we talk of scientific things we talk about them in the way the discipline works. We should not avoid scientific terminology but try to connect it whenever possible to common metaphors and language. We should use pictures and stories.

We need also to know that science contains many words that ask for thought and action on the part or the students. Sentences with words like *compare, evaluate, infer, observe, modify,* and *hypothesize* prompt students to solve problems. We can only teach good science by realizing that language and intellectual development go hand in hand and that one without the other is mostly meaningless.

SCIENCE NOTEBOOKS

Many science educators have lately touted science notebooks as an aid to students involving themselves more in the discourse of science (Campbell and Fulton 2003). Their use has also shown promise in helping English language learners (ELLs) in the development of language skills as well as learning science concepts and the nature of science.

NATIONAL SCIENCE TEACHERS ASSOCIATION

Science notebooks differ from science journals and science logs in that they are not merely for recording data (logs) or reflections of learning (journals), but are meant to be used continuously for recording experimentation, designs, plans, thinking, vocabulary, and concerns or puzzlement. The science notebook is the recording of past, and present thoughts and predictions and are unique to each student. The teacher makes sure that the students have ample time to record events and to also ask for specific responses to such questions as, "What still puzzles you about this activity?"

For specific ideas for using science notebooks and for information on the value of using the notebooks in science, see *Science Notebooks: Writing About Inquiry* by Brian Campbell and Lori Fulton (2003). You can assume that science notebooks are a given in what I envision as an inquiry-oriented classroom. While working in an elementary school years ago, I witnessed some minor miracles of children writing to learn. The most vital lesson for us as teachers was the importance of asking children to write each day about something that still confused them. The results were remarkable. As we read their notebooks, we witnessed their metacognition, and their solutions through their thinking "out loud" in their writing.

The use of science notebooks should be an opportunity for the students to record their mental journey through their activity. Using the stories in this book, the science notebook would include the specific question that the student is concerned with, the lists of ideas and statements generated by the class after the story is read, pictures or graphs of data collected by the student and class, and perhaps the final conclusions reached by the student or class as they try to solve the mystery presented by the story.

Let us imagine that your class has reached a conclusion to the story they have been using and have reached consensus on that conclusion. What options are open to you as a teacher for asking the students to finalize their work? At this juncture, it may be acceptable to have the students actually write the "ending" to the story or write up the conclusions in a standard lab report format. The former method, of course, is another way of actually connecting literacy and science. Many teachers prefer to have their students at least learn to write the "boiler plate" lab reports, just to be familiar with that method, while others are comfortable with having their students write more anecdotal kinds of reports. My experience is that when students write their conclusions in an anecdotal form, while referring to their data to support their conclusions, I am more assured that they have really understood the concepts they have been chasing rather than filling in the blanks in a form. In the end, it is up to you, the classroom teacher, to decide. Of course, it could be done both ways.

As mentioned earlier, a major factor in designing these stories and follow-up activities is based upon one of the major tenets of a philosophy called *constructivism*. That tenet is that knowledge is constructed by individuals in order to make sense of the world in which they live. If we believe this, then the knowledge that each individual brings to any situation or problem must be factored into the way that person tries to solve that problem. By the same token, it is most important to realize that the *identification* of the problem and the way the problem is *viewed* are also factors determined by each individual. Therefore it is vital that the adult facilitator encourage the students to bring into the open, orally and in writing, those ideas they already have about the situation being discussed. In bringing these preconceptions out of hiding, so to speak, all of the children and the teacher can begin playing with all of the cards exposed and alternative ideas about topics can be addressed. Data can be then analyzed openly without any hidden agendas in childrens' minds to sabotage learning. You can find more about this process in the series *Uncovering Student Ideas in Science: 25 Formative Assessment Probes*, vols.1–4 (2005, 2007, 2008, 2009).

The stories also point out that science is a social, cultural, and therefore human enterprise. The characters in our stories usually enlist others in their investigations, their discussions, and their questions. These people have opinions and hypotheses and are consulted, involved, or drawn into an active dialectic. Group work is encouraged, which in a classroom would suggest cooperative learning. At home, siblings and parents may become involved in the activities and engage in the dialectic as a family group.

The stories can also be read to the children. In this way children can gain more from the literature than if they had to read the stories by themselves. A child's listening vocabulary is usually greater than his or her reading vocabulary. Words that are somewhat unfamiliar to them can be deduced by the context in which they are found. Or, new vocabulary words can be explained as the story is read. We have found that children are always ready to discuss the stories as they are read and therefore become more involved as they take part in the reading. So much the better because getting involved is what this book is all about; getting involved in situations that beg for problem finding, problem solving, and construction of new ideas about science in everyday life.

HELPING YOUR STUDENTS DURING INQUIRY

How much help should you give to your students as they work through the problem? A good rule of thumb is that you can help them as much as you think necessary as long as the children are still finding the situation problematic. In other words, the children should not be following your lead but their own lead. If some of these leads end up in dead ends, then that aspect of scientific investigation is part of their experience too. Science is full of experiences which are not productive. If children read popular accounts of scientific discovery, they could get the impression that the scientist gets up in the morning, says, "What will I discover today?" and then sets off on a clear, straight path to an elegant conclusion before suppertime rolls around. Nothing could be further from the truth! But it is very important to note that a steady diet of frustration can dampen students' enthusiasm for science.

Dead ends can be viewed as signaling a need to develop a new plan or ask the question in a different way. Most important, dead ends should not be looked upon as failures. They are more like opportunities to try again in a different way with a

NATIONAL SCIENCE TEACHERS ASSOCIATION

clean slate. The adult's role is to keep a balance so that motivation is maintained and interest continues to flourish. Sometimes this is more easily accomplished when kids work in groups. Most often nowadays, scientists work in teams and use each other's expertise in a group process,

Many people do not understand that the scientific process includes luck, personal idiosyncrasies, and feelings, as well as the so-called *scientific method*. The term *scientific method* itself sounds like a recipe guaranteed to produce success. The most important aid you can provide for your students is to help them maintain their confidence in their ability to do problem solving using all of their ways of knowing. They can use metaphors, visualizations, drawings, or any other method with which they are comfortable to develop new insights into the problem. Then they can set up their study in a way that reflects the scientific paradigm including a simple question, controlling variables, and isolating the one variable they are testing.

Next, you can help them to keep their experimental designs simple and carefully controlled. Third, you can help them to learn keep good data records in their science notebooks. Most students don't readily see the need for this last point, even after they have been told. They don't see the need because the neophyte experimenter has not had much experience with collecting usable data. Until they realize that unreadable data or necessary data not recorded can cause a problem, they see little use for them. The problem is that they don't see it as a problem. Children don't see the need for keeping good shadow length records because they are not always sure what they are going to do with them in a week or a month from now. If they are helped to see the reasons for collecting data and that these data are going to be evidence of a change over time, then they will see the purpose of being able to go back and revisit the past in order to compare it to the present. In this way they can also see the reasons for keeping a log in the first place.

In experiences we have had with children, forcing them to use prescribed data collection worksheets has not helped them to understand the reasons for data collection at all and in some cases has actually caused more confusion or amounted to little more than busy work. On one occasion while circulating around a classroom where children were engaged in a worksheet-directed activity, an observer asked a student what she was doing. The student replied without hesitation, "step 3." Our goal is to empower students engaged in inquiry to the point where they are involved in the activity at a level where all of the steps, including step 3, are designed by the students themselves and for good reason—to answer their own questions in a logical, sequential, meaningful manner. We believe it can be done but it requires patience on the part of the adult facilitators and faith that the children have the skills to carry out such mental gymnastics, with a little help from their friends and mentors.

One last word about data collection. After spending years being a scientist and working with scientists, one common element stands out for me. Scientists keep on their person a notebook that is used numerous times during the day to record interesting items. The researcher may come across some interesting data that may not seem directly connected to the study at the time but he or she makes some notes about it anyway because that entry may come in handy in the future. Memory is viewed as an ephemeral thing, not to be trusted. Scientists' notebooks are a treasured and essential part of the scientific enterprise. In some cases they have been considered legal documents and used as such in courts of law. There is an ethical expectation that scientists record their data honestly. Many times, working with my mentor, biologist Skip Snow in the Everglades National Park Python Project, I have seen Skip refer to previous entries when confronted with data that he thinks may provide a clue to a new line of investigation. Researchers don't leave home without notebooks.

WorkinG WiTH enGLiSH LanGuaGe Learner (eLL) PoPuLaTionS

Now, suppose that members of your class are from other cultures and have a limited knowledge of the English language. Of what use is inquiry science with such a population and how can you use the discipline to increase both their language learning and their science skills and knowledge?

First of all, let's take a look at the problems associated with learning with the handicap of limited language understanding. Lee (2005) in her summary of research on ELL students and science learning, points to the fact that students who are not from the dominant culture are not aware of the rules and norms of that culture. Some may come from cultures in which questioning (especially of elders) is not encouraged and where inquiry is not supported. Obviously, to help these children cross over from the culture of home to the culture of school, the rules and norms of the new culture must be explained carefully and visibly, and the students must be helped to take responsibility for their own learning. You can find specific help in a recent NSTA publication by Ann Fathman and David Crowther (2006) entitled *Science for English Language Learners: K–12 Classroom Strategies.* Also very helpful is another NSTA publication, *Linking Science and Literacy in the K–8 Classroom*, especially Chapter 12, "English Language Development and the Science-Literacy Connection"(Douglas and Worth 2006). Add to this array of written help two more books: *Teaching Science to English Language Learners: Building on Students' Strengths* (Rosebery and Warren 2008) and *Science for English Language Learners: K–12 Classroom Strategies* (Fathman and Crowther 2006). Finally, an article from *Science and Children* (Buck 2000) entitled "Teaching Science to English-as-Second Language Learners" has many useful suggestions for working with ELL students.

I can summarize as best as I can a few ideas and will also put them into the teacher background sections when appropriate.

Experts agree that vocabulary building is very important for ELL students. You can focus on helping these students identify objects they will be working with in their native language and in English. These words can be entered in science

notebooks. Some teachers have been successful in using a teaching device called a "working word wall." This is an ongoing poster with graphics and words that are added to the poster as the unit progresses. When possible, real items or pictures are taped to the poster. This is visible for constant review and kept in a prominent location, since it is helpful for all students, not just the ELL students.

Many teachers suggest that the group work afforded by inquiry teaching helps ELL students understand the process and the content. Pairing ELL students with English speakers will facilitate learning since often students are more comfortable receiving help from peers than from the teacher. They are more likely to ask questions of peers as well. It is also likely that explanations from fellow students may be more helpful, since they'll probably explain things in language more suitable to those of their own age and development.

Use the chalkboard or whiteboard more often. Connect visuals with vocabulary words. Remember that science depends upon the language of discourse. You might also consider inviting parents into the classroom so that they can witness what you are doing to help their children to learn English and science. Spend more time focusing on the process of inquiry so that the ELL students will begin to understand how they can take control over their own learning and problem solving.

The SIOP model (Echevarria, Vogt, and Short 2000) has been earning popularity lately with teachers who are finding success in teaching science to ELL students. SIOP is an acronym for Sheltered Instruction Observation Protocol. It emphasizes hands-on/minds-on types of science activities that require ELL students to interact with their peers using academic English. You can reach the SIOP Institute website at *www.siopinstitute.net*. While it is difficult to summarize the model succinctly, the focus is on melding the use of academic language with inquiry-based instruction. Every opportunity to combine activity and inquiry should be taken and all of the many types of using language be stressed. This would include writing, speaking, listening, and reading. There is also a strong emphasis on ELL students being paired with competent English language speakers so that they can listen and practice using the vocabulary with those students who have a better command of the language.

In short, the difference between most other ESL programs and Sheltered Instruction is that in the latter, the emphasis is on connecting the content area learning and language learning in such a way that they enhance each other rather than focusing on either the content or the language learning as separate entities. In many programs it is assumed that ELL students cannot master the content of the various subjects because of their lack of language proficiency. Sheltered Instruction assumes that given more opportunities to speak, write, read, talk and listen in the context of any subject's language base, ELL students can master the content as well as the academic language that goes with the content.

Teachers also need to be more linguistically present during classroom management tasks. They need to talk with students to make sure they are interpreting their inquiry tasks and learning how to explain their observations and conclusions in their new language. The teacher's role includes making sure students are focused by reminding them to write things down and to help them discuss their findings in English. As I said before, it is not only the ELL students who need to work on their academic language but all students who need to learn that science has a way of using language and syntax that is different than other disciplines. All students can benefit from being considered Science Language Learners.

And now, on to the stories that I hope will inspire your students to become active inquirers and enjoy science as an everyday activity in their lives.

references

Buck, G. A. 2000. Teaching science to English-as-second language learners. *Science and Children* 38 (3): 38–41.

Calkins, L. M. 2000. *The art of teching reading.* Boston: Allyn and Bacon.

Campbell, B., and L. Fulton. 2003. *Science notebooks: Writing about inquiry.* Portsmouth, NH: Heinemann.

Cervetti, G. N., P. D. Pearson, M. Bravo, and J. Barber. 2006. Reading and writing in the service of inquiry-based science. In *Linking science and literacy in the K–8 classroom,* ed. R. Douglas and K. Worth, 221–244. Arlington, VA: NSTA Press.

Douglas, R., and K. Worth, eds. 2006. *Linking science and literacy in the K–8 classroom.* Arlington, VA: NSTA Press.

Echevarria, J., M. E. Vogt, and D. Short. 2000. *Making content comprehensible for English language learners: The SIOP model.* Needham Heights. MA: Allyn and Bacon.

Fathman, A., and D. Crowther. 2006. *Science for English language learners: K–12 classroom strategies.* Arlington, VA: NSTA Press.

Gee, J. P. 2004. Language in the science classroom: Academic social languages as the heart of school-based literacy. In *Crossing borders in literacy and science instruction: Perspectives on theory and practice,* ed. E. W. Saul, 13–32. Newark, International Reading Association.

Joyce, J. 1922. *Ulysses.* Repr., New York: Vintage, 1990. Page reference is to the 1990 edition.

Keeley, P., F. Eberle, and C. Dorsey. 2008. *Uncovering student ideas in science, volume 3: Another 25 formative assessment probes.* Arlington, VA: NSTA Press.

Keeley, P., F. Eberle, and L. Farrin. 2005. *Uncovering student ideas in science, volume 1: 25 formative assessment probes.* Arlington, VA: NSTA Press.

Keeley, P., F. Eberle, and J. Tugel. 2007. *Uncovering student ideas in science, volume 2: 25 more formative assessment probes.* Arlington, VA: NSTA Press.

Keeley, P., and J. Tugel. 2009. *Uncovering student ideas in science, volume 4: 25 new formative assessment probes.* Arlington, VA: NSTA Press.

Lee, O. 2005. Science education and student diversity: Summary of synthesis and research agenda. *Journal of Education for Students Placed At Risk* 10 (4): 431–440.

Padilla M. J., K. D. Muth, and R. K. Padilla. 1991. Science and reading: Many process skills in common? In *Science learning: Processes and applications*, ed. C. M. Santa and D. E. Alvermann, 14–19. Newark, DE: International Reading Association.

Palincsar, A. S., and S. J. Magnusson. 2001. The interplay of firsthand and text-based investigations to model and support the development of scientific knowledge and reasoning. In *Cognition and instruction: Twenty-five years of progress*, ed. S. Carver and D. Klahr, 151–194. Mahwah, NJ: Lawrence Erlbaum.

Postman, N. 1979. *Teaching as a conserving activity*. New York: Delacorte.

Reiss, M. J. 2002. Reforming school science education in the light of pupil views and the boundaries of science. *School Science Review* 84 (307).

Rosebery, A. S. and B. Warren, Eds. 2008. *Teaching science to English language learners: Building on students' strengths*. Arlington, VA: NSTA Press.

Winokur, J., and K. Worth. 2006. Talk in the science classroom: Looking at what students and teachers need to know and be able to do. In *Linking science and literacy in the K–8 classroom,* ed. R. Douglas and K. Worth, 43–58. Arlington, VA: NSTA Press.

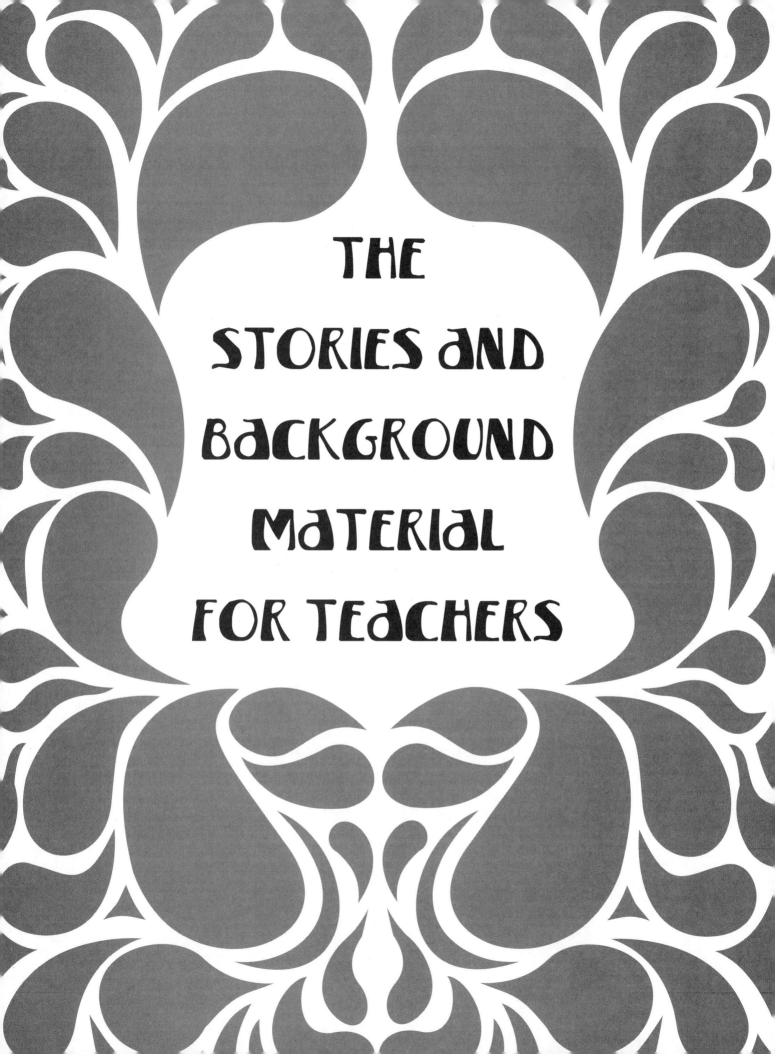

THE STORIES AND BACKGROUND MATERIAL FOR TEACHERS

PHYSICAL SCIENCE AND TECHNOLOGY MATRIX

Stories

Basic Concepts	The Magic Balloon	Bocce, Anyone?	Grandfather's Clock	Neighborhood Telephone System	How Cold Is Cold?
Energy	X	X	X	X	X
Energy Transfer	X	X	X	X	X
Conservation of Energy		X			X
Forces	X	X	X		
Gravity	X	X	X		
Heat	X				X
Kinetic Energy		X	X		
Potential Energy		X	X		
Position and Motion		X	X		
Sound				X	
Periodic Motion			X	X	
Waves				X	
Temperature	X				X
Gas Laws	X				
Buoyancy	X				
Friction		X	X		
Experimental Design	X	X	X	X	X
Work		X	X		
Change of State					X
Time		X	X		

Basic Concepts	The Magnet Derby	Pasta in a Hurry	Iced Tea	Color Thieves	A Mirror Big Enough
Forces	X				
Properties of Matter	X	X	X	X	
Energy	X	X	X		
Changes in State					
Heat and Temperature		X	X		
Structure of Matter			X		
Properties of Materials	X				
Light Energy				X	X
Molecules	X	X	X		
Changes of State			X		
Chemical Bonds		X	X		
Energy Spectrum				X	X
Color Spectrum				X	
Thermodynamics		X	X		
Reflection				X	X
Refraction				X	
Energy Transfer	X	X		X	X
Temperature		X			

continued

Basic Concepts	Warm Clothes?	The Slippery Glass	St. Bernard Puppy	Florida Cars?	Dancing Popcorn
Forces	X		X	X	X
Experimental Design	X	X	X	X	X
Scientific Inquiry	X	X	X	X	X
Properties of Matter	X	X	X	X	X
Energy	X	X		X	X
Changes in State		X			
Properties of Materials	X			X	X
Heat and Temperature	X	X			
Structure of Matter		X		X	X
Properties of Materials	X			X	X
Molecules	X	X		X	
Changes of State		X		X	
Chemical Bonds				X	X
Chemical Change				X	
Thermodynamics	X	X			
Energy Transfer	X	X			
Temperature	X	X			
Changes in Weight and Mass			X	X	
Buoyancy					X
Density					X

Basic Concepts	Sweet Talk	Cooling Off	Party Meltdown	The Crooked Swing	The Cookie Dilemma	Stuck!
Melting	X		X			
Dissolving	X					
Temperature	X	X	X			X
State Change	X	X	X			
Mixtures	X	X			X	
Solvent	X					
Solute	X					
Heat	X	X	X		X	X
Thermal Energy	X	X	X		X	X
Thermometers		X				
Calorimeters		X				
Conduction		X	X			X
Equilibrium		X	X			
Thermal Conductivity			X			X
Periodic Motion				X		
Problem Solving	X	X	X	X	X	X
Model Building		X		X		
Problem Analysis	X	X	X	X	X	X
Creativity				X	X	
Systems	X	X	X	X	X	X
Chemical Reactions					X	
Friction						X
Static Friction						X
Kinetic Friction						X
Net Force						X
Force						X
Interaction	X	X	X	X	X	X

CHAPTER 5
GRANDFATHER'S CLOCK

It was tall and skinny. Once it had been carried through the doors between the porch and the living room, it sat almost wedged between the floor and ceiling. It had a lovely face and delicate hands. In a way, it looked almost human and not a piece of furniture. The word *beautiful* came to Mary's mind. Her parents called it a grandfather's clock but her grandparents had not owned it as far as she knew. It had come to them from an aunt of her dad's who had

died recently and willed the clock to them. Mary's parents were quite excited about it—something about its being 200 years old and in the family for a long time and other stuff. Grownups seemed to think old things were really cool. Mary couldn't quite figure out why old things were cooler than brand-new things, but whatever! The grandfather's clock was now in a place of honor, sitting against the wall and looking really big in their small house.

The clock was made of dark wood with a long narrow window in front. This window could be opened and inside there was a kind of metal pole that hung down from somewhere near the top of the clock. You could touch the pole. It had a brass dish about the size of a small saucer attached to it at the very bottom end. Mary's parents called the pole thing a pendulum. When you pulled the pendulum to one side and let it go, it kept swinging back and forth and the clock part up top made tick-tock noises. If it went long enough, you could see the hands on the face of the clock move. You also had to wind the clock with a key about once a week so the pendulum would go on swinging and the hands would go on moving. The hands of course told the time the old-fashioned way, not like the neat digital face they had on other clocks. Mary guessed that the clock was pretty special to be working so well after 200 years of ticking and tocking. She had a digital alarm clock that hadn't lasted a year before it broke.

Two weeks passed and Mary made an observation. "Mom," she said, "the grandfather's clock is always running slower than the other clocks in the house."

"I noticed that too, Mary," replied her mother. "We have to move the hands ahead every day but it always runs slow. The next day we have to do it again and it never keeps good time. We looked for a button or switch to make it go faster but can't find any."

"The pendulum seems to make the clock go. Maybe it needs to swing faster," offered Mary. "But, how do we do that?"

"Maybe the dish on the bottom of the pendulum is too heavy," suggested Mom. "If it's too heavy, it could slow down the swing time."

"Or the pendulum swings too far from side to side—it takes too long to make a swing. If we could make it take shorter swings, it would go faster."

Mary shared her problem with her teacher, Ms. Patel, the next day. "It's a beautiful old clock," complained Mary, "but it doesn't keep good time, so in a way, it's useless."

"Why don't you set the clock to go faster?" asked Ms. Patel.

"How? We can't find any switches or buttons!" replied Mary. "We think the long pole that comes down from the top has something to do with how fast the clock goes but we can't seem to make the pole change speed."

"That pole and the bob on the bottom is called a pendulum," Ms. Patel explained to the whole class. "They swing in regular patterns but we have to know more about them in order to change how they move.

"Let's make some pendulums out of string and washers," suggested Ms. Patel. "We can test these and see if we can find ways to speed them up or slow them down. So, for a start," she said as she drew the pendulum on the board, "What parts of the pendulum can we change? And how can we find out if changing these parts is what makes a difference in how fast they swing?"

Later that week, after experimenting with the pendulums in class, Mary went home and fixed the clock. Now it keeps perfect time but if it doesn't someday, Mary and her family know just how to fix it. It really is simple—when you know how.

NATIONAL SCIENCE TEACHERS ASSOCIATION

PURPOSE

The main purpose of studying the pendulum in this story is to provide a vehicle for finding and sorting out variables and designing a study for discovering the variable that controls the period (the time for a back-and-forth swing) of the pendulum. The physics of the pendulum is much too sophisticated for young children and will wait for later years. On the other hand, it will come as a surprise to most students, and possibly to adults, that the only variable that makes a difference in the period of the pendulum is the length of the pendulum. The period is defined as the time it takes for the pendulum to make one complete swing, forth and back.

If possible obtain the October 2006 issue of *Science and Children* and read the featured article "Inquiry on Board." This article by Helen Buttemer shows how, using easily constructed visual aids, you can visually guide the planning, conducting, and analyzing of experiments such as the one required in this story. Dr. Buttemer makes the set up and design of an experiment clear to students of all ages by putting variables on sticky notes and moving them through the design process so that students can participate in the process and see the results. It will make a difference in your students' understanding of experimental design. I cannot recommend it highly enough.

RELATED CONCEPTS

- Periodic motion
- Time
- Variables
- Fair tests
- Analysis
- Period of the pendulum
- Hypothesis
- Controls
- Data
- Conclusions

DON'T BE SURPRISED

This activity will bring out many preconceptions including (1) the weight of the pendulum affects the period and (2) the size of the swing affects the period. Another outcome of the activities may be the discovery that the pendulum may be used as a timing device. It seems so counterintuitive that the weight does not affect the period that your students may not believe their own data. The investigation may have to be done as a demonstration and any deviation may be an excuse for them to challenge the result. Their expectation will be that the further the pendulum swings or the heavier the pendulum bob is, the shorter the period.

CONTENT BACKGROUND

Mary's solution to taming the unruly grandfather's clock is a very simple one. The pendulum must be shorter in order to swing more often in a given period of time.

Actually the word *period* is an important one here since the time taken for the pendulum to make one swing forward and back to its original position is called its period.

When children are ready for terminology they may be introduced to the terms *independent* or *manipulated variable* (the variable that is modified, e.g., the length of pendulum, the weight of the bob, or the amplitude of the swing). The *dependent* or *observed variable* is the variable that is measured for possible change. In this case it is the period of the pendulum. Children in grades 5–8 are ready for this kind of terminology.

The only adjustment needed to lessen the period is shortening the pendulum. In a clock, the pendulum bob, the weight at the end of the pendulum, is raised to shorten the period or lowered to increase the period. In effect, this adjustment changes the center of gravity of the entire system having the same effect as changing the length of the rod. With the shortening of the pendulum, the period is also shortened and the pendulum system takes less time to swing to and fro. Since the pendulum is attached to the clock gears, the more swings in a given time period causes the gears to move more quickly and the hands of the clock to move more rapidly—therefore we say that the clock speeds up. The lowering of the bob would have the opposite effect, slowing down the mechanism and the clock. The pendulum length is actually measured from the pivot point to the center of mass of the pendulum. If one is using washers for a bob, the center of mass is probably in the center of the washer, or close enough to this point for all practical purposes.

The pendulum is one example of a system that exhibits what we call periodic motion. Periodic motion simply means that the motion of objects in a system moves in a predictable way, which is usually cyclical in nature. Other examples would be a vibrating object such as a guitar string or tuning fork, the Moon's motion around the Earth, the Earth's motion around the Sun, or the Earth's rotation on its axis. Therefore, learning about periodic motion has implications for many natural phenomena. It is a big idea or conceptual scheme, which can be used in many situations to help us understand models, which in turn explain the world around us. In the story "Where are the Acorns?" the movement of shadows during the day or over the seasons is used as an indicator of what appears to be the periodic motion of the sun as it appears to move across the daytime sky from dawn to sunset. Constellations exhibit periodic motion in the northern and southern hemispheres. We have constellations that only appear in the winter and others that are only seen in the summer. The constellations appear to move in predictable patterns across the sky during the night due to the rotation of the Earth. Planets such as Venus and Mars move predictably among the stars because they have their own periodic motion around the Sun. One of the most important aspects of periodicity is that it helps us to predict happenings and to build models of the universe, which in turn help us to explain how things work.

It might be important here to reemphasize the term *system*. A system is a collection of interconnected parts (or objects) that interact with each other. In many animal bodies we have organs that make up digestive systems, circulatory

NATIONAL SCIENCE TEACHERS ASSOCIATION

systems, nervous systems, and so on. In plants there are tissues that constitute water conducting systems, leaves, and roots. In the universe, we have solar systems, intergalactic systems. In nature, we have ecosystems and in weather we have the atmosphere. They all have in common the fact that the system is a whole made up of parts and that these systems behave according to certain rules. The most important rule is that if you change one part of the system, the entire system responds and changes in some way. For example, if in an ecosystem a plant or animal is removed, the entire system is changed to accommodate its removal. If a predator is removed, its prey will increase in number and perhaps eat more vegetation, which in turn will affect the food supply for other animals. You will find that looking at nature as a series of systems can be very useful.

From the story line, it becomes apparent that the students need to work with pendulums and find out what can be done to the pendulum system to change the number of swings the pendulum makes in any given time period or the period of the pendulum. If you as the teacher do this activity before trying it with the students, you will want to figure out how you will identify and test the variables involved. From the story, the clues can be identified from the conversation between Mary and her mother. Identified were the length of the pendulum, the weight on the pendulum bob, and the distance the pendulum swings. In physics, the latter would be called the amplitude of the swing. What we now have is a set of variables that have to be tested against the problem from the story of how to change the pendulum's period. The period is usually defined as the time it takes for the pendulum to swing from one side and back to that side again—i.e. back and forth. Since the back-and-forth swing of the clock's pendulum has been tentatively identified as the keeper of the time on the clock, the number of swings in any given time period must be changed by modifying the pendulum system. A system is defined as a group of objects interacting with each other. In this case, the system includes the pendulum bob and the connecting rod. When you make a pendulum, I suggest that you use a tongue depressor, available from your doctor's office or from most pharmacies, a thin string about 50 cm long, a paper clip and some washers, available from your workshop or a local hardware store. Figure 5.1 shows the pendulum system and its parts.

You will notice that the tongue depressor has been cut so that there is a split running lengthwise for about 2–3 cm. The string slides into this slot, and it can be

Figure 5.1 The pendulum system

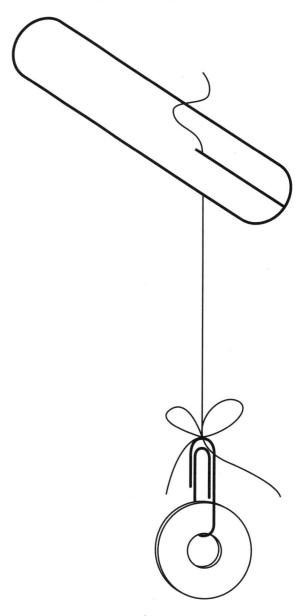

pulled up and down to change the length of the string easily. The clip is bent to make a hook so that the washers can be added and subtracted easily, and the clip is tied to the other end of the string. The tongue depressor is then taped to the desk or table, sticking out far enough so that the string does not rub against the table and swings freely.

Now that you have the pendulum, you must decide how each of the variables relates to the period of the pendulum. This of course is the purpose of the inquiry and will result in the answer for Mary as to how to "set" her clock. You must find a way to test each of the variables while keeping the others unchanged. Let us suppose that you are going to test the effect of the weight of the bob. Your hypothesis would be either, "The weight of the bob will change the period of the pendulum" or "The weight of the bob will not change the period of the pendulum." This means that the length of the string and the size of the swing must be kept constant while you are testing the effect of the weight of the bob. You might decide to let the pendulum swing for 15 seconds and see how many periods the pendulum makes. You will probably want to repeat your experiment five or more times to be sure that any error you might make would be nullified. You could take the average of the five trials and throw out any data that were exceptionally offtrack. Next you would add a washer or two and repeat the experiment. Your result might be surprising! There would be no difference, no matter how many washers you added. Your conclusion would be that the mass of the bob does not affect the period of the pendulum. Your evidence would be in your data and the analysis of those data would bear out your conclusion.

Next you might try to see if the amplitude of the swing has any effect. Again you state your hypothesis. You keep the number of washers and the length of the string constant and try different spots from which to release the bob. Again you try each spot five times and record your results. Surprise again? No difference in the period regardless of where you release the bob. Logically, the pendulum must swing faster in order to make a longer round-trip in the same amount of time. That leaves only one variable left to try, the length of string. You state your hypothesis regarding the length of string and period change and then do the experiment using the same design for acquiring data. This time, you see some differences. The shorter the string, the more swings you count in 15 seconds. The longer the string, the fewer swings you get in 15 seconds. Your conclusion would be that the length of the string affects the period of the pendulum. Your data back up your conclusion. You can now complete the story and solve Mary's problem. Actually, the pendulums of grandfather's clocks do not have a way of changing the length of the rod, but you can shorten or lengthen the pendulum system by raising or lowering the bob, which in essence does the same thing as changing the length of the pendulum since physicists have found that the real length of the pendulum is measured from the pivot point to the center of the bob. Looking back, you have managed to isolate the variables in the system and found a way to test each of the variables individually while keeping the other variables constant. The data were analyzed and conclusions made using the data to corroborate the conclusions. The

new understanding was then applied to the situation in the story, which amounts to an application of learning to a new situation. All steps of the inquiry process have been covered. See Chapter 1 again to review the essentials of the inquiry process for students.

related Ideas From The National Science Education Standards (Nrc 1996)

K–4: Abilities Necessary to Do Scientific Inquiry
- Ask a question about objects, organisms, and events in the environment.
- Plan and conduct a simple investigation.
- Employ simple equipment and tools to gather data and extend the senses.
- Use data to construct a reasonable explanation.
- Communicate investigations and explanations.

5–8: Abilities Necessary to Do Scientific Inquiry
- Identify questions that can be answered through scientific investigations.
- Design and conduct a scientific investigation.
- Use appropriate tools and techniques to gather, analyze, and interpret data.
- Think critically and logically to make the relationships between evidence and explanations.

related Ideas From Benchmarks For Science Literacy (aaas 1993)

K–2: Scientific Inquiry
- People can often learn about things around them by just observing those things carefully, but sometimes they can learn more by doing something to the things and noting what happens.
- Describing things as accurately as possible is important in science because it enables people to compare their observations with those of others.
- When people give different descriptions of the same thing, it is usually a good idea to make some fresh observations instead of just arguing about who is right.

3–5: Scientific Inquiry
- Results of scientific investigations are seldom exactly the same, but if the differences are large, it is important to try to figure out why. One reason

for following directions carefully and for keeping records of one's work is to provide information on what might have caused the differences.

• Scientists do not pay much attention to claims about how something they know about works unless the claims are backed up with evidence that can be confirmed with a logical argument.

6–8: Scientific Inquiry

• If more than one variable changes at the same time in an experiment, the outcome of the experiment may not be clearly attributable to any on of the variables. It may not always be possible to prevent outside variables from influencing the outcome of an investigation but collaboration among investigators can often lead to research designs that are able to deal with such situations.

USING THE STORY WITH GRADES K–4

Constructing and testing the pendulums is the main activity in following up on this story. Ms. Patel suggests to the class that they should make and test pendulums to help Mary solve her problem, which is to make the clock tell the correct time. The suggestions for making simple pendulums are given in the content background section above.

We refer you to the *National Science Education Standards* essay on pendulums (NRC 1996, pp. 146–147) for an excellent look at how one teacher uses the task.

This story however, leads into solving the problem of how to fix the clock. Mary needs to find a way to speed the clock up since it loses minutes each day. She has deduced that the pendulum has something to do with the accuracy of the clock and now must find a way to change the period of the pendulum.

Help the children to identify the variables listed in the story. The clues lie in the conversation between Mary and her mother. Both the distance of the swing and the weight of the bob are mentioned as possible problems. Help the children find the third variable, the length of the pendulum, by looking at the pendulums they have built and looking at how many variables could be changed. Once the three have been identified, the design of the experiment can begin. If you can obtain a copy of the *Science and Children* article "Inquiry on Board," the use of Inquiry Boards will help your students understand the use of variables and controls (Buttemer 2006).

Here is your opportunity to conduct a scientific discourse. The children have built the pendulum systems and need to talk about the variables, the fair tests they need to conduct, and agree on the amount of time to use for counting swings. Many will suggest a whole minute, but you may be able to convince them after one trial that one minute is too long and that a shorter time period would be just as accurate. You might want to talk with them about possible errors that can be made (e.g., counting, starting the counting at the same time as the release, and how many swings would constitute a real "difference.") For example, if the

numbers of washers are tripled and a difference of one swing is noticed, would that be enough of a difference to count? You will probably want to talk about how many trials are necessary to be sure you have good data. And of course, you may try to figure out how each of the trial data is going to be recorded. You could use a graphic organizer or worksheet if you feel your students need it. If they can be involved in the design of the sheet, you can avoid children filling in blanks without knowing why they are doing so. Much of this can be recorded in their science notebooks if you give them time to do so and remind them of the various things you have discussed.

My experience is that four students make up a good experimenting group for this activity. One will release the pendulum and say, "go," the second will count the swings, the third will read the clock and say "stop," and the fourth will record the data. When getting materials, the materials can be in different parts of the room and each member of the group can be assigned a part to be retrieved, thus eliminating traffic problems.

Measuring can be a problem for younger children. If your students cannot use a ruler or tape yet, it might be a good time to teach them. Barring their readiness for such a task, you might have them measure from the bottom of the tongue depressor to the middle of the washer hole according to tapes or strings you have made up in advance. I suggest three different lengths to give reasonable data, but in a pinch, two lengths will make the point.

It helps if you have a secondhand clock on the wall or can obtain one and place it where everyone can see. With much younger children, you may have to be timekeeper and have the students do their experimenting in unison. You may want to have a student demonstrate the process and all students count swings just for practice.

Now you are ready for groups to actually experiment. If your students are very independent, you can tell them to test all three variables at their leisure. Remind them to write in their science notebooks a hypothesis for each variable, including results, conclusions, and evidence. If your students need a bit of organization, tell them that the class is going to test, say, weight first and then complete that segment before going on to the next variable. Together you can discuss with the class that they need to state a hypothesis for each variable, record this in their science notebooks, run the tests, draw conclusions, and justify their conclusions on the basis of the data. You may be free, if you are not timekeeper, to rove among the groups and observe their work and help those groups who need some direction.

After all of the data are in and each group has come up with their conclusions, it is time to share as a class. The discourse here can be centered on their findings and how they can use the information they have garnered to see how Mary might have solved her problem. If there are discrepancies in the findings, you can invite the disagreeing parties to perform their experiments again with the class as judge. Usually, little mistakes are picked up and a consensus can be reached. Now they are ready to finish the story and some of their creative literacy

can be used. You might instruct them to finish the story complete with data to substantiate the way Mary could fix her clock. This can go in their science notebooks or in another form you prefer. In conclusion, I would suggest that you go over their procedure with the students so that they think about what they did and stress the vocabulary involved in problem solving and inquiry. You might even challenge them to provide evidence to show that they are able to build a pendulum that will measure 30 complete swings in one minute and thereby building a timepiece.

USING THE STORY WITH GRADES 5–8

I suggest that you read the background material for grades K–4 as well as this section since there are a great number of similarities in the procedure. Your students, being more sophisticated and able to work on their own more than the younger students, will usually give you more options and perhaps a bit more freedom to observe their experimenting, during which time you can assess their growth by watching and listening to their communication with others in their group. I suggest that you work with groups of four just as in the suggestions listed above. The materials and the pendulums would be identical to those used by the younger students. Your students will also be able to measure lengths with rulers and tapes and keep more sophisticated records in their science notebooks. You can tell them that scientists usually measure to the middle of the bob, which will be the middle of the hole in the washers you use. The procedure is basically the same as for younger students with modifications you feel are justified due to the difference in maturity. I have found however, that if older students have not been involved in inquiry before, they sometimes need just as much guidance as do the younger ones, at least for a while. They too have to be reminded about controlling variables and may be introduced to the terms independent or manipulated variable (the variable that is deliberately modified, e.g., the length of pendulum, the weight of the bob, or the amplitude of the swing). The dependent or responding variable is the variable that is measured for possible change, and the controlled variables—the variables that we intentionally keep the same so we can be sure that the manipulated variable alone is responsible for any change in the dependent variable. In this case it is the period of the pendulum that is the dependent or responding variable. Children in grades 5–8 are usually ready for this kind of terminology. It will also contribute to their ability to read literature about experiments with understanding.

You may want to use graphic organizers with your students if it seems necessary but be sure that they keep track of their work in their science notebooks so that they have a record of their thinking and their activity. They are now in a position to finish the story and talk about and write about how Mary fixed her clock to keep good time. If you are fortunate enough to have a small pendulum clock, the

students can try out their solutions on the clock (e.g., make it go faster or slower). Barring this, find a musical metronome, which can do the same thing. I suggest that, as in the case of the younger students, you ask your students to construct a pendulum that keeps time at a given rate. This will offer you another chance at an assessment of their learning.

related BOOKS anD NSTa Journal articles

Buttemer, H. 2006. Inquiry on board. *Science and Children* 43 (2): 34–39.

Driver, R., A. Squires, P. Rushworth, and V. Wood-Robinson. 1994. *Making sense of secondary science: Research into children's ideas.* London and New York: Routledge Falmer.

Keeley, P. 2005. *Science curriculum topic study: Bridging the gap between standards and practice.* Thousand Oaks, CA: Corwin Press.

Keeley, P., F. Eberle, and L. Farrin. 2005. *Uncovering student ideas in science: 25 formative assessment probes* (vol. 1). Arlington, VA: NSTA Press.

Keeley, P., F. Eberle, and J. Tugel. 2007. *Uncovering student ideas in science: 25 more formative assessment probes* (vol. 2). Arlington, VA: NSTA Press.

references

American Association for the Advancement of Science (AAAS). 1993. *Benchmarks for science literacy.* New York: Oxford University Press.

National Research Council (NRC). 1996. *National science education standards.* Washington, DC: National Academies Press.

CHAPTER 6

THE CROOKED SWING

alan and Serena were walking home from school when they came upon a new garden swing in their next-door neighbor's yard. The swing was attached to the limb of a large tree. (Look closely at the drawing above so that you can see the way the swing was hung.) The two kids could not resist trying it out so they asked their neighbors, an older couple named Mr. and Ms. King, who were out doing yard work, if they minded. Ms. King answered their request with a kindly smile.

"Certainly you may use it. But I think you should know that we've found a problem with it. You'll see when you try it. Maybe you can help us to solve the problem."

"Thank you. We'll do our best."

Allan sat on the swing on one side, and drew it back and let it swing for a while.

"Hey, I see the problem," he said. "It swings crooked, not back and forth like a normal swing. Maybe if you got on with me, Serena, the extra weight will help."

Serena got on the swing next to him and the result was the same. The swing would just not swing straight.

"Hey," she said, "I wonder if it has anything to do with the swing being a kind of pendulum? We've been studying them in school. Maybe there is something wrong with it."

"Well, there's a way to make the swing higher off the ground. We can shorten the chains and see if that will help," said Allan.

"Okay," said Serena, and they tried to shorten the swing by raising it a few links of chain on both sides.

"Now let's try it," said Allan.

They did and got the same results.

"Rats," said Serena," I thought that might do it. I guess I need to learn a little more about pendulums. I thought I knew enough, but this is different in some way. Maybe we ought to try to make a model of this swing and see what makes it go crooked."

In a few days, they again knocked on their neighbor's door and said, "We think we know what your problem is with the swing. And we think we can help you fix it."

(The author wishes to thank Dr. Alan Feldman of the University of South Florida for the idea of the crooked swing story.)

NATIONAL SCIENCE TEACHERS ASSOCIATION

PURPOSE

This story has two purposes. One is to apply what is known about pendulums to a new problem, and the other is to use technical skills to solve a problem. The swing operates on the principles of periodic motion and the crooked branch, upon which the swing is hung, presents a technical problem looking for a solution.

RELATED CONCEPTS

- Periodic motion
- Model building
- Creativity
- Problem solving
- Analysis of problems
- Engineering-product improvement

DON'T BE SURPRISED

Students may not see the relationship between what they know about pendulums and the problem in the way the swing is hung from the crooked branch. People often have difficulty seeing a problem as a connection of parts. The swing is a system and the relationship between the parts of the system is relevant to solving the problem.

CONTENT BACKGROUND

Students need to know something about pendulums in order to see the problem of the crooked swing. The swing is a *system* made up of the chair, the chains that support it and the tree limb from which the chains are suspended. This is, in essence, a coupled pendulum, each end of the swing being a simple pendulum and responding to the laws of *periodic motion*. Periodic motion is any motion that repeats itself and has an identical time interval called a *period*. The period is defined as the time it takes for a regularly occurring motion to complete one cycle. This definition includes the motion of the planets around the Sun, the movement of shadows throughout a day and the pendulum in a grandfather's clock. It could also include waves in water, a bouncing ball, or the vibrations of a tuning fork. Obviously it also includes a swing, as in this case, and it is the periodic motion of the two ends of the swing that must be synchronized in order for them to move together. Another way to put it is that the periods of the two ends of the swing must be equal for the swing to move in a straight path. If the period of one pendulum on one end of the swing is not the same as the other, one end will swing faster/slower than the other, resulting in a crooked path.

Here is a quick review about pendulums. Check out the story called "Grandfather's Clock" (chapter 5 of this book), in which a girl tries to find out how to get her new clock to keep time correctly. This story and teacher material can be

of great value to you in preparing to teach this concept. A *pendulum* is a system consisting of a point where a rod or string is attached; at the end of the rod or string is a weight called a *bob*. Thus, the system swings back and forth when energy is applied to the pendulum so that it swings in a consistent arc. The variables that can be changed are: the weight of the bob, the length of the pendulum from swing point to the center of the mass of the bob, and the height of the release point of the swing (called *amplitude*). The vital questions about pendulums are: does the weight of the bob, the size of the arc of the swing, or the length of the system have any effect upon the period of the pendulum? It turns out that only the length of the pendulum changes the period. This is the principle behind the workings of a grandfather's clock or any pendulum clock. There is usually a small threaded nut at the bottom of the bob that can be manipulated to raise or lower the bob, changing the period of the pendulum and therefore affecting the timekeeping mechanism of the clock. Lengthening the pendulum will slow it down and shortening it will speed it up.

The term *system* is an important scientific concept. A system is a group of related objects or parts that interact with each other. We have examples in our body: circulatory and respiratory systems; in astronomy: planetary and intergalactic systems; and we have examples in nature: soil and plant tissue systems and the larger *ecosystem*. One important aspect of a system is that all parts are interconnected so that a change in one part of the system has an effect on all other parts of the system. For instance in the Everglades, aquarium fish have been added, sometimes unwittingly, to the natural ecosystem and thus have changed the ecology. These fish—oscars, cyclids, tilapia, and other exotic species—have disrupted the food chain and the environment so that the native fish populations have suffered. Emphasizing this point of interconnectedness with your students is very helpful because it is a very important and all-encompassing conceptual scheme that can increase understanding across the curriculum, even with nonscientific systems like politics and finance.

Systems are classified as open or closed. *Open systems*, such as the Earth, solutions, and ecosystems, allow substances to enter or leave the environments (which are probably systems in their own right). In a *closed system*, the materials that make up the system are enclosed in some way so that matter cannot enter or leave. An example of a closed system would be a nail in a moist environment enclosed in a container. Here, the only elements available to the objects in the system are those in the jar. You can get a better understanding by looking at two probes from *Uncovering Student Ideas in Science, Volume 4* (Keeley and Tugel 2009). "Is It a System?" will help students understand more of what constitutes a system and "Nails in a Jar" will show students how a closed system can be defined and used in a classroom as well as in developing a world view. In "Nails in a Jar," you are asked to predict whether, in a closed jar (closed system) rusting nails will cause the system to gain, lose, or conserve weight. In an open system, the nails would gain weight since elements from the outside would add substance to the nails, but in a closed system, only those elements in the jar can be involved in the chemical reaction. Therefore, the mass is conserved and there is no change in the weight of the system.

related ideas from the national science education standards (nrc 1996)

K–4: Abilities Necessary to Do Scientific Inquiry

- Ask a question about objects, organisms, and events in the environment.
- Plan and conduct a simple investigation.
- Employ simple equipment and tools to gather data and extend the senses.
- Use data to construct a reasonable explanation.
- Communicate investigations and explanations.

5–8: Abilities Necessary to Do Scientific Inquiry

- Identify questions that can be answered through scientific investigations.
- Design and conduct a scientific investigation
- Use appropriate tools and techniques to gather, analyze, and interpret data.
- Think critically and logically to make the relationships between evidence and explanations.

related ideas from Benchmarks for science literacy (aaas 1993)

K–2: Scientific Inquiry

- People can often learn about things around them by just observing those things carefully, but sometimes they can learn more by doing something to the things and noting what happens.
- Describing things as accurately as possible is important in science because it enables people to compare their observations with those of others.
- When people give different descriptions of the same thing, it is usually a good idea to make some fresh observations instead of just arguing about who is right.

3–5: Scientific Inquiry

- Results of scientific investigations are seldom exactly the same, but if the differences are large, it is important to figure out why. One reason for following directions carefully and for keeping records of one's work is to provide information on what might have caused the differences.
- Scientists do not pay much attention to claims about how something they know about works unless the claims are backed up with evidence that can be confirmed with a logical argument.

- If more than one variable changes at the same time in an experiment, the outcome of the experiment may not be clearly attributable to any one of the variables. It may not always be possible to prevent outside variables from influencing the outcome of an investigation but collaboration among investigators can often lead to research designs that are able to deal with such situations.

USING THE STORY WITH GRADES K–4

It is important that the children have an opportunity to look at the picture of the swing closely so that they can assess the parts of the system and note anything that does not look normal. If you can either draw the main parts of the swing system on the board or copy the picture, it will help them to analyze the problem. You may want to refer to the *National Science Education Standards* (NRC 1996, pp. 146–147) essay on pendulums to see how one teacher has a class explore pendulum systems. With elementary age children, it is probably best to have them explore simple pendulums first. Consider using the story "Grandfather's Clock" (chapter 5) before pushing on to "The Crooked Swing."

With younger children, you will have to consider whether or not they possess the skills to count and keep records, although all they need to do is count the number of swings within a set time. Young children do play on swings that are pendulums. If these can be modified to shorten both of the supporting chains of one swing so that two swings next to each other can be compared, the idea of two different periods can be illustrated. Then the children can build their own pendulums and investigate their properties. (*Note:* Tire swings are more simplified forms of pendulums since they are suspended from only one cord, therefore, they can never swing crooked.)

A wonderful article on helping students learn how to design inquiries is "Inquiry on Board," in *Science and Children* (Buttemer 2006). It is available online to members of NSTA. This article shows how variables can be identified and moved along a series of posters to form questions and finally to design an investigation. The crooked swing provides a wonderful opportunity for you to help your children look at a pendulum as a system and to identify the separate parts. Asking them which parts could be changed without changing any of the others at the same time will begin to help them see how one goes about setting up an investigation.

My favorite way of setting up inquiry is to create a chart called, "Our Best Thinking Until Now," and ask the children to make statements about which of the variables might change how many times the pendulum will swing back and forth in one minute. Ask for reasons and write their predictions on the chart. Then change the statements to questions and explain that all of these questions can be answered by investigating them. Help them to design investigations that control the variables they are not testing. After testing the pendulums and recording their

results in their science notebooks, you can discuss what they have found. Tell them they can go back to the chart and change any part of their statements that the data have shown need changing. This helps them realize that scientists can learn from predictions that are not correct as well as those that are, and that it is okay to change your mind when confronted with data that convinces you that you should.

If you decide to tackle the problem of the crooked swing with very young children, it is doubtful that they will focus their attention on the crooked branch and see this as the root of the problem. However, teaching is full of surprises! This can be demonstrated on the playground if the chains of the swing can be changed so that one side is longer than the other. But this results in a swing seat that is not horizontal, which may divert children from the point. The neat thing about the crooked swing problem presented above is that the swing itself remains horizontal just like any other porch swing that behaves itself. This fact stresses the importance of the lengths of the two support chains.

Upper elementary children are capable of making working models of the problem and should be encouraged to draw pictures of these models in their science notebooks. I always have materials on hand that can be used to make models. Scraps of wood, string, washers, and tape are usually enough for building working models at their desks. I find that working in groups on this problem is useful since several hands may be necessary to hold parts of the model in place while the testing goes on. Also, in this part of the problem-solving process, more minds at work mean more ideas to be tested.

USING THE STORY WITH GRADES 5–8

Students in the middle grades are perfectly capable of looking at the swing picture, developing strategies to model the problem and find some solutions. They may not have had a chance to work with simple pendulums before and would benefit from working with some now before they try to apply pendulum theories to the new problem. They could follow the ideas suggested above and find out the variable that changes the period of the pendulum through direct experience. They may also need a review in setting up an investigation and controlling variables. It should not take more than one class period to prepare them to consider the problem of the crooked swing. As suggested above, they will benefit greatly by drawing the problem situation in their science notebooks and then working with a real model of the swing. Students seem to work much better in groups both because they need each other's help in manipulating materials and because they need to discuss ideas in a group.

Some will immediately see that the problem lies with the fact that the branch angles upward and will go on to suggest solutions. Most will have had experience with porch swings that were hung from horizontal ceilings, and will want to build a new structure on the limb. Some will suggest building a new free-standing structure on the ground from which to hang the swing. Others will find more creative ways

of hanging the swing or finding ways to make the two suspending chains equal in length. Encourage this creativity by letting them brainstorm possible solutions. A colleague of mine taught me that when a student came up with a solution, I should answer in a positive way, such as, "Great idea! That's *one* way." It works. If you frame the problem in such a way that you ask for multiple solutions, you will find that students will not quit so easily. A reward for the most solutions might encourage them to look at the problem in several ways rather than in just one.

related books and NSTA Journal articles

Keeley, P. 2005. *Science curriculum topic study: Bridging the gap between standards and practice.* Thousand Oaks, CA: Corwin Press.

Keeley, P., F. Eberle, and C. Dorsey. 2008. *Uncovering student ideas in science, volume 3: Another 25 formative assessment probes.* Arlington, VA: NSTA Press.

Keeley, P., F. Eberle, and L. Farrin. 2005. *Uncovering student ideas in science, volume 1: 25 formative assessment probes.* Arlington, VA: NSTA Press.

Keeley, P., F. Eberle, and J. Tugel. 2007. *Uncovering student ideas in science, volume 2: 25 more formative assessment probes.* Arlington, VA: NSTA Press.

Keeley, P., and J. Tugel. 2009. *Uncovering student ideas in science, volume 4: 25 new formative assessment probes.* Arlington, VA: NSTA Press.

Konicek-Moran, R. 2008. *Everyday science mysteries: Stories for inquiry-based science teaching.* Arlington, VA: NSTA Press.

Konicek-Moran, R. 2009. *More everyday science mysteries: Stories for inquiry-based science teaching.* Arlington, VA: NSTA Press.

Konicek-Moran, R. 2010. *Even more everyday science mysteries: Stories for inquiry-based science teaching.* Arlington, VA: NSTA Press.

references

American Association for the Advancement of Science (AAAS). 1993. *Benchmarks for science literacy.* New York: Oxford University Press.

Buttemer, H. 2006. Inquiry on board. *Science and Children* 34–39.

Keeley, P., and J. Tugel. 2009. *Uncovering student ideas in science, volume 4: 25 new formative assessment probes.* Arlington, VA: NSTA Press.

Konicek-Moran, R. 2008. *Everyday science mysteries: Stories for inquiry-based science teaching.* Arlington, VA: NSTA Press.

National Research Council (NRC). 1996. *National science education standards.* Washington, DC: National Academies Press.

CHAPTER 7

THE MAGIC BALLOON

It was a wonderful balloon! After spending at least 15 minutes arguing about the balloons for Andy's ninth birthday party, Abby and Paul finally agreed on this balloon, which had "Happy Birthday" spelled out in multicolored fireworks on both sides. It was one of those Mylar jobs, which had to be filled with the gas that made them float for weeks. It also made them try to escape into the clouds if you let go of the string.

The lady at the balloon counter attached it to a tank of gas, turned the knob and the balloon expanded and tugged at her hands. The silver envelope filled with the gas and became slick and smooth without wrinkles. "I'll give you lots of gas," said the saleswoman, "so it will last a long time."

"Thanks," said Abby, "It's a present for a birthday party."

"Be sure to hold on to the string tightly," the lady said as she tied a pretty ribbon around the neck of the balloon.

Clutching the floating silver sphere, the two proudly walked toward the exit with the prize trailing them like a floating dog that had been told to "heel."

It was January and a frosty one at that. Temperatures had been hovering around zero for a week. Abby and Paul stopped at the door and zipped up their jackets and pulled their ski caps down over their ears. Their big sister, Ruth was driving them today and was doing some shopping for herself. Ruth finally met them at the exit door and they all ran through the frosty night to the chilly car.

Once they were strapped in, Ruth started the engine. "Turn on the heat!" commanded Paul in a shivering voice.

"Geez! Wait a bit for this old engine to warm up!" muttered Ruth. "Anyway, with this old car, we'll be home before it gives off any heat." Ruth had just earned her driver's license and their parents were allowing her to use their older car. It had its problems, one of which was a poor heater. But it ran, and it was a safe car.

Abby, holding onto the balloon, glanced up at it as they pulled out of the parking lot and onto the main road.

"Uh, oh!" she said. "We got a bad balloon! It must be leaking." At the next red light, Ruth turned around and saw that the balloon was all crinkly and was not floating like it had before. Paul too, looked disappointed at its condition.

"Better take it back now," he said. "We'll never get to come back again tonight and the party's tomorrow."

"Oh, all right," said Ruth as she reluctantly turned the car around and started back to the mall. In a few minutes they were back and Ruth decided to double-park at the entrance while Paul and Abby returned the balloon. It looked pretty sick by now.

The two children made their way back to the counter but the saleswoman was not there. They looked up at the deflated balloon. They looked at some other balloons they might substitute for the deflated one and after about five minutes, she returned.

"Can I help you with something?" she asked.

"Our balloon is leaking," said Abby.

"Yeah," added Paul. "We'd like a new one."

The woman looked at the balloon and said, "What's wrong? It looks perfectly fine to me!"

Paul and Abby looked up and to their utter amazement saw that she was right. The balloon was as full and plump as it had been when they bought it.

"But, but..." stammered Paul. "Just a while ago it was half flat looking and wrinkled and it wasn't floating or..."

"Did you take it outdoors?" interrupted the lady.

"Sure, we were taking it home," offered Abby.

"That may be a clue to what happened," said the lady winking at them. "Trust me, take it home and see what happens. You won't be disappointed. It's a magic balloon that is always plump when it is indoors."

Reluctantly, the two children went out to the car. Abby turned to Paul and said, "I don't buy the magic stuff, but it sure did leak and refill again once we went inside. What could happen to the stuff inside to make it shrink?"

"At least it seemed to shrink!" said Paul puzzled. "Let's take it home and see what happens. She said to trust her."

With that, the two got into the car and Ruth drove them home. They watched the balloon very carefully the rest of the trip and well into the evening and again the next morning.

Purpose

This is a story that has meaning for anyone who has ever seen a parade with floating balloons or has gone to a celebration where balloons were present. Floating always seems like magic because it appears to be defying the law of gravity. The helium-filled plastic envelopes that reach for the heavens fascinate babies to adults. For this story, the main purpose is to explore the relationship between temperature and pressure of gases, but it may spill over into the concepts of floating and density in older children. It also asks questions about gas being a form of matter that has mass and takes up space. Basically, it revolves around a law developed by French chemist/physicist Jacques Charles in 1787 now known as Charles' law. We'll take a look at how it explains a lot of apparent mysteries concerning balloons and objects that float in the air and hope it stimulates your students to ask a lot of good questions about this phenomenon. Incidentally, in 1783 Jacques Charles ascended to the altitude of 914 meters in a hydrogen balloon of his design. When he landed just outside of Paris, terrified peasants destroyed his balloon. Fortunately, he wasn't hurt. Here was a man, way ahead of his time!

related concepts

- Forms of matter
- Volume
- Density
- Temperature
- Gases
- Float and sink
- Forces
- Energy

Don't Be surprised

Most children and even some adults have a difficult time understanding that gases take up space and that they have mass. They seem to understand that the balloon inflates due to the increase in the amount of air you blow into it or helium that is put into it. Many will balk at the idea that "free" air around them has mass since they walk around in it all day and don't feel its impact on their bodies. They may believe that the gas is warmer since they have been told so often that warm air rises.

In the literacy area, I strongly recommend the book *Le Ballon Rouge* (*The Red Balloon*) by Albert Lamorisse (1956). The story follows a lonely little boy and a red balloon in their mutual friendship in Paris. There is also a movie from which the book was made. The movie is short and has no dialog. The story is a metaphor for friendship and loneliness and should open the door to a lively discussion, whether read to the children or shown as a movie. It is a classic in either form.

National science teachers association

CONTENT BACKGROUND

If you have ever had the opportunity to experience what the kids in the story have, you might have noticed the same reaction of the balloon to changes in temperature. If not, you can make it happen right in your own kitchen and be prepared for what your students bring to your class after hearing the story. If you were to put a balloon filled with any gas, even that from your lungs, into the refrigerator or freezer for a short time, you will notice that the balloon takes up less space; has less volume after being chilled. It is much more fun with a helium filled balloon because it adds the dimension of floating and provides another property to observe. The balloon will not pull at the string as much after being chilled and may appear wrinkled due to the lack of volume the gas takes up in the Mylar envelope. Given that most classrooms do not have refrigerators, you may want to try this story during the cooler part of your school year so that the outdoors can do the cooling. Most students will ask questions about the gas in the balloon and these questions will give you an insight into their preconceptions, most of which will not jibe with the scientific explanation. For example, working with the questions raised in the story may give them some insight into the behavior of gases since they will be able to see changes in the shape of the balloons. Most of these observations cannot be explained adequately without accepting the concept that gases actually possess mass and take up space.

Older students may also be more interested in why the helium balloon floats and how much weight it can pull to the ceiling. Others may want to see if they can put enough weight on the string to allow the balloon to float and yet not rise to the ceiling. Can it be done? Try it and see.

Picture in your mind that the balloon is filled with molecules of gas, which constantly strike the surface of the inside of the balloon and push it into an inflated state. When the balloon is subjected to differences in temperature, the amount of motion of these molecules changes. For example, when the temperature of the gases in the balloon is raised, the molecules move faster and faster and constantly strike the inside surface of the balloon with greater force and the balloon expands since it is stretchable and pliable. Conversely, when the temperature of the gas inside the balloon is cooled, the molecules move more slowly and thus strike the balloon's surface with a lesser force and the balloon deflates accordingly. This is what happened to the balloon as the children went outside into the cold winter air. It reversed itself when they went back into the warm store and waited for the salesperson.

Students may also wonder why the balloon filled with helium floats on the air in the room. Also related to the inflation size of the balloon is the fact that the balloon filled with a gas that is less dense than the surrounding air will receive an upward, buoyant force on it by the surrounding air and this pushes it upward. By density we mean the amount of mass an object has in relation to its volume. Density is a property of any substance. No matter what the size of a piece of, say, lead, its density is the same. In a larger piece of any given substance, the mass obviously increases but the ratio of mass to volume, or density, remains the same. Think of

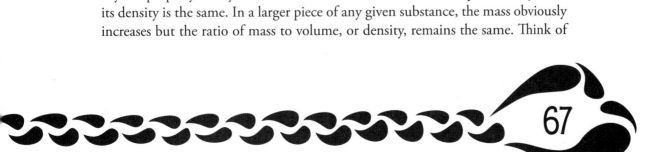

the balloon and the helium inside it as a closed system. Nothing gets in or out but the gas inside the balloon can exert more pressure on the elastic balloon and make it swell and take up more space. The gas inside can also exert less pressure on the elastic balloon, and make it take up less space. As the size of the balloon/gas system decreases, its combined density increases since it still weighs the same but now takes up less space. Thus, it receives less force in an upward direction and succumbs to the force of gravity. This is the same principle that explains why things float or sink in water. If you have ever tried to push an inflated ball down into the water, you can feel the force of the water pushing upward. Think of a balloon floating in the atmosphere that is pushing it upward in the same way. The larger the ball, the more force you can feel. Think of the difference between pushing a tennis ball under water and a large beach ball. The secret is in the relationship between the volume and the mass of the object and that of the "liquid" in which it is floating.

Most helium-filled balloons will slowly lose helium through the Mylar and eventually lose enough volume so that they no longer float. This phenomenon is something that just about everyone has witnessed but is not directly related to this story.

Hot-air balloons follow the same principle. As the air is heated, it expands due to its increased pressure, filling the bag with air. The pressure of the molecules in the heated air is also increased and forces the bag to billow out and take up more space. At some point, the upward force exceeds the mutual pull of gravity and the balloon rises. In order for the balloon to stay aloft, the pilot must also keep the air warm by lighting the flame in the cockpit or basket. Should the air cool and the pressure in the bag decrease, the balloon would slowly sink toward the Earth. In fact, when the pilots want to land, they open a valve in the top of the balloon releasing air and decreasing the volume.

Should some of you wish to delve more deeply into the physics of the gas laws, you will find some interactive material at the following website: *www.chm. davidson.edu/ChemistryApplets/GasLaws/Gasconstant.html.*

NATIONAL SCIENCE TEACHERS ASSOCIATION

related ideas from the national science education standards (nrc 1996)

K–4: Properties of Objects and Materials
- Objects have many observable properties, including size, weight, shape, color, temperature, and the ability to react with other substances. Those properties can be measured using tools, such as rulers, balances, and thermometers.
- Materials can exist in different states—solid, liquid, and gas. Heating or cooling can change some common materials such as water from one state to another.

5–8: Properties and Changes of Properties in Matter
- A substance has characteristic properties, such as density, a boiling point, and solubility, all of which are independent of the amount of the sample.

related ideas from benchmarks for science literacy (aaas 1993)

K–2: The Structure of Matter
- Objects can be described in terms of the materials they are made of (clay, cloth, paper, etc.) and their physical properties (color, size, shape, weight, texture, flexibility, etc.).
- Things can be done to materials to change some of their properties, but not all materials respond the same way to what is done to them.

3–5: The Structure of Matter
- Heating and cooling cause changes in the properties of materials. Many kinds of changes occur faster under hotter conditions.

6–8: The Structure of Matter
- Equal volumes of different substances usually have different weights.
- Atoms and molecules are perpetually in motion. Increased temperature means greater average energy of motion, so most substances expand when heated.

USING THE STORY WITH GRADES K-4

Children in the early years normally are not ready for excursions into density but are certainly capable of noticing the difference in the shape and size of party balloons in different temperatures. You may use either helium balloons or common balloons inflated with regular air. If you were fortunate enough to have a difference between indoor and outdoor temperatures in your region in the fall or winter, this would be a good time to try this story. If not, placing the balloons in a refrigerator or freezer for a while will result in the same shrinking. You may get questions about what further heating will accomplish. Holding the balloon in a warm place will have an effect as well. You might hold it carefully over a warming plate (careful, not too close!) or hold it under a stream of warm water. Younger children, though they have a difficult time believing that air has mass and takes up space around them, are ready to accept that a gas will blow up a balloon and that it is inside the balloon. It is possible, but difficult to weigh an air-filled balloon before and after inflation on a scale such as a triple-beam balance. The difference will be small but it does show a difference in mass due to the air that has been added. Depending on the age level, you may also want to ask them if they think that the shrunken balloon will weigh less, more, or the same as the original balloon. They may be surprised to note that mass does not change in a closed system. Some may realize that if nothing is added or taken away, the result in mass is the same before and after cooling. If you can get a helium balloon, the result of the activity will be more dramatic but regular balloons react the same as far as size is concerned. Variables to investigate may include time in the cooler; size of the balloon; thickness of the rubber in the balloon; color of the balloon; and temperature differences, which can be accomplished by comparing freezer with refrigerator cooling. Many opportunities for controlling variables exist here and experience in talking through the experimental designs is also a valuable part of the activity. If you are using helium-filled balloons, you can time the differences it takes for the balloon to rise from the floor to the ceiling. For this you would need a stopwatch. And don't forget to have the children write in their science notebooks!

I recommend your reading Bill Robertson's *Science and Children* article entitled "Why Does Air Expand When You Heat It and Why Does Hot Air Rise?"

Latex can be a serious allergen, so it would be prudent to send a note home before this lesson to confirm that all students can handle the balloons safely.

USING THE STORY WITH GRADES 5-8

Many of the same kinds of questions will probably arise from the older children. The fact that the balloon reacts so readily to temperature gives fast feedback for experiments. These children need a great deal of work with talking about science and designing experiments around gas volume and temperature. If they are capable of measuring the circumference of balloons before and after chilling, graphing

of their results is a must. Some teachers have had success in attaching a strip of paper around the diameter of the balloon. When cooled, the paper might fall off the balloon or if heated, the paper might tear if the balloon stretches enough. The graph could match time in the freezer and circumference of the balloon (the paper or string). Also, if there is a thermometer in both the freezer and the refrigerator, you can graph temperature with circumference. Remember also the option of warming the balloon further to measure differences. Once again, I recommend your reading Bill Robertson's *Science and Children* article entitled "Why Does Air Expand When You Heat It and Why Does Hot Air Rise?"

Now comes the question of floating in the atmosphere and overcoming the force of gravity with an upward force. Density is a difficult concept for many students to understand, mainly because they have to keep in mind two properties of a substance at once. These are volume and mass, not only of the object in question but also of the medium in which they are floating or sinking. Help them think of the atmosphere as a "liquid" in which the balloon floats. Its mass/volume ratio is less than that of an equal amount of room air, by volume, when it floats. When its mass/volume ratio becomes more than an equal amount of air by volume, it does not float. This is because the volume decreases due to the reduction in temperature or the natural loss of gas over time. You can feel the resisting force when you push down on a helium-filled balloon. It feels the same as pushing a hollow ball under water. This kinesthetic addition to learning can be powerful for many students. Even though the water's density makes this upward force greater than that of air, the feeling is so similar that most students get the point.

You might also be interested in giving your students a probe ("Comparing Cubes" or "Floating High or Low") from *Uncovering Student Ideas in Science, Volume 2* (Keeley, Eberle, and Tugel 2007). Either or both probes will give you a good idea about where your students are in their understanding of density.

Your students might also be interested in inquiring how much mass a balloon can lift off the ground and how the balloon's change in volume relates to this ability. This is a fairly indirect way of looking at the balloon's volume but comparing the heated balloon's or room temperature balloon's lifting power to the cooled balloon's lifting power can be done and graphed easily.

RELATED BOOKS AND NSTA JOURNAL ARTICLES

Burns, J. 2007. Bubbles on a soda can: A demonstration of Charles Law. *Science Scope* 30 (5): 60–64.

Driver, R., A. Squires, P. Rushworth, and V. Wood-Robinson. 1994. *Making sense of secondary science: Research into children's ideas.* London and New York: Routledge Falmer.

Keeley, P. 2005. *Science curriculum topic study: Bridging the gap between standards and practice.* Thousand Oaks, CA: Corwin Press.

Keeley, P., F. Eberle, and L. Farrin. 2005. *Uncovering student ideas in science: 25 formative assessment probes* (vol. 1). Arlington, VA: NSTA Press.

Keeley, P., F. Eberle, and J. Tugel. 2007. *Uncovering student ideas in science: 25 more formative assessment probes* (vol. 2). Arlington, VA: NSTA Press.

Robertson, B. 2006. Why does air expand when you heat it and why does hot air rise? *Science and Children* 44 (1): 60–62.

references

American Association for the Advancement of Science (AAAS). 1993. *Benchmarks for science literacy.* New York: Oxford University Press.

Keeley, P., F. Eberle, and J. Tugel. 2007. *Uncovering student ideas in science: 25 more formative assessment probes* (vol. 2). Arlington, VA: NSTA Press.

Lamorisse, A. 1956. *Le Ballon Rouge* (*The Red Balloon*) Films Montsourise.

National Research Council (NRC). 1996. *National science education standards.* Washington, DC: National Academies Press.

Robertson, B. 2006. Why does air expand when you heat it and why does hot air rise? *Science and Children* 44(1): 60–62.

NATIONAL SCIENCE TEACHERS ASSOCIATION

CHAPTER 8
BOCCE, ANYONE?

Leo loved to play bocce, a game that has been popular for over 7,000 years. It is said that the Egyptians played it using polished round stones. Leo had a lovely, flat, green lawn in back of his house and the whole family played at least several times a week. The game is played with a set of four balls, or *bocce*, which are rolled toward a smaller ball called the *pallino*. Whichever player has a bocce that is closest to the pallino, scores points. There are of course rules for playing and scoring. The bocce balls are about 4½ inches (11.4 cm) in diameter and weigh about 3 pounds (1.26 kg). The pallino is only 1¾ inches (4.5 cm) in diameter. The pallino is first thrown from a line on one end of the bocce field and the players then roll their bocce from the same line to get as close as they can to it. At the beginning of each round the pallino is thrown and ends up in different places for each round.

Leo had a best friend named Paul and Paul would have liked to play too but there was a problem. Paul had special needs because he was in a wheelchair and had limited use of his hands as well as his legs. Leo wanted to play bocce with Paul, but Paul was unable to roll the ball. Both boys thought and thought about how they could play bocce together because they spent hours together every day after school and on weekends.

One day when Leo was out practicing his bocce, they had an idea. What if, instead of rolling the bocce by hand, he rolled the ball down a ramp? Could they aim the ramp and do something to the ramp so that the bocce balls would roll different distances? Would it work? Only one way to find out, so they found a plywood board in the garage and got some bricks to prop it up and tried releasing the bocce from the top of the board.

"I could do that," Paul thought, " 'cause I can reach the top of the board and let the ball roll toward the pallino." They agreed on a rule that they had to release the ball from the top of the board (they would now officially call it a ramp) and not push it but just let it roll out onto the lawn. They would both use the ramp in the same way. If it became necessary, Leo would follow Paul's directions on moving the ramp up or down or to one side or the other.

But now they had another problem. Neither of them had much experience with ramps and they had to figure out how to aim it and how to get the ball to go as far as they wanted it to go. And then, to make matters even more complicated, Paul's cousin Amy decided to get Paul some bocce balls of his own and they were sure that Paul's weighed more than Leo's. Naturally, Paul wanted to use his own. Would that make a difference? Only way to find out was to try, and so they did. They solved their problems and had many hours of bocce together and both of them got so good that Paul and Leo were about even in games won. I wonder what they found out and how they got the bocce balls to go just where they wanted them to go?

NATIONAL SCIENCE TEACHERS ASSOCIATION

PURPOSE

Rolling objects are always fascinating for children. This story gives children an opportunity to find patterns in the process of rolling objects down ramps. Shades of Galileo! Since he was one of the first to actually do investigations by what "natural philosophers" of his day would have called "playing," he opened a new era in science investigations.

RELATED CONCEPTS

- Force
- Kinetic energy
- Gravity
- Ramps (simple machines)
- Velocity
- Friction

- Potential energy
- Work
- Momentum
- Speed
- Acceleration
- Inertia

DON'T BE SURPRISED

The physics of motion is beset with rules often described as, "under ideal conditions." Well, in the real world it is usually impossible to create ideal conditions and so we have to be a little circumspect when it comes to recreating the results of ideal laws. Yet, we still are able to revisit many of the laws of motion and draw some conclusions based on these laws developed by Sir Isaac Newton in the 17th century. Many of your students will believe the common misconception that heavy objects travel fArther than light objects when rolled down a ramp. On some surfaces (after they leave the ramp) they do, if the surface is smooth and provides little friction. They may also believe that heavier balls travel faster down a ramp than lighter balls and therefore reach the end of the ramp first, which is not true. This follows the common misconception that if two objects of different masses are dropped (in the absence of air resistance differences), the more massive one will strike the ground first.

The balls arrive at the same time if released at the same time. But don't give it away to the kids before they have a chance to figure it out for themselves by experimenting with objects! The boys in the story, and your students, are in for a surprise when they begin rolling objects down a ramp. There are so many questions that will be raised for them to test that they could be busy for some time.

CONTENT BACKGROUND

Isaac Newton (1642–1727) said that an object will continue to do whatever it is doing unless it is acted on by something and that something we call a *force*. Actually, what he really said was that "Every body continues in its state of rest, or of uniform

motion in a straight line, unless it is compelled to change that state by forces impressed upon it." But the first statement is easier to remember. It is known as Newton's first law of motion or sometimes as the *law of inertia*. Inertia is the property of all objects that causes the object to resist change. The amount of inertia in any object is dependent on its mass. The more mass an object has, the more difficult it is to start it in motion, change its direction, or stop it from moving. Whether an object is standing still or moving at a high rate of speed, only a force will change its position or its motion. A lot of what the object does depends upon its position. If you are holding a ball in your hand and release it, the ball and the earth are attracted to each other by the force of gravity and since the Earth is so much more massive, the ball does the falling toward the center of the Earth. This is something we have all experienced since the days when we would throw our strained carrots out of the high chair just to see them hit the floor. Newton was clever enough to work out the mathematics of it and form general rules, defining forces and how they work. Forces are pushes and pulls, kicks, blows, punches, and so on, some working through direct contact and others through a distance, without touching. Kicking a soccer ball is an example of direct contact and gravity and magnetism are examples of non-touching forces acting through a distance. For this reason students may believe that force and energy are synonymous.

Many people, including a majority of children, believe that after an object is put into motion by a force, such as throwing a ball into the air, a force needs to continue acting on the object to keep it moving. This is a common misconception. Physicists like to work with ideas that can be quantified and so like to use the term *momentum*. Actually once an object is in motion it has momentum which is related to its mass and its velocity. An object with more mass or more velocity will have more momentum. Think about the difference between stopping a moving locomotive and a moving tennis ball if both are travelling at the same speed. Also consider a small bullet travelling at a high rate of speed. Since both mass and velocity (speed in a direction) are related here, a small bullet going at a tremendous speed has a great deal of momentum and can cause a great deal of damage to anything that stops its motion. You may have felt the sting when you caught a swiftly thrown ball. The mass was small but the velocity was large, thus the pain.

So what is the difference between inertia and momentum you may be asking. Well, inertia is mainly determined by the mass of the object, which in turn explains an object's resistance to change. More mass, more resistance. Momentum is this mass in motion in a specific direction and thus is defined as mass × velocity. For example, if someone kicks a soccer ball, the ball has a velocity and a mass. The goalie feels this momentum when she makes a save. The soccer ball however never changes its mass throughout the episode. The momentum was the only thing that changed when the ball was caught or deflected.

Balls placed at the top of a ramp will have the force of gravity pulling on them straight down, which will cause them to move down the ramp. But another force is usually also at work, friction. There is friction from the air they pass through and also from the surface of the ramp itself. The amount of this friction will depend on the smoothness of the balls and the smoothness of the ramp itself.

National Science Teachers Association

There are also two types of energy at work in the implications of this story, potential energy and kinetic energy. Potential energy describes the energy that exists in the balls because of their position and due to the fact that they had been moved to the top of the ramp against the force of gravity. This endowed them with the potential to do work. This energy was transformed into kinetic energy, the energy of motion, as they move down the ramp.

But physics is based on ideal laws and they state that in an ideal situation, bocce balls should travel the same distance once they leave the ramp regardless of mass. (Friction is a force because it is capable of altering motion). In the classroom, children can compare the different results by rolling two solid balls of different masses down a ramp that empties out onto either a carpet or a slippery floor surface. The heavier ball will experience more friction on a carpet and the two balls should roll almost the same distance before stopping. However, when the balls leave the ramp onto a slippery surface such as a linoleum, tile, or wooden floor, there will be less friction and the more massive ball will probably travel farther. Friction is less on a slippery surface than on a carpeted surface. This difference is actually a way to show the effect of friction and how it can affect the behavior of rolling or sliding objects.

Galileo first experimented with rolling objects on ramps in the 16th and 17th century because it helped him to explain what happens to falling objects. It turned out that falling objects and rolling objects behave the same and rolling balls down ramps allowed Galileo to have more control over the speed of the balls so that he could measure their motion more easily. Both dropped and rolled balls are affected by the force of gravity in a similar way and move from a higher to a lower position, following the same laws of gravity that Newton later explained.

I cannot possibly explain the whole of the physics of motion here. If you want to really find a good source on this topic, I suggest that you obtain copies of Bill Robertson's books *Force and Motion* and *Energy*, from his *Stop Faking It!* Series (2004, 2005) available from NSTA press. These books in the series will help you to become a more confident teacher of these topics.

related ideas from the National Science Education Standards (NRC 1996)

K–4: Position and Motion of Objects

- The position of an object can be described by locating it relative to another object or the background.
- An object's motion can be described by tracing and measuring the position over time.
- The position and motion of objects can be changed by pushing or pulling. The size of the change is related to the strength of the push or pull.

5–8: Motions and Forces

- The motion of an object can be described by its position, direction of motion and speed. That motion can be measured and represented on a graph.
- An object that is not being subjected to a force will continue to move at a constant speed and in a straight line.
- If more than one force acts on an object along a straight line, then the forces will reinforce or cancel one another, depending on their direction and magnitude. Unbalanced forces will cause changes in the speed or direction of an object's motion.

related ideas from Benchmarks for science literacy (aaas 1993)

K–2: Motion

- Things move in many different ways, such as straight, zigzag, round and round, back and forth, and fast and slow.
- The way to change how something is moving is to give it a push or pull.

3–5: Motion

- Something that is moving may move steadily or change its direction. The greater the force, the greater the change in motion will be. The more massive an object is, the less effect a given force will have.
- How fast things move differs greatly. Some things are so slow that their journey takes a long time; others move too fast for people to even see them.

6–8: Motion

- In the absence of retarding forces such as friction, an object will keep its direction of motion and its speed. Whenever an object is seen to speed up, slow down, or change direction, it can be assumed than an unbalanced force is acting on it.

USING THE STORY WITH GRADES K-4

As usual, after reading the story to the class, ask them what they already know about how far rolling objects will travel after going down a ramp, and record these on the "Best Thinking" chart. They will probably bring up the idea of rolling different weights of balls before you need to suggest it. It is important to use two balls that differ only in mass. A good example would be a metal ball and a wooden or glass marble with the same diameter. With young children it is a particularly

great opportunity to talk about fair investigations and to help them to identify and control the many variables involved. Some teachers find it useful to demonstrate the "wrong" methods to the children and ask them if what she is doing is fair. For example, if you push one ball and release the other or let one go before the other, the children will immediately cry "foul." The height of the ramp or length of the ramp must be controlled and then questions should pop up about what differences the height or angle of the ramp might cause. If you have access to the teachers' manual of the unit "Balls and Ramps," from the *Insights Program,* published by Kendall/Hunt, you might want to read it for some insight into what the children might suggest trying. Lessons 11 through 13 are particularly pertinent to this story. The unit as written is designed for first grade. The extent to which you are willing to take the children's questions and the curiosity of the children themselves will dictate how long you continue on this journey into the physics of motion. Remember to include time for recording their findings in their science notebooks and plenty of time for discussion of their activities and results. The vocabulary you decide to include will again depend on the class' willingness to learn and use new words. Introducing the vocabulary in the context of the activity will help the children make the connection between word and context.

I suggest that you read the next section for your own benefit so that you can see where the concept is going over the years. It will help you understand more about the physics of motion even though you will probably not use the ideas directly with your students at this time.

USING THE STORY WITH GRADES 5–8

I suggest you read the section above about using the story with grades K–4. After reading the story, ask the class to pair up and share with their partner what they think the boys will have to do to make the bocce go where they want them to go. Record the results of these conversations on the "Best Thinking" chart and if possible turn them into questions. It is more likely that the older children will scoff at the boys' naiveté, but you should ask them to provide some examples from their experience or some evidence to support their opinions. The combination of the pair-share activity and the recording of their ideas should provide enough doubt to merit some experimental design to prove their points. The main points addressed by the story are inertia forces and momentum. You may want to find out what forces they think are acting on the balls at various points down the ramp. Some students will identify gravity pulling the ball downward and friction where the ball meets the ramp or even friction from the air. Most will think that at the bottom of the ramp a force is still "in" the ball. This is a common misconception, even among adults. But, as you may know, at this point, the only force acting on the rolling ball is friction, which now begins to change the motion of the ball and bring it to a halt. To paraphrase Newton, an object only changes its motion (or lack of it) when a force affects it. What the ball has at the bottom of the ramp is *momentum*, a word

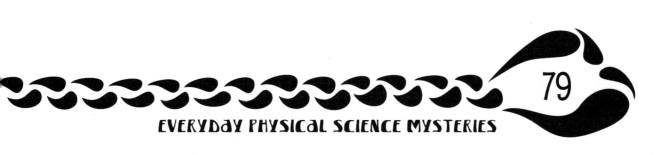

coined to account for the continued motion of the ball as it spends its allotment of kinetic energy as it battles friction, which tries to slow it down.

Students know that it is harder to stop a moving bowling ball than it is to stop a moving tennis ball. They also know that it is harder to push a bowling ball into motion than it is a tennis ball. Physicists call this property of an object inertia. Inertia is the tendency of an object to keep on doing what it is doing, sitting on a couch or moving at 1,000 miles per hour. This brings us to the famous equation, $F = ma$, where, F = force, m = mass, and a = acceleration. Acceleration is defined as any change of motion or direction. Thus, slowing down, to a physicist, is as much acceleration as going faster. Such is the confusing language of science and the even more confusing everyday language, where drivers call the gas pedal an accelerator, which makes our cars go faster. Acceleration can also mean changing direction so when you turn on a curve, you are accelerating!

But let's go back to the $F = ma$ equation. If you make a simple algebraic change in the equation by dividing both sides by m, you find that $a = F/m$ or in other words the amount of acceleration a moving object has is directly proportional to the force applied and inversely proportional to the mass of the object. Plainly stated, this means that the acceleration of an object increases if you apply a bigger push and decreases if you use the same amount of push on a heavier object. This explains the bowling ball/tennis ball phenomenon mentioned above.

Again, it is best to use two balls of different mass but of the same diameter. When the balls reach the end of the ramp, the heavier ball will have more momentum and by the same token it will be subject to more friction once it touches the floor it rolls upon. The lighter ball will have less momentum but will be subject to less friction once it touches the floor. The harder the ball presses on the floor, the more friction can be expected. But, on a carpeted floor, the friction will be more pronounced than on a slick floor due to the rougher, thicker pile of the carpet. The heavier ball will experience more friction due to its greater mass and the lighter ball less, due to its lesser mass. Thus the balls should go about the same distance, once leaving the ramp. On the smoother surface, like a slippery floor, the amount of frictional force is less effective and the more massive ball with its greater momentum will travel farther than the lighter ball, despite Newton's "ideal law of physics." Paul and Leo will have to consider these ideas when they adjust the ramp to control the bocce and consider the frictional function of the grass.

Basically, what has happened here is that you have allowed the students to voice their preconceptions about moving and rolling objects; you then help them to design experiments to test these theories; they obtained their results and discussed them as a class; you explained the ideas of forces from the point of view of the physicist; they worked together to integrate their results with Newton's laws of motion; and then they tried to apply their new understanding by manipulating the several variables. More potential energy is added to the balls by increasing the height and angle of the ramp, since you must raise the balls higher. Different frictional forces are observed by trying different surfaces at the base of the ramp. The students have tested hypotheses, gained information about physical laws from the

teacher and then accommodated their prior thinking to new situations using the ideas gained through both learning about the laws and evaluating them through experimentation.

Students may notice that the heavier and lighter balls both reach the end of the ramp at the same time and this may confuse them. They may even ignore the "ties" and concentrate on the situations where one ball does reach the end of the ramp slightly before the other. You must make them consider the ties as data. Students at any age may consider this acitivity as a race and concentrate on the "winner" and ignore the fact that the ties are data that tell them that there really is no winner. This means of course that many trials, perhaps 10, must be run so that data can be accumulated for analysis.

One can only conclude that the balls are caused to move, equally down the ramp by the force of gravity regardless of their mass. This has been shown over and over again by dropping two balls of different masses and noticing that they hit the floor at the same time. Try it and you will see. How can this be? I prefer to explain it in terms of inertia. The heavier ball resists the force of gravity more than the lighter ball because it has more inertia or resistance to moving. In essence, they balance out and reach the floor at the same time. It is actually more complicated than that but at this grade level it should be enough to leave the students pondering this strange but universal phenomenon. They should in the meantime have gained a much better understanding of the phenomenon of motion and forces.

An added activity might be to have the children invent games using balls and ramps, perhaps providing targets at which to aim the balls. They may think of others but it will give them a chance to apply their knowledge in their own ways.

related books and nsta journal articles

Adams, B. 2007. Energy in motion. *Science and Children* 44 (7): 30–35.

Education Development Center. Balls and ramps. *Insights.* Kendall/Hunt: Dubuque, IA.

Keeley, P. 2005. *Science curriculum topic study: Bridging the gap between standards and practice.* Thousand Oaks, CA: Corwin Press.

Keeley, P., F. Eberle, and L. Farrin. 2005. *Uncovering student ideas in science: 25 formative assessment probes* (vol. 1). Arlington, VA: NSTA Press.

Keeley, P., F. Eberle, and J. Tugel. 2007. *Uncovering student ideas in science: 25 more formative assessment probes* (vol. 2). Arlington, VA: NSTA Press.

King, K. 2005. Making sense of motion. *Science Scope* 28 (6): 22–26

McCarthy, D. 2005. Newton's first law: A learning cycle approach. *Science Scope* 28 (5): 46–49.

Robertson, W. C. 2002a. *Energy: Stop faking it! Finally understanding science so you can teach it.* Arlington, VA: NSTA Press.

Robertson. W. C. 2002b. *Force and motion: Stop faking it! Finally understanding science so you can teach it.* Arlington, VA: NSTA Press.

Robertson, W. C. 2007. What exactly is energy? *Science and Children* 44 (7): 62–63.

Science on Display. 2000. Roller coasters: Thrilling physics. *Science Scope* 24 (1): 56–57.

Stroup, D. 2003. Balloons and Newton's third law. *Science Scope* 27 (5): 54.

Van Hook, S., and T. Hoziak-Clark. 2007. Spring into energy. *Science and Children* 44 (7): 21–25.

references

American Association for the Advancement of Science (AAAS). 1993. *Benchmarks for science literacy.* New York: Oxford University Press.

National Research Council (NRC). 1996. *National science education standards.* Washington, DC: National Academies Press.

Robertson, W. C. 2002. *Energy: Stop faking it! Finally understanding science so you can teach it.* Arlington, VA: NSTA Press.

Robertson. W. C. 2002. *Force and motion: Stop faking it! Finally understanding science so you can teach it.* Arlington, VA: NSTA Press.

CHAPTER 9
COOLING OFF

Juan and Esteban were doing their homework at the kitchen table on a weekend afternoon. Juan was reading the problem out loud as he often did. "If you had a half cup of water in a Styrofoam cup at 25°C and added it to another half cup of water in a Styrofoam cup at the same temperature, what would be the temperature of the whole cup of water?"

He paused to think a moment. "You know, Steve, it seems to be common sense that if you added the same temperature water to the cup, the temperature would stay the same. But that seems to be too easy."

"Yeah, you're right. That must be a trick question. You can't trust teachers not to pull a fast one on you," said Esteban.

"Maybe you add the two temperatures together so that it comes out to be 50°C."

"I guess that might work. But 50°C seems awfully hot! Somehow that doesn't sound right. I know how to *cool* off my cocoa. I just add cold milk, but I know it isn't the same temperature as the hot cocoa 'cause the milk just came out of the refrigerator."

"Right," said Juan, "and then you just have to add a little bit to cool off the cocoa."

"Now, look at the next problem. It asks us to predict the temperature of mixing two different amounts of water at the same temperature," said Esteban. "That seems like the same problem as the other one but now we have to think about the amounts."

"I can just imagine that things are going to get tougher as we go along! See. Look at the next problem. They want us to predict what the temperature would be after we mix equal amounts of water with different temperatures. I can see where this is going!"

"Well, does the amount of water make a difference?" asked Juan. "I think the temperature does, but then thinking about the amount of water messes up my brain."

"Maybe we can just do the mixing of the water and get the answers right from the thermometer."

"Hey, good idea, dude!" said Esteban. "We have everything we need to answer these questions right here in the kitchen. Then we can figure out a way to predict the answers to the other problems without having to measure everything! At least I think we ought to be able to do it. Tell you what, you use those aluminum cups over there, and I'll use these glass cups and we'll just find out by doing it. We don't have any Styrofoam cups, but what difference could that make?"

NATIONAL SCIENCE TEACHERS ASSOCIATION

PURPOSE

The main purpose of the story is to help students understand the dynamics of heat energy transfer. Another purpose is for them to understand how to make predictions and gather and graph results from experimental data.

RELATED CONCEPTS

- Heat
- Thermal energy
- Calorimeters
- Equilibrium

- Temperature
- Thermometers
- Conduction
- Graphing

DON'T BE SURPRISED

Your students will probably not be able to distinguish between heat and temperature as concepts. It took over 2,000 years for humankind to understand the difference, but your students have your guidance and the result of many centuries of research to come to a conclusion acceptable to the current scientific community. They may also not comprehend that heat is a transfer of energy from a body that has a higher amount of thermal energy to one that has less. And it is entirely possible that even at the middle school level, students will not realize that the scientific community stresses the fact that it is heat (thermal energy) that moves and not cold (the lack of or possession of lower thermal energy).

Children have many misconceptions about heat and temperature. For one thing, children may think that heat emanates from things that warm us, like mittens and blankets. An article about this misconception (Watson and Konicek 1990) is available online at *www.exploratorium.edu/ifi/resources/workshops/teachingforconcept.html.*

CONTENT BACKGROUND

The two boys in the story are typical students who try to solve the teacher who gave the homework rather than the problem itself! Actually, children, when presented with problems that have several numbers, often resort to adding them together (or subtracting, multiplying, or dividing them) without giving thought to the actual situation being presented. When children believe that heat and temperature are synonymous, the problems presented by the homework in the story are difficult to solve.

Heat

Children and adults alike think of heat as merely a number; the higher numbers mean hot and the lower ones, cold. Heat and cold are separate entities that fight it out in a substance until one wins. We often add to this confusion by telling them

to close doors to "keep the cold out." Sloppy use of language conflicts with the language of physics. We are dealing with the laws of thermodynamics here in this story and as complex as that sounds, the reasoning is quite simple. Heat is defined as the transfer of kinetic energy from a warmer body to a cooler one. Heat is often called *thermal energy* and is a property of all matter since there are always moving molecules in matter. While physicists tell us that absolute zero is reached when no more heat can be extracted from matter, they have not been able to reach that point in the laboratory. They've come close, but there's been no cigar.

We've all been raised on the statement "energy can be neither created nor destroyed," the first law of thermodynamics, and this makes sense. Energy can, however, be converted from one form to another. And it can be moved from one place to another: through conduction (touching), radiation (from radiating bodies like the Sun or an electric heater), and convection (through currents that move it around).

In the case of conduction, kinetic energy from moving atoms and molecules in one substance pass on their energy to other atoms and molecules in another substance by bouncing into them and giving them a "kick," transferring energy as they do. This transfer will continue until both giver and receiver have reached equilibrium. In fact, it never really stops because the amount of heat exchanged will continue since the temperatures of the bodies involved are constantly changing.

When you stand in the sunlight or near a stove that is giving off heat radiation, you can feel the infrared energy waves reaching you and warming you. All bodies radiate heat to some extent and do not need air as a medium to transfer it. We have evidence of this since the Sun, our source of radiational heat, sends its thermal energy to Earth through almost completely empty space.

To describe convection, it helps to consider an example. If you have a pot of water on the stove and turn on the burner beneath it, the pan will absorb heat from the burner and transfer it by conduction to the water at the bottom of the pan. As the water warms, it becomes less dense than the rest of the water and rises to the top of the pan. The cooler water at the top sinks down to take its place, and is in turn warmed so that it too rises. Meanwhile, the water that rose previously has cooled somewhat, so it sinks and then warms, and so on. A circular current is set up until all of the water shares an equal amount of thermal energy. The same thing can happen in a room, since physicists consider air to behave like a fluid. Convection does not occur in solids.

Temperature

Temperature measures changes in heat. It is a completely arbitrary number that depends entirely on which scale one is using. There are three main temperature scales in use today, the Fahrenheit, Celsius, and Kelvin scales. Each is named for its originator and thus is capitalized:

- Fahrenheit for Gabriel Fahrenheit in 1719 (boiling point of water: 212°F, freezing point: 32°F)

NATIONAL SCIENCE TEACHERS ASSOCIATION

- Celsius for Anders Celsius in 1742 (boiling point of water: 100°C, freezing point: 0°C)
- Kelvin for Lord Kelvin of Scotland in 1848, (absolute zero is 0 K, (−273°C), boiling point of water: 373°C, freezing point of water: 273°C)

Note: *Absolute zero* is defined as the temperature at which no heat can be extracted, or in some circles, the point at which all molecular motion ceases. As we noted before, this temperature has never been reached even in controlled laboratory settings.

Thermometers only became useful for measurement of changes in temperature when Santorio Santorio (1611) added a scale to an instrument called a thermoscope, invented by Galileo in 1596. This had only given indications of a rise or fall in temperature due to the expansion of the substance in which it was immersed. During the following centuries, other instruments to measure heat called *thermometers* were developed, but unless scientists adopted some sort of an agreed-upon *scale* or *calibration* the measurements from these were useless. In 1724, Fahrenheit developed the scale that is still in use today in a very few countries, based on events that were familiar to people and that could frame reference points (like the freezing and boiling points of water). In science, the Celsius scale, which is based on the freezing point of water being 0° and boiling point 100°, thus making calculation easier, is considered the standard scale and was adopted as such in 1948. Lord Kelvin's scale was formed to take absolute zero into account. So the thermometer and the measurement of temperature was less an invention than a series of developments and improvements over the years. They have evolved.

When a thermometer is placed in a liquid or under the tongue, it is really registering its *own* temperature since it has come in contact with molecules that are transferring kinetic energy. In essence, it is a snapshot of the kinetic energy in any given substance in a specific part of the container that holds the substance. It does *not* measure the *total* energy of the substance. An example of what this means follows. A cup of boiling water (100°C) and a single drop from that cup both have the same temperature. I would be willing to place one single drop of that water on my hand without fear of scalding myself. I would not be willing to pour the entire cup of boiling water on my hand, even though both the drop and the cup of water have the same temperature. The amount of heat in the cup of water far exceeds the amount of heat in the drop of water because there is more of it. The heat from the entire cup of water would do serious damage to my hand whereas the single drop would merely cause a pinprick of feeling. This is why measurement of heat is better done with the concept of *calories* or *joules*, which I will explain below. (CAUTION: Do not try this with children! Use it as an example but caution them not to play with boiling liquids in any form. Accidents can happen!)

Oftentimes children, and even adults, confuse heat and temperature because when the heat or kinetic energy in a substance changes, the temperature changes. But temperature measures just kinetic energy, while heat measures the total energy of a substance, including potential energy (more about this below). It was not until Joseph Black, a Scottish scientist explained the difference between heat and temperature in

1761 that science could finally move forward. When scientists thought that the two were synonymous, they were at a loss to explain many phenomena. The discoveries and theories of Joseph Black led the way to progress in the area of thermodynamics.

Measuring Heat

First, let me say again, that all matter is made up of constantly jostling molecules and atoms. Their motion means that there is kinetic energy present in all matter (the energy of motion is known as *kinetic energy*). You cannot see this motion any more than you can see the molecules themselves, but, according to the present theory, all matter is made up of these moving particles, a sort of hidden energy. The more motion, the more heat.

What we refer to loosely as heat is actually *thermal energy*. Thermal energy is the sum total of the energy in any given substance, including the *kinetic* energy in the molecules and atoms and the *potential* energy in the substance (although this can get very complicated and we won't get too deep here). It is very common to refer to a substance as containing heat, but this is incorrect. Matter does not contain heat, but it does have moving molecules: molecular kinetic energy and the potential for more molecular movement if necessary. Heat flows from one thing to another and it is that kinetic energy that is being transferred. This may seem picky but it is an important distinction in thermodynamics. When there is contact between two objects, heat always flows from the substance that has more kinetic energy to the substance that has less. In other words, heat flows from warmer matter to cooler matter. It continues to do so until both bits of matter are at the same temperature. It is then that we can say that they have reached equilibrium.

Thermal energy is measured in an agreed-upon unit called a *calorie*. One calorie is defined as the amount of heat required to raise the temperature of one gram of water to one degree Celsius. If you see the Calorie spelled with a capital C, it is a kilocalorie and is the amount of heat required to raise the temperature of one kilogram of water, one degree Celsius. You may have also seen heat energy measured in *British Thermal Units* or *btu's*. This is the amount of thermal energy needed to heat 1 pound of water to 1 degree F. (Interesting note: The *joule* is now considered to be the international unit of thermal energy, except in the United States. A joule is the force of one Newton moving an object one meter, but this translates into energy as well. Once again, we won't go too deep here—it's just important that you get an idea of the current terminology.)

You may be familiar with the calorie in measuring the food that you eat. Any food has the potential of releasing heat, particularly when it combines with oxygen, either in a flame or in your blood stream. Various kinds of food have different caloric values, which are determined by burning them in a *calorimeter*, an instrument that determines how many grams of water can be raised one degree Celsius, or more important to us, put unwanted pounds on our bodily frames.

We all know that when we touch objects in a room that some feel warmer or cooler than others. If they have been in the same environment for a long time, they have all come to equilibrium and are the same temperature. Yet, when we touch

NATIONAL SCIENCE TEACHERS ASSOCIATION

something, metal for instance, it feels cooler than wood or cloth. Some materials transfer heat more readily than others. Some accept heat more readily than others and by the same token give it up more easily. When we touch an object that transfers heat easily, heat from our bodies flows into that object and our hands feel cooler than when we touch something that does not transfer heat easily. In other words, our hands are not good thermometers—they are easily fooled. By the same token, you cannot feel your own forehead to see if you have a fever since your hand and head are probably the same temperature and no heat flows. If your hands are cold, heat from your forehead will flow to your hand but this is not an indication of the true temperature of your body.

Another example of this difference in heating and cooling capacity is found in your refrigerator. Juices in aluminum cans cool much faster than those in glass containers. Physicists say that aluminum has a lower *specific heat* than glass (*specific heat* is—loosely—a measure of the capacity of substances to hold heat). The aluminum cans allow heat to leave the juice easily while the glass containers don't allow heat to leave quite so fast. However, the reverse is true as well. Once out of the refrigerator, the aluminum cans of juice will absorb heat much faster and have a warmer temperature sooner than glass.

Water has a very high specific heat because it takes a great deal of heat energy to raise its temperature. It loses its heat slowly, which makes it a perfect medium for hot water bottles because the water in the rubber container keeps feet warm for a longer time.

Either way, the laws of thermodynamics are part of your everyday life. Thermal energy and the way that it moves is important in many ways. It is best that we understand it and use our knowledge to save money and energy.

related ideas from the National Science Education Standards (NRC 1996)

K–4: Properties of Objects and Materials

- Objects have many observable properties, including size, weight, shape, color, temperature, and the ability to react with other substances. Those properties can be measured using tools, such as rulers, balances, and thermometers.
- Objects are made of one or more materials, such as paper, wood, and metal.
- Objects can be described by the properties of the materials from which they are made, and those properties can be used to separate or sort a group of objects or materials.

K–4: Light, Heat, Electricity, and Magnetism

- Heat can be produced in many ways such as burning, rubbing and mixing one substance with another. Heat can move from one object to another.

5–8: Transfer of Energy

- Energy is a property of many substances and is associated with heat, light, electricity, mechanical motion, sound, nuclear energy, and nature of a chemical change. Energy is transferred in many ways.
- Heat moves in predictable ways, flowing from warmer objects to cooler ones until both reach the same temperature.

related ideas from Benchmarks for science Literacy (aaas 1993)

K–2: Energy Transformations

- The Sun warms the land, air, and water.

3–5: Energy Transformations

- When warmer things are put with cooler ones, the warm ones lose heat and the cool ones gain it until they are all the same temperature. A warmer object can warm a cooler one by contact or at a distance.
- Some materials conduct heat much better than others. Poor conductors can reduce heat loss.

6–8: Energy Transformations

- Heat can be transferred through materials by the collision of atoms or across space by radiation. If the material is fluid, currents will be set up in it that aid the transfer of heat.
- Energy appears in different forms. Heat energy is in the disorderly motion of molecules.

USING THE STORY WITH Grades K–4

I prefer to find out what my students already think about mixing things of different temperatures and usually give the probe, "Mixing Water," from *Uncovering Student Ideas in Science, Volume 2* (Keeley, Eberle, and Tugel 2007). This probe asks students to predict the resulting temperature when two tumblers containing the same amount of water at different temperatures are mixed. This will tell you if your students are merely manipulating numbers or are aware that the resulting temperature will be somewhere between the high and low temperatures of the two tumblers.

For younger students, a modified probe might ask if the temperature of the mixture will be different than either of the originals. After trying it out with temperatures that are not dangerous to the children's safety, such as room temperature

with cool water, ask them how they think the resulting temperature happened. You can introduce them to the word *heat* and talk about its being transferred from the water in one glass to the water in the other. Since the resulting mixture was warmer than the colder water, you might try to elicit from them that the heat traveled from the warmer to the cooler water.

By asking them to list the things that they know heat up and cool down, you can make a list of objects with which they have had direct experience. Our experience is that the list will look something like this:

- Water heats up when it is in the sunshine.
- Sand heats up when it is in the sunshine.
- Our house heats up when it is in the sunshine.
- Metal things heat up when they are in the sunshine.
- Things cool off when they are in the refrigerator.
- Some things cool off faster or heat up faster than others.

Taking this list and turning the statements into questions that are investigable is a simple task, e.g., Does water heat up when it is in the sunshine? Do some things cool off or heat up faster than others? This sets the stage for investigations, predictions and conclusions. Read the *Science and Children* article "Heating Up, Cooling Down" (Damonte 2005) for more ideas on how to involve students in the mystery of how different materials take in heat energy and transfer it to other things. The author looks at common materials like sand and water to make suggestions about inquiry into heat and especially specific heat differences.

Older elementary students, because they can read and interpret thermometers can quantify the changes in such investigations. Perhaps you have digital thermometer probes that you can use to recover data on temperature change over time. If not, simple thermometers with data recorded in science notebooks will generate wonderful discussions. You can also take the opportunity to introduce them to graphing their results. More will be said about that in the next section for middle school. You may even want to try the calorimeter activity described below with older children.

USING THE STORY WITH GRADES 5–8

Having recently spent a day with a group of talented middle school teachers from Springfield, Massachusetts, investigating the topic of heat and heat transfer, I am prepared to discuss some of the activities and ideas that excited them and which they plan to use in their inquiry activities in their classes. Middle school children have skills that allow them to collect data and graph the results. However, sometimes it is necessary for the teacher to help them interpret graphs. This "teachable moment" often occurs when they have plotted their data and are confused by the result.

After the students have had a chance to try a few different scenarios like those listed in the story, you can ask them if they have any ideas about the direction in which heat moves. This simple calorimeter activity can measure heat transfer from one insulated container to another. The diagram (Figure 9.1) shows how the setup is arranged. Materials for this activity are:

- Two insulated (Styrofoam) cups with foam tops made from scrap foam material. The foam should have two slits, one for a thermometer and the other for the aluminum bar described below.
- One aluminum "bar" made from a folded strip of aluminum foil long enough for the ends of the bar to be immersed in water in both cups.
- Two thermometers long enough to reach the water in each container and also long enough to be read without removal from the container.
- Two cups of 100 cc of water at temperatures approximating 60°C and 30°C, 100 cc of each will be placed in the two separate cups.
- One chart for recording the temperatures of each thermometer at two-minute intervals.
- A copy of the probe for each student.
- A copy of the setup diagram for each group of students.

You will need to heat some water to approximately 60°C for one cup and use room temperature water of approximately 25–30°C for the other. I suggest that children work in groups of three or four. When you are ready to begin, have the students pour the water into the two containers as shown, then put the cover, the aluminum bars and thermometers into place. Have the students take an initial temperature reading in each cup; then record that and the temperatures in each cup at two-minute intervals, keeping the data on a data sheet for use later when they graph their results.

But, before the activity explain to them what they are going to be doing, observing, and finally graphing. Tell them that they are going to see if the energy in one cup influences the temperature of the water in the other cup via the bar that connects them. Then, before the students begin the activity, ask them to take the probe I have written. (See Figure 9.2, p. 94.) It asks them to predict what a graph of their findings will look like. Ask them to discuss their predictions and give reasons for their choices.

Those who understand what is about to happen will lean toward choice (B) because they will predict that the cooler water will be warmed by the heat traveling from the warmer cup via the aluminum bridge. They may still be confused as to why the lines in (B) never meet, but once they perform the activity they will probably touch the aluminum bridge and feel the heat. This is heat that is lost to the atmosphere and so does not make it into the cooler cup. This means that all of the heat energy in the warm cup does not make it into the cooler cup and the actual temperature at equilibrium will be somewhere in between the temperatures shown as the lines in the graph level off and do not change. It would be somewhere around 45°C if no heat were lost. It also shows that it is the heat that is moving since the bridge gets warm and not cool. The class discussion here is very important since it gives those with misconceptions the chance to voice their ideas and to listen to others. I have found that students are more likely to listen to expressed ideas and modify their own if they are from a peer rather than a teacher.

Figure 9.1 Setup for the calorimeter activity. The bar that is embedded in each Styrofoam cup is made from folded aluminum foil wrap. The cups have foam or other insulation on top and the bar and thermometers are inserted through slits in the foam tops.

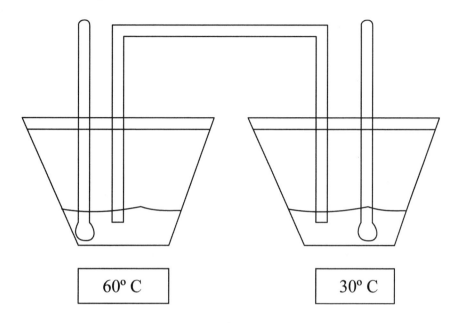

60º C   30º C

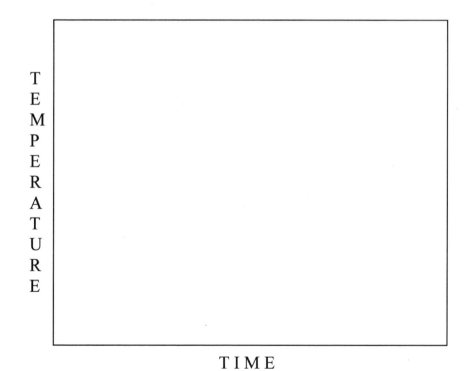

TEMPERATURE

TIME

Figure 9.2 Four students were using two Styrofoam cup calorimeters to find out how heat is conducted from one calorimeter to another. Each cup had water at a different temperature. In one Styrofoam cup, there were 100 cc of wate at 90°C and in the other, the same amount of water at 30°C. An aluminum bar connected the two cups and the water they held. A thermometer was inserted in each cup to record the temperature. Readings of the temperatures were recorded every two minutes and were plotted on a graph, time against temperature. Below are four pictures of possible graphs after 30 minutes of recording. Which of the four graphs do you think most depicts the one the students created after plotting their data? Circle the letter you choose and explain your choice.

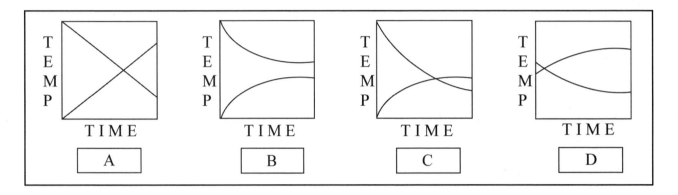

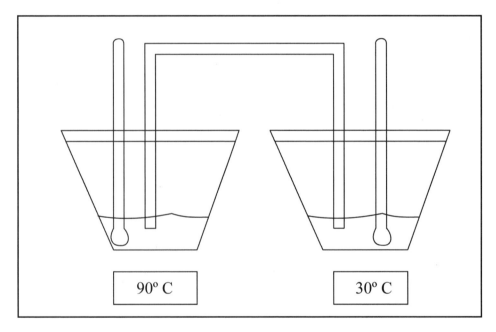

You will notice that the correct graph is the one where the lines never meet but reach equilibrium before the lines touch. It is (B) on the probe. The others are not correct because in (A) and (C) they show the lines crossing, which could never happen due to the impending equilibrium or (D) they start at the same place and both lose and gain heat at the same rate.

This activity improves both the conceptual understanding of heat transfer and students' ability to produce and interpret graphs. They can then finish the story by having the boys come to a conclusion about mixing water. I predict that some student will suggest mixing the two cups of water to see what the resulting temperature is without the aluminum bar setup.

If you would like to continue this investigation, challenge the students to create a setup that will cut down the heat loss due to the inefficiency of the system they just used. This will lead them into the area of finding materials that reduce heat loss, insulators. They will then likely come closer to achieving a graph that is more like ideal conditions.

For a look at how one teacher combined activities on heating and cooling and introduced the idea of specific heat as insulators, see the *Science Scope* article "To Heat or Not to Heat" (May and Kurbin 2003) in the journal archives at *www.nsta.org*.

RELATED BOOKS AND NSTA JOURNAL ARTICLES

Childs, G. 2007. A solar energy cycle. *Science and Children* 44 (7): 26–29.

Konicek-Moran, R. 2008. *Everyday science mysteries*. Arlington, VA: NSTA Press.

Konicek-Moran, R. 2009. *More everyday science mysteries*. Arlington, VA: NSTA Press.

REFERENCES

American Association for the Advancement of Science (AAAS). 1993. *Benchmarks for science literacy*. New York: Oxford University Press.

Damonte, K. 2005. Heating up, cooling down. *Science and Children* 42 (9): 47–48.

Keeley, P., F. Eberle, and J. Tugel. 2007. Mixing water. In *Uncovering student ideas in science, volume 2: 25 more formative assessment probes*, 83–89. Arlington, VA: NSTA Press.

May, K., and M. Kurbin. 2003. To heat or not to heat. *Science Scope* 26 (5): 38–41.

National Research Council (NRC). 1996. *National science education standards*. Washington, DC: National Academies Press.

Watson, B., and R. Konicek. 1990. Teaching for conceptual change: Confronting children's experience. *Phi Delta Kappan* 71 (9): 680–685.

CHAPTER 10
WARM CLOTHES?

Put on your warm coat and mittens," shouted Mom from the living room just as Ian was about to head out the door on his way to school. He knew better than to argue; besides it was windy and cold outside. So Ian reached into the closet and pulled out his fleece-lined jacket and his wool mittens. For good measure he grabbed his ski hat, which was wool too.

"Might as well be really warm if I'm going to look like a preschooler," thought Ian.

But actually when he put the coat and mittens on in the hallway, they felt pretty cold.

"I guess it takes a little time for them to warm up," he thought. "Yeah, and probably it needs to be really cold for them to start putting out heat."

And so Ian headed out the door and down to the school bus stop. There was no hurry since he was a bit early, and he had to stand at the bus stop for a while with the other kids. He was delighted to see that most of them were dressed as warmly as he was. They all had fun blowing out breath and watching it form clouds as it left their mouths and noses.

He did notice that his hands were now quite warm. The rest of him felt pretty cozy too despite the cold wind that blew down the street to where the children stood waiting for the bus.

"I guess I was right," he said to Paulo, who was standing next to him.

"Right about what?" asked Paulo.

"Mittens and coats take a while to start putting out heat after you put them on. They were really cold in the closet, but now that I've had them on for a while, I can feel the heat."

"Mittens and coats put out heat? What are you talking about, dude?" said Paulo. "You got some sort of electric mittens or something?"

"Nah, just ordinary wool mittens, like everybody else's," explained Ian.

"Then what's all this stuff about mittens putting out heat?"

"Well, my mom made me put them on and called them my 'warm clothes,' so I guess they must put out a lot of heat to keep me warm."

"Maybe you can put them in the oven and bake a pie after school," teased Paulo.

"That sounds dumb, but now that you mention it, I wonder where they *do* get their energy to make me feel warm. They were just sitting there in the closet and felt cold until I wore them for a while. Then they started to put out heat and warm me up."

Paulo just laughed and said, "I could tell you where the heat comes from, but maybe you have to figure it out for yourself."

When he got to school, he asked his teacher who never seemed to want to answer questions. Instead, he asked Ian if he could design a test to see if mittens and other "warm clothes" really put out heat.

"Yeah, I think I can," said Ian.

NATIONAL SCIENCE TEACHERS ASSOCIATION

purpose

Do your students believe that an insulating substance such as wool can actually produce heat? Our research says that many children do, especially the younger ones. This story is designed to motivate your students to let you know what they believe and then for them to be able to test their theories in the classroom. Even though they may be convinced that the piece of clothing does not produce a change in temperature, they may still hold onto a belief that warm clothing does generate heat. Only time and experience will convince them otherwise. The purpose of this story is to give them an opportunity to gain that experience.

related concepts

- Heat
- Insulation
- Energy
- Temperature

DON'T BE Surprised

We have found that children up to fourth grade may be convinced that wool mittens, jackets or coats, sleeping bags, rugs, blankets, and other things used to keep them warm are actually involved in the production of heat. This is a belief that is difficult to change as children may believe that if only enough time were allowed, the heat would appear. They will probably design an investigation to compare thermometers placed inside clothing with thermometers at room temperature and will expect dramatic temperature differences. When these changes in temperature do not occur, they will blame their experimental design and attempt to repeat the test with changes in variables. It also is difficult to get children to recognize their own bodies as heat sources. See the article by Watson and Konicek (1990) in *Phi Delta Kappan* to see how one teacher handled this situation (link provided in References).

CONTENT BackGround

Heat is defined as the *transfer of energy* from a warmer object to a cooler object. Heat sources are those objects that can produce thermal energy by themselves through *radiation*. Radiation occurs when a body emits energy into the surrounding area by sending it out in the form of electromagnetic waves or particles. Examples are the Sun, lightbulbs, stoves, radioactive materials, and metabolizing organisms such as humans. Heat sources may also be any substance that has more *heat energy* in it than anything in the surrounding space.

When heat energy is introduced into a mass, it causes the molecules of that body to move faster, producing an increase in temperature. This is why a pot of water heats up when it is in direct sunlight or on a lighted stove burner. The

molecules of water begin to vibrate more rapidly. A thermometer inserted into the water would show a rise in temperature.

In many situations, it is important to retain heat, or to prevent it from entering a substance or area. Homes are *insulated* with materials that diminish the amount of heat that can pass through it or excite its molecules. This includes materials like rock-wool insulation, foam, and air. Think of a Styrofoam cooler. It is the *movement* of energy or heat that is significant. The insulating material does not allow heat to move easily, either in or out. It keeps homes cool in the warm seasons and warm in the colder seasons.

The same thing is true of the mitten, the coat, the scarf, the sleeping bag, and the underwear. They all reduce the rate of heat transfer. For this reason, we wear clothes (certainly also for modesty's sake) that keep our body's heat from escaping into the atmosphere. In colder climates, mittens and coats may be imperative to prevent that precious body heat from leaving and causing us discomfort, or even more dire consequences. If a person is immersed in cooler surroundings such as water or even cold air, the heat leaves the body at a rapid rate if the body is not insulated. This may cause *hypothermia*, a condition where the body's temperature drops so low that its ability to function is slowed or, worse, stopped to the point of death.

There are clothes that do produce warm temperatures but these clothes are equipped with either a power supply, usually a rechargeable battery, as a source of energy or a chemical pack that produces heat. But the more usual case, say a mitten, does not provide heat generation but, instead, insulation. The mitten worn on the hand traps the heat energy produced by the body and given off by the hand. This allows the heat to warm the thin layer of air between hand and mitten. If a thermometer were to be placed in the mitten while it was being worn, the temperature would be close to the body temperature of the wearer. Some heat does escape so the temperature would not be the same as the internal temperature of the wearer, but it normally would be warm enough for comfort.

One often gets advice to dress for cold weather in layers. Not only does this allow for modification of the layers if the outside temperature should change, but it provides a layer of air between each layer that in turn adds to the insulation made available to the body, since air under the right conditions is a good insulator.

NATIONAL SCIENCE TEACHERS ASSOCIATION

reLaTeD IDeas FROM THe NaTIONaL SCIeNCe eDUCaTION STaNDARDS (NrC 1996)

K–4: *Light, Heat, Electricity, and Magnetism*
- Heat can be produced in many ways, such as burning or rubbing one substance with another. Heat can move from one object to another by conduction.

5–8: *Transfer of Energy*
- Energy is a property of many substances and is associated with heat, light, electricity, mechanical motion, sound, nuclei, and the nature of a chemical. Energy is transferred in many ways.
- Heat moves in predictable ways, flowing from warmer objects to cooler ones, until both reach the same temperature.

reLaTeD IDeas FROM BeNCHMARKS FOR SCIeNCe LITeRaCY (aaaS 1993)

3–5: *Energy Transformations*
- Heat is produced by mechanical and electrical machines and any time one thing rubs up against another.
- When warmer things are put with cooler ones, the warm ones lose heat and the cools ones gain it until they are all at the same temperature.
- Poor conductors can reduce heat loss.

6–8: *Energy Transformations*
- Energy cannot be created or destroyed, but only changed from one form into another.
- Energy appears in different forms. Heat energy is the disorderly motion of molecules.

USING THE STORY WITH GRADES K-4

Once the story is read, you'll probably find that your students identify with Ian and will want to design a way to test the theory. Your class will probably be divided in their opinions. You might want to think about administering the probe "The Mitten Problem," from *Uncovering Student Ideas in Science, Volume 1*, by Keeley, Eberle, and Farrin (2005). It is not entirely necessary to do so, as this chapter's story will help you to elicit student views. We have found, however, that with some classes, the probe helps reluctant children isolate a method for developing a test. As usual, I suggest starting a chart containing their ideas as "Our Best Thinking."

Most children will agree on placing a thermometer in an article of clothing and another thermometer next to it, then waiting for a negotiated amount of time before comparing temperature readings. This plan will be modified as the tests (and I emphasize the *tests*, plural) go on. Be prepared to do many tests as the class modifies its ideas as to what causes the temperature in the mitten—or whatever item they use for the experiment—to remain the same. Help them design a test that is fair. Make sure that the two thermometers read the same before the experiment begins.

You should be prepared to use different items such as mittens, gloves, sleeping bags, coats, rugs, or wool hats to satisfy the children's need to test various items. Students may also insist that you put things in plastic bags to "keep the cold (or the draft) out."

Of course, none of these will make any difference. Nor will the place that the experiments are conducted affect the outcome, since the two thermometers will be next to each other. Be advised that there may be a slight variation of a degree now and then, but you can discuss with the children the ideas of significant differences and whether small changes like that are due to little errors in procedure or in the equipment. After all, those who expect differences in a "heat-producing object" will expect at least double-digit differences.

One or two of the students will be like Paulo and know the science concept; a few others will predict that the mitten will insulate the thermometer from the room heat. Over time, this will not occur. You may even have students set up experiments and allow lots of time before reading the thermometers. Children who have used older oral thermometers to take their temperatures will focus a lot on time since it has been their experience that they had to leave the thermometer in their mouths for at least three minutes, so "time must be important." We have had children who stubbornly insisted that if we left the thermometers in the test situation for a year, there would certainly be a difference.

As I suggested earlier, you may really appreciate the article "Teaching for Conceptual Change," by Watson and Konicek (1990). It tells how one teacher carried out the lessons over several days before giving the children a new idea to test (i.e., that the mitten kept body heat from escaping). As the article states, the children thought of putting thermometers under their caps to test the idea and "went out to recess with an experiment under their hats."

Although the students will eventually submit to the fact that the temperature shown by the thermometer in the article of clothing and the one outside the article will not change, they still may not have a clue as to why. Talking about what kinds of things they know produce heat will eventually include the human body. You may want to capitalize on this lead to ask them if they see any relationship between the experiments they have been doing and the fact that the human body is a heat source. Some students will still resist and this is normal. It may take a while before they put the ideas together and understand the role of the insulators they wear to keep themselves warm. You have, at least, opened the door to their curiosity and provided them with experiences that will eventually bring them to a scientific conclusion.

USING THE STORY WITH GRADES 5–8

Your students, being older, will probably not be as inclined to believe that warm clothes actually heat the body. However, you may find that some of them are still on the edge of understanding the concept. You have the opportunity to have all of your students take sides in the Ian-Paulo debate and actually provide one or the other of the characters with the evidence that will turn the tide. They should be instructed to find a way to convince each of the characters that one is right and the other mistaken. You may even consider a drama where various students act the roles of Ian and Paulo and engage in a debate (friendly please). They will need to provide concrete evidence to support their arguments. This will lead to actual experimentation. You can consider teams to design and do the research.

Even if everyone in the class believes that temperatures in and out of the mitten will be the same, reasons for their beliefs may differ. It will be helpful to you to know what your students believe conceptually about heat production and insulation, as well as about the human body as a heat source. Actually any object or mass that is warmer than its surroundings can be a heat source. You might ask your students if an ice cube can be a heat source. (It can, if the environment around it is colder than the cube!) All substances contain some heat. That heat is transferred to any material that is cooler than it is. Although this is not the usual circumstance under which ice is used, it can be a great discussion generator, because ice, which normally absorbs heat in drinks, could actually be a heat source and send heat radiating to a surrounding area to cause that area to become warmer. Students who can understand this certainly understand the second law of thermodynamics.

RELATED BOOKS AND NSTA JOURNAL ARTICLES

Damonte, K. 2005. Heating up and cooling down. *Science and Children* 42 (9): 47–48.

Driver, R., A. Squires, P. Rushworth, and V. Wood-Robinson. 1994. *Making sense of secondary science: Research into children's ideas.* London and New York: Routledge Falmer.

Keeley, P. 2005. *Science curriculum topic study: Bridging the gap between standards and practice.* Thousand Oaks, CA: Corwin Press.

May, K., and M. Kurbin. 2003. To heat or not to heat. *Science Scope* 26 (6): 38–41.

references

American Association for the Advancement of Science (AAAS). 1993. *Benchmarks for science literacy.* New York: Oxford University Press.

Keeley, P., F. Eberle, and L. Farrin. 2005. *Uncovering student ideas in science: 25 formative assessment probes, vol. 1.* Arlington, VA: NSTA Press.

National Research Council (NRC). 1996. *National science education standards.* Washington, DC: National Academies Press.

Watson, B., and R. Konicek. 1990. Teaching for conceptual change: Confronting children's experience. *Phi Delta Kappan* 71 (9): 680–684. *www.exploratorium.edu/IFI/resources/workshops/teachingforconcept.html*

CHAPTER 11
PARTY MELTDOWN

Kelsey and her friends were having a party—a big party! There were to be 12 girls, lots of noise and music, pizza, chips, cake, and soda. Fortunately there would be plenty of ice since Kelsey and Lucy had been making ice all day in preparation for the drinks. They had borrowed ice cube trays from everyone in the neighborhood and filled the freezer with the trays full of water. By the time the girls began to arrive, the freezer had done its job and there was plenty of ice. They then put the ice cubes into any kind of bowls they could find. Some were metal and others were plastic or glass. They all went into the freezer to keep cold.

Kelsey was in the kitchen getting more bowls of ice out of the freezer when Elizabeth popped her new Justin Beiber CD into the player. As soon as he was recognized, everyone screamed with excitement and ran into the family room to dance. This, of course, included Kelsey, who in the rush left two bowls of cubes out on the kitchen counter.

Much later, when it was time for more soda and more ice, the girls returned to the kitchen to find the two bowls sitting there where they had been forgotten.

"Hey, one bowl is full of ice-cold water but no ice," Nicole exclaimed, "but the other one still has some ice in it. Bet you forgot to put the metal one in the freezer."

"No way," Kelsey responded. "We took them out at the same time and forgot them when we went in to dance!"

"Puh-lease!" said Nicole. "That's why one is water and the other is still half frozen. Get real, Kelse!"

"Oh, forget it!" exclaimed Kelsey. "Just grab whatever ice is left and let's get back to the party."

The next day, as Kelsey, Lucy, and Sara were cleaning up after the party, the two bowls were still on the counter and Kelsey reminded Lucy of what had happened the night before.

"Duh," said Lucy. "The ice cubes in the plastic bowl get colder in the freezer than the cubes in the metal tray and since they were colder, they melted slower."

"That's crazy, the ice cubes were all the same temperature," said Sara, who often had strong opinions. "The metal bowls are shiny and shiny stuff gets hotter than dull stuff like plastic. So the shiny bowl got hotter and melted the ice. All of your cooking pans are shiny. Think that's just luck?"

"Metal things just naturally get hotter quicker," said Kelsey. "It has nothing to do with shiny or dull! Don't you remember how hot metal things get out in the Sun? The metal bowl took up heat from the room air and melted the ice."

"Who cares!" laughed Lucy. "Let's get the dishes washed and get out of this kitchen!"

They did just that, but inside Kelsey's head, the question remained. Who was right? Or were any of them? Did any theory make more sense than another?

NATIONAL SCIENCE TEACHERS ASSOCIATION

PURPOSE

This story will allow students to become aware that some materials give up and take in thermal energy at different rates. A second purpose is to understand how two different substances having the same temperature can feel as though they have different temperatures because of the various rates of the movement of thermal energy between the hand and the substance.

RELATED CONCEPTS

- Heat
- Thermal energy
- Conduction
- Thermal conductivity
- Temperature
- Change of state (melting)

DON'T BE SURPRISED

Students often focus more on the visible properties of objects, like shininess, than the material of which they are actually made. Many will side with Lucy and hold conflicting opinions that even though the ice cubes were in the freezer together, the cubes in the plastic bowl got colder than the ones in the metal bowl. It is not uncommon for students to hold conflicting opinions without realizing it.

CONTENT BACKGROUND

Heat is transferred as energy (thermal energy) from warmer objects to cooler objects by one of three different processes: conduction, convection, or radiation. In this story we are dealing with the process of heat transfer by conduction. Conduction involves the molecules or atoms of one substance coming in contact with their counterparts in another substance. In this instance, the girls argued about the ice cubes that were touching the metal and plastic bowls. An additional conduction of heat took place when the surface of the bowls contacted room-temperature air.

Not all substances conduct thermal energy equally. Some materials such as metals conduct energy more efficiently than nonmetals. They are said to have a greater *thermal conductivity*. Thermal energy by conduction involves touching. The molecules of the warmer substance are moving faster with more energy than the molecules of the cooler substance. When the molecules from the warmer substance collide with the molecules of the cooler substance, some of that energy is transferred to the slower molecules causing them to move faster. They, in turn, interact with their cooler neighbor molecules and transfer some of their energy along until the molecules all have pretty much the same amount of energy. We can gauge with a thermometer or sense with our bodies the average of this thermal activity—what we call an object's *temperature*. Thus, temperature is a measure of the average amount of energy in a system but is not a measure of the total amount of energy in that system.

This form of energy transfer is the basis of warming and cooling used in everyday life. Heat energy moves from the warmer to the cooler until both substances or areas are in equilibrium (or are the same temperature). You will notice that I did not say that they have the same amount of energy because that will depend upon the mass of either of the systems involved. A swimming pool at room temperature will have much more heat in it than a cup of boiling tea. Their temperatures are very different, but the swimming pool holds a great deal more energy due to its greater mass.

Another way to look at this relationship to mass and temperature is to think of a cup of boiling tea and all of the energy in that cup. You would probably not mind having a drop of that tea land on your hand but you certainly would not want the entire cup. They are both the same temperature, yet the cup has much more energy and could do much more damage to your hand if the whole cup were to be spilled on it. A drop might sting for a moment but would not do any damage.

In the story, the girls placed the ice cubes in separate bowls in the freezer which we can presume had a constant temperature. If the bowls were in the freezer for a reasonable amount of time, everything would then have the same temperature, freezer air, ice, and bowls alike. They were removed from the freezer to the counter and subjected to room temperature air. Since thermal energy moves from the warmer to cooler, we can assume that the energy in the room air, by conduction, transferred to the bowls and then again by conduction to the ice cubes.

Now, this is where the differences in thermal conductivity come in. The metal bowl has a greater thermal conductivity than the plastic, meaning the molecules of the metal transfer thermal energy faster than the plastic. Therefore, the thermal energy reaches equilibrium with the ice in the metal bowl before equilibrium is reached in the plastic bowl. So, the plastic bowl still had ice in it, while the metal bowl had water from melted ice.

One of the most puzzling things in everyday life is that when we touch a metal object in a room, it feels colder than a wooden or plastic object in the same room. Both objects have been in the room for some time and and therefore should be the same temperature. Yet, the metal feels colder. Think about this before you read on.

Heat flows from our body to the metal and wood because of the difference in temperature. We are warmer than room temperature (unless we happen to be in a sauna). Heat leaves our body at a faster rate when in contact with the metal than it does when in contact with the wood. Thus, it feels like the metal is cooler. So, we are fooled into believing that the metal is cooler.

It is interesting to note that the greater the temperature difference between two substances, the faster the temperature change toward equilibrium. This temperature difference is often referred to as ΔT or *delta T.* Your cup of tea will cool off faster when it is at a higher temperature than if it is at a lower temperature. This makes perfectly logical sense since the higher energy molecules bouncing around there are, the more likely they will leave the surface of the tea and take heat away from the drink.

When I was a kid, I grew up during the time, before the Salk vaccine, when parents' worst fear for their children was the disease polio. Every time there was a suspicion of a fever, parents worried. Countless times, my parents put their foreheads

against mine to see if I had a fever. If my forehead was warmer than theirs, the heat from my body would be very evident to their cooler bodies. The same principal causes thermometers to work in that they absorb heat from or give up heat to the substance into which they are placed. With exposure to heat, the liquid in the thermometer will expand through conduction and with exposure to cooler substances, the liquid inside will contract as it gives up heat. So you see, heat transfer via conduction is everywhere in our world and can explain so many everyday mysteries.

related ideas from the national science education standards (nrc 1996)

K–4: Properties of Objects and Materials

- Objects have many observable properties, including size, weight, shape, color, temperature, and the ability to react with other substances. Those properties can be measured using tools, such as rulers, balances, and thermometers.
- Objects are made of one or more materials, such as paper, wood, and metal.
- Objects can be described by the properties of the materials from which they are made, and those properties can be used to separate or sort a group of objects or materials.

K–4: Light, Heat, Electricity, and Magnetism

- Heat can be produced in many ways such as burning, rubbing, and mixing one substance with another. Heat can move from one object to another.

5–8: Transfer of Energy

- Energy is a property of many substances and is associated with heat, light, electricity, mechanical motion, sound, nuclear energy, and nature of a chemical change. Energy is transferred in many ways.
- Heat moves in predictable ways, flowing from warmer objects to cooler ones until both reach the same temperature.

related ideas from benchmarks for science literacy (aaas 1993)

K–2: Energy Transformations

- The Sun warms the land, air, and water.

3–5: *Energy Transformations*

- When warmer things are put with cooler ones, the warm ones lose heat and the cool ones gain it until they are all the same temperature. A warmer object can warm a cooler one by contact or at a distance.
- Some materials conduct heat much better than others. Poor conductors can reduce heat loss.

6–8: *Energy Transformations*

- Heat can be transferred through materials by the collision of atoms or across space by radiation. If the material is fluid, currents will be set up in it that aid the transfer of heat.
- Energy appears in different forms. Heat energy is in the disorderly motion of molecules.

USING THE STORY WITH GRADES K–4

Very young children will be able to understand the changes of state in substances like water when it goes from liquid to ice or liquid to gas, or vice versa. I like to give young children an ice cube in a plastic tray and ask them to engage in an ice cube race to see who can melt the ice cube fastest without touching it. Witnessing the change of state is paramount for understanding this concept when they are older. Children of early grades never seem to tire of watching state changes and can be introduced to the idea of heat energy coming into play in these changes.

In this case, you might ask children to choose from several different kinds of trays made of different materials on which to place their ice cubes. This imbedded formative assessment will tell you which children are aware that certain kinds of trays that are better conductors of heat and will make a difference in how fast their ice cube melts. If they choose a good conductor of heat, they will have a head start on melting their ice cube regardless of what else they do to speed up the melting.

NSTA members can access online the article "Heating Up, Cooling Down" (Damonte 2005) from the NSTA website. This article looks at the difference in *specific heat capacity* of three substances: sand, water, and soil. Specific heat capacity is the amount of heat needed to raise the temperature of a substance. Every substance has its own specific heat capacity. A given amount of water, for example, requires five times more heat to raise its temperature than the same amount of sand, and by the same token, gives off heat five times more slowly. You may have noticed this if you have walked across a sandy beach on a hot day. The heat transfer to your feet was instantaneous and painful because the sand heated up more quickly than the water where you probably sought relief!

Upper elementary students can follow the story as it develops and duplicate the situation. This will convince them that the problem is plausible. Then they can test containers made of different substances to see the variation in the rate of melting. Of course, you must help them list the results and keep all of the variables controlled.

For a quick and dramatic introduction to the issue of heat transfer, you can place an ice cube on an inverted metal can, and another on an inverted plastic, or better yet, Styrofoam cup of the same size (it helps if you remove any paper label on the can so that more surface area can be exposed to the air). The can will pick up the heat from the air in the room much more quickly than will the cup, and the ice cube on the can will begin to melt almost immediately while the other cube will remain in its frozen state for much longer. The discussion that follows should bring out the fact that the ice cubes were placed on two different materials. You could ask, "What do you think would happen if you wrapped your hands around both cups?" This is the time to introduce the terminology of *heat energy* and *transfer* (*conduction*), to the students because the vocabulary will be in context with the situation. Your students should now be able to finish the story of the mystery of the two bowls of ice cubes.

USING THE STORY WITH GRADES 5–8

Middle school students may also want to duplicate the story to verify the outcome. However, a good discussion should precede the repeat of the story so that you can assess their conceptions of heat and heat transfer. Listening to your students as they talk is a wonderful way to understand their thinking, and it can guide you toward the next steps. Some of the ideas listed in the section for K–4 may be useful, and the article by Damonte (cited on p. 110) would also be of help to you in attempting to move the students toward a better undertanding of the concepts involved. Since students at this age are familiar with thermometers, the difference between heat energy and temperature will be even more accessible to them. The drop vs. the cup of boiling water I talked about in the Content Background section will help to make the distinction more real.

Using the can and Styrofoam cup activity mentioned above can also be a discussion stimulator. However, the story is an investigable activity in itself and will give the results that allow the students to finish the story. They can try the various suggestions made by the girls about shiny, dull (plastic), metal, and other holders and the idea of how cold the ice can get if it is placed in the freezer. If you place a thermometer in the water before you freeze the ice in the ice cube tray, it can give you the internal temperature of the ice cubes. Students will find that the ice cubes will all be the same temperature as the surrounding air in the freezer regardless of the container. This negates Sara's and Lucy's claims, but Kelsey's idea should prove to be true.

A very interesting extension using ideas about heat and heat transfer is described in the *Science Scope* article "Science Sampler: A Slice of Solar" (Galus 2003). The author asked her students to design solar ovens to cook an apple slice using their recently acquired knowledge of heat transfer while using common everyday materials. This kind of activity helps students to solidify their knowledge through application.

In 2010, there was an International Boiling Point Project in which students from all over the world entered data on what factors they found influenced the boiling point of water. Although the project may not continue further, the website holds a great deal of information that might be useful to you in teaching about heat, heat transfer, and state change. The website is *www.ciese.org/curriculum/boilproj/*.

related BOOKS and NSTA JOURNAL articles

Keeley, P. 2005. *Science curriculum topic study: Bridging the gap between standards and practice.* Thousand Oaks, CA: Corwin Press.

Keeley, P., F. Eberle, and C. Dorsey. 2008. *Uncovering student ideas in science, volume 3: Another 25 formative assessment probes.* Arlington, VA: NSTA Press.

Keeley, P., F. Eberle, and L. Farrin. 2005. *Uncovering student ideas in science, volume 1: 25 formative assessment probes.* Arlington, VA: NSTA Press.

Keeley, P., F. Eberle, and J. Tugel. 2007. *Uncovering student ideas in science, volume 2: 25 more formative assessment probes.* Arlington, VA: NSTA Press.

Keeley, P., and J. Tugel. 2009. *Uncovering student ideas in science, volume 4: 25 new formative assessment probes.* Arlington, VA: NSTA Press.

Konicek-Moran, R. 2008. *Everyday science mysteries: Stories for inquiry-based science teaching.* Arlington, VA: NSTA Press.

Konicek-Moran, R. 2009. *More everyday science mysteries: Stories for inquiry-based science teaching.* Arlington, VA: NSTA Press.

Konicek-Moran, R. 2010. *Even more everyday science mysteries: Stories for inquiry-based science teaching.* Arlington, VA: NSTA Press.

May, K., and M. Kurbin. 2003. To heat or not to heat. *Science Scope* 26 (5): 38–41.

references

Damonte, K. 2005. Heating up, cooling down. *Science and Children* 42 (9): 47–48.

Galus, P. 2003. Science sampler: A slice of solar. *Science Scope* 26 (8): 56–57.

International Boiling Point Project. 2010. *www.ciese.org/curriculum/boilproj/*

NATIONAL SCIENCE TEACHERS ASSOCIATION

CHAPTER 12

HOW COLD IS COLD?

Kristin filled her glass with ice cubes from the freezer, all the way up to the top. She then filled the glass with lemonade and sat down to drink it. The day was hot and muggy and Kristin did not take long to finish her drink. When she was finished she dumped almost a full glass of ice cubes into the sink.

Kristin's father had been watching the entire scene. "You know, Krissy," he said, "you don't have to waste all of that ice. Why do you put so much ice into your glass?"

"I like my lemonade really cold," she responded, "and the more ice I put in, the colder the lemonade gets."

"Are you sure about that?" asked her dad.

"Of course," answered Kristin. "It makes sense. More cold ice makes a cold drink, well … colder."

"Maybe," said her dad "more ice might make it cool down faster, but would it really make it colder? Look! You threw away almost all of the ice!"

"It was cold enough, so I drank it all down. I can't help it if all of the ice didn't melt. Besides, if I let all of the ice melt, the lemonade would have gotten colder and colder and maybe too cold to drink. There was a lot of cold in the ice that had to go into the drink and the more ice, the more cold there was to cool the drink."

"I don't know," mumbled her dad. "Something doesn't quite make sense here. Could the lemonade get colder than the ice that's in it?"

"Well, I think so," Kristin replied cautiously. "Or maybe not. I don't really know. More ice would keep on making it colder as long as there was still ice, wouldn't it?"

"We need to do some experimenting," said her dad. "We need a hypothesis or two. It looks like we have a least a couple of questions here."

NATIONAL SCIENCE TEACHERS ASSOCIATION

PURPOSE

Heat and cold are often difficult concepts for children to understand. First, our everyday sloppy language gives them a predisposition to such common misconceptions as cold being a substance that moves from place to place. How often have we told others to "Close the door, you're letting the cold in?" Our colloquial language often reinforces the existence of "cold energy," when it is scientifically acceptable to refer only to heat as a form of energy that is transferred from a warmer object to a cooler one and that cold is an absence of heat.

Secondly, the story tries to set the stage for discussions and inquiry into the nature of temperature and heat and to the fact that heat exchange is the cause of what scientists call a *phase* change—when something goes from liquid to solid or vice versa. In essence this may be the students' first encounter with the laws of thermodynamics.

This story actually has its origin in a personal event that happened to my family while we were living in Africa. Our highly prized and ancient refrigerator labored daily against the oppressive 43°C degree temperature and did so valiantly just to maintain an internal temperature low enough to preserve our food. Making ice in the refrigerator was a luxury and we used it sparingly, all except our teenage daughter who is personified as Kristin in the story. Her insistence on using large quantities of ice for her drinks led to many confrontations between Kristin and me, which are literally very close to the dialog in the story.

RELATED CONCEPTS

- Energy
- Temperature
- Thermal energy
- Cooling
- Solid
- Phase change
- Energy transfer
- Heat
- Melting
- Freezing
- Liquid
- Physical change

DON'T BE SURPRISED

Your students may well believe that cold is something that moves from colder places into warmer places and cools them off. Air conditioners blowing out cold air may add to this idea. They may believe that cold is an entity that moves much like a wind or an object. Who can blame them when we use language that emphasizes that belief? It would follow that they would believe that more ice would add to the transfer of more cold into the lemonade. Kristin thought that the more ice there was in the glass, the colder the drink would become for that very reason. They will be surprised when they find out that once a drink with ice cubes reaches a certain temperature, the continued presence of ice in the drink will not lower the temperature further.

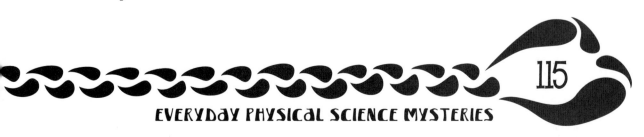

CONTENT BACKGROUND

If you have ever filled your glass with ice to cool your drink, you will have noticed that the drink never got "too cold to drink!" Even if you forgot your drink only to return later and find the ice almost gone, you will have noticed that it is still drinkable, temperature-wise. It might certainly have been diluted and watery due to the melting of the ice, but the temperature was still within the comfort zone for drinking. How can this be when we think: There was a lot of cold in the ice that had to go into the drink and the more ice, the more cold there was to cool the drink. Should it not have gone on giving its cold to the drink, making it colder and colder?

Could it be that instead of the cold going into the drink, the heat from the drink might be going into the ice? Is this what makes ice melt? If the drink were very warm, would the ice melt faster? These wonderings can be made into testable questions and might lead you as the teacher to try out some ice experiments yourself before working with the children. Before using this story with the children I recommend that you obtain a copy of *Science Matters* by Hazen and Trefil and read Chapter 2 on energy. Their explanation of energy, in this case heat energy, will benefit you greatly and give you the confidence you need to lead your students through their inquiries. Basically here it is in a nutshell:

Thermal energy, temperature, and heat are entirely different things to a physicist. *Thermal energy* is the total amount of kinetic energy in a substance. The amount of thermal energy in a substance is determined by the amount of kinetic energy created by the amount of bouncing around of all of the molecules that make up the substance. A thermometer can only measure the thermal energy of the molecules that bounce off it and certainly not all of the molecules in a substance, but you can assume that the thermometer would register the same if it is placed anywhere in the container of the substance you are measuring.

Temperature is a human-devised concept that measures the difference in this thermal energy among various objects on arbitrary temperature scales such as Fahrenheit, Celsius, or Kelvin scales. It tells us the average amount of thermal energy in any substance.

Heat is usually defined as the transfer of energy from an object that is hot to one that is cooler.

Every substance has some thermal energy in it unless it has somehow miraculously reached the temperature of absolute zero, a temperature impossible to attain even in a laboratory. Absolute zero is theoretically reached when no more thermal energy can be extracted from a substance. The larger the substance, the more thermal energy is present. Two ice cubes have twice the thermal energy as one ice cube! You might be very willing to have a small droplet of boiling water placed on your hand but not a pot of boiling water. Why not? Because there is much more heat in the pot of water than in the droplet despite the fact that they are the same temperature! Here lies the difference between heat and temperature. These ideas may seem counterintuitive to many of you, but don't let that scare you away from physics. Instead, let it intrigue you and entice you to learn more.

Thermal energy is attributed to the motion of molecules in any substance. More molecular activity means greater thermal energy and less activity means less. So, when you heat or cool something, you are changing the activity level of its particles. Remember, heat is referred to as the energy that can be transferred from one substance to another. By adding energy to any substance, the amount of thermal energy it contains can be increased, by transferring it from the donor, such as the Sun, electricity, burner, or nearby higher energy source to the receiver. Heat energy can be transferred from the warmer to the cooler by one of three methods, by conduction, radiation, or convection. You have felt the result of *conduction* when you put a spoon into a hot cup of liquid and then touched the spoon. The heat energy is transferred directly from the collision of the atoms in the liquid to the atoms in the spoon to you. You may also have felt the transfer of energy by *radiation* if you stood close to a fire or an electric heater or lamp. The energy of the heat source is in the form of infrared energy (a high energy part of the light spectrum), which in turn excites your heat sensors and you feel heat. In *convection*, the atoms in a liquid or gas set up a current of rising and falling atoms, which eventually bring everything in the substance to the same temperature. It all boils down to the laws of thermodynamics and in this case, the second law. We can summarize the second law of thermodynamics by saying that heat energy moves spontaneously from a warmer area to a cooler area. An interesting phenomenon about conduction is that some substances conduct heat better than others. For instance, if you touch metal, it feels cooler than other substances in a room. This is because the heat from your body transfers more quickly to the metal and it feels cooler to you. If the metal has been in the room for a long time, it will have the same temperature as the rest of the objects in the room. Your body will be fooled into thinking that the metal is cooler when it is really not.

Kristin has formed a common misconception about energy that includes cold as a form of energy that can move from one place to another. Secondly, she has reckoned that there is an unlimited supply of this "cold" in the ice that can continue to move into the drink and continue to drop the temperature until the ice is gone. In her mind, the "cold" in the ice disappears into the drink until it is all used up. If this were true, it would be entirely possible for the drink to become colder than the temperature of the ice itself. We know this to be untrue from experience. The heat in the drink will transfer into the ice causing it to melt. The drink will never get any colder than the temperature of the ice in it. Since the ice and the drink will become the same temperature and heat can only flow from warmer to cooler there will be no heat transfer. Only if the liquid in the drink warms to a temperature higher than the ice will heat continue to flow. In other words, heat can flow from one substance to another if there is a temperature difference between the two.

This can be tested with the aid of a thermometer and a glass of ice water. The heat in the drink changes the phase of the ice from solid to liquid by increasing the energy in the atoms in the ice as it melts. Mind you, the temperature of the ice cubes will not change as long as the cubes remain in solid form, but the heat energy from the drink will eventually change the state of water from solid (ice) to liquid. And, the resulting temperature of the ice drink will never go below that of the temperature of any given ice cube in the drink. The amount of heat in the drink, transferred to the cubes will eventually result in temperature equilibrium between the ice and the drink. When equilibrium has been reached, the temperature will go no lower. In essence, when the ice and drink have reached the same temperature, there can be no further flow of energy since everything is the same temperature. Otherwise, the law of thermodynamics that states that heat flows from the warmer substance to the cooler substance would be broken (or at least repealed!). So far, that has never happened. And I anticipate that in your work with the students, the law will be upheld.

related ideas from the National Science Education Standards (NRC 1996)

K–4: *Properties of Objects and Materials*
- Materials can exist in different states—solid, liquid, and gas. Some common materials such as water, can be changed from one state to another by heating or cooling.

K–4: *Light, Heat, Electricity, and Magnetism*
- Heat can be produced in many ways such as burning, rubbing, or mixing one substance with another. Heat can move from one object to another.

5–8: *Transfer of Energy*
- Energy is a property of many substances and is associated with heat, light, electricity, mechanical motion, sound, nuclear energy, and the nature of a chemical change. Energy is transferred in many ways.
- Heat moves in predictable ways, flowing from warmer objects to cooler ones until both reach the same temperature.

related ideas from Benchmarks for Science Literacy (AAAS 1993)

K–2: *The Structure of Matter*
- Heating and cooling cause changes in the properties of materials. Many kinds of changes occur faster under hotter conditions.

3–5: *Energy Transformations*

- When warmer things are put with cooler ones, the warm ones lose heat and the cool ones gain it until they are all the same temperature. A warmer object can warm a cooler one by contact or at a distance.

6–8: *Energy Transformations*

- Heat can be transferred through materials by the collision of atoms or across space by radiation. If the material is fluid, currents will be set up in it that aid the transfer of heat.
- Energy appears in different forms. Heat energy is in the disorderly motion of molecules.

USING THE STORY WITH GRADES K–4

This story can be used with the K–4 grades quite easily since Kristin's age is not clearly evident from the reading. As seen in the Standards and Benchmarks, the expectations for K–4 are that students will be able to distinguish between things that are warm and cold and to realize that when warm things are placed next to cool things, the cool things become warmer and the warm things become cooler. Also implicit in the expectations is the fact that substances can change from one state to another.

Actually, the story works better with third or fourth graders than with younger students although the discussion of the situation can give you a good insight into your students' thoughts about heat and the transfer of heat at any level. Most children by the time they come to school have had experience with ice and freezing and melting. They have also had time to develop incomplete conceptions about what is happening in this process. It might be best to focus on the melting of the ice cube for younger children and see what they already know about the phenomenon. An ice cube-melting race is a good way to involve the children and to see what they know about the process. Give each child an ice cube in a small dish and ask them to do what they can to make it melt as quickly as possible. They cannot touch it with any part of their bodies or take it to any other part of the room but are free to do anything else. Some will blow on the cube and others will wave their hands over the cube while others may move it back and forth with a pencil or pen. While you move about the room, you can ask them why they are doing what they are doing.

You may also want to administer one of probes on melting from *Uncovering Student Ideas in Science,* volumes 1 or 2 (Keeley, Eberle, and Farrin 2005; Keeley, Eberle, and Tugel 2007). "Ice Cubes in a Bag" is in volume 1 and "Ice Cold Lemonade" is in volume 2. Young children are not adept at reading thermometers and this limits their ability to conduct temperature studies. You can of course demonstrate and read the thermometer for them but this is secondhand science. It is a wonderful opportunity to teach them about temperature changes, and there are digital thermometers

that can be used for this purpose. Don't pass up the opportunity to have a class discussion about the story so that you can become aware of your students' ideas about heat and freezing and melting.

For the third and fourth graders the story should make sense and if they are able to use thermometers, the questions raised by Kristin and her dad can be tested. The students should discover that the temperature reaches equilibrium as soon as the liquid and the ice in the glass are at the same temperature. After this point, no matter how much ice is left in the glass, the temperature will remain the same since the flow of energy from warm to cool cannot take place since there is no difference. There will however, be a constant flow of energy from the liquid to the ice since the energy from the room will affect the liquid and the ice will absorb the excess heat as needed to maintain the equilibrium. After the ice all melts, the liquid will gradually move in the direction of the room temperature and the students will notice that the temperature will rise as it does so. Their explanations of these phenomena will provide an enlightening conversation for you and for the students. Be sure to bring the room temperature to the attention of the students by asking them how high they think the drink temperature will go. All of these findings should be put into their science notebooks and the conclusions and explanations as well. Your students might want to finish the story in their books now as well. If you need a prompt, you might ask them to predict what Kristin will say to her dad after she has experimented as they have done, backing up her response by using their findings.

USING THE STORY WITH GRADES 5-8

Middle school students should have skills in reading thermometers but do not expect them truly to understand the difference between temperature as read on the thermometer and the concept of heat, which is a complete abstraction. This is because in everyday life, we measure differences in energy by temperature even though energy is much different. Students therefore often confound the two. In fact the Standards documents suggest that at this age the time and effort spent in trying to teach students the difference is not worth it. Overall, the most important lesson to be learned here is that the energy moves from a higher energy source to a lower energy source, and it is the heat that is transferred and not the "cold." I would also add here that it is important to realize that it takes energy to change a solid to a liquid and a liquid to a gas and that energy does not necessarily change the temperature of the substances involved. To wit, adding heat to boiling water, once it is at a full boil, does not raise the temperature of the water. It will remain at 100°C at sea level. The added energy goes into continuing the phase change from liquid to gas and will continue to do so until the liquid is entirely evaporated.

I suggest using the story with grades 5–8 as a stimulus for discussion and then for the design of experiments to find out the answer to Kristin's dilemma. The discussion will probably produce ideas that can be placed on the "our best thinking" chart and can be changed to questions and eventually hypotheses. The role of the

teacher is to help focus the students' thinking on designing experiments that will answer their questions or support or not support their hypotheses.

For example, students may suggest putting thermometers in several glasses of water and then add varying amounts of ice to each one so they can monitor the temperature changes they anticipate as the ice melts. Should the containers all be made of the same material? Should the ice cubes be as much the same size as possible? Should the ice cubes come from the same tray? How should data be recorded? Will they graph them? When is the experiment over; when the ice is completely melted in all, some, one? The design depends, of course, on the hypothesis and the students should be helped to make the tests as fair as possible. Once the data are in, there may be small discrepancies. Small differences may be tempting for students to make their point. Your role might be to ask, how much difference in a measurement is significant? For example, suppose a student puts five ice cubes in one glass and one in another, and hypothesizes that the glass with five cubes will result in a lower temperature. The thermometer in the five-cube glass registers one degree cooler than the one-cube glass. One would expect if there were to be a difference, it would be more than one degree. Where could the difference come from? Perhaps the reading was faulty or perhaps the thermometers are not synchronized or perhaps the timing of the reading was different. Redoing the experiment as a class demonstration with all possibilities covered would be a reasonable solution to that problem. Remember, the stories and this book are about inquiry. There is not always a clear path to discovery and understanding. Having the students talk it all out will reap huge rewards. Then again, there may not be total agreement from all students. This is part of science too. Read the article "Teaching for Conceptual Change," by Watson and Konicek (1991) to see how one teacher handled situations like this. During the discussion, always ask the student who makes a conclusion statement to verify the statement with evidence. Science goes deeper than opinions and your role is to remind the students of this fact. You may possess one of the computer-assisted probes that will measure the temperatures accurately and even graph the changes on the computer screen as they occur. I do not discourage the use of these but ask you to consider how your students might benefit from collecting data and doing their own graphing. Following this, the probe apparatus might solidify the concept and the students could say that the apparatus "agreed with their findings." See the subtle difference there?

I sincerely believe that at the end of the experiments and discussion, your students and perhaps, even you, will have a new and clearer idea about energy transfer and about the process in which knowledge is gained.

related Books and NSTA Journal articles

Ashbrook, P. 2006. The matter of melting. *Science and Children* 43 (4): 18–21.
Damonte, K. 2005. Heating up, cooling down. *Science and Children* 42 (9): 47–48.

Driver, R., A. Squires, P. Rushworth, and V. Wood-Robinson. 1994. *Making sense of secondary science: Research into children's ideas.* London and New York: Routledge Falmer.

Keeley, P., F. Eberle, and L. Farrin. 2005. *Uncovering student ideas in science: 25 formative assessment probes, volume 1.* Arlington, VA: NSTA Press.

Keeley, P., F. Eberle, and J. Tugel. 2007. *Uncovering student ideas in science: 25 more formative assessment probes, volume 2.* Arlington, VA: NSTA Press.

Line, L., and E. Christmann. 2004. A different phase change. *Science Scope* 28 (3): 52–53.

May, K., and M. Kurbin. 2003. To heat or not to heat. *Science Scope* 26 (5): 38.

Purvis, D. 2006. Fun with phase changes. *Science and Children* 43 (5): 23–25.

Robertson, W. C. 2002. *Energy: Stop faking it! Finally understanding science so you can teach it.* Arlington, VA: NSTA Press.

references

American Association for the Advancement of Science (AAAS). 1993. *Benchmarks for science literacy.* New York: Oxford University Press.

Keeley, P. 2005. *Science curriculum topic study: Bridging the gap between standards and practice.* Thousand Oaks, CA: Corwin Press.

Keeley, P., F. Eberle, and L. Farrin. 2005. *Uncovering student ideas in science: 25 formative assessment probes, volume 1.* Arlington, VA: NSTA Press.

Keeley, P., F. Eberle, and J. Tugel. 2007. *Uncovering student ideas in science: 25 more formative assessment probes, volume 2.* Arlington, VA: NSTA Press.

National Research Council (NRC). 1996. *National science education standards.* Washington, DC: National Academies Press.

Watson, B., and R. Konicek. 1990. Teaching for conceptual change: Confronting children's experience. *Phi Delta Kappan* 71 (9): 680–684.

NATIONAL SCIENCE TEACHERS ASSOCIATION

CHAPTER 13
DANCING POPCORN

Shantidas was reading a science magazine when she spotted something that looked like fun. It was called "dancing popcorn" and the article gave directions but did not tell her what was going to happen. This was unusual since most of these kinds of articles told you the whole story, which was kinda fun but didn't really let you figure anything out for yourself. Shantidas liked figuring things out for herself. She loved science and liked to do projects that didn't have easy answers attached to them.

This activity called for using a small glass of a clear carbonated soda like Sprite or 7-Up. You were supposed to put a few popcorn kernels in the glass and then observe what happened. Shantidas followed the instructions and sat back to observe. The popcorn kernels sank right to the bottom of the glass, but bubbles began to form all over them.

In a few moments some of the popcorn kernels began to rise to the surface, and then just as quickly they sank to the bottom where the process began all over again.

"Okay," she thought, "the bubbles on the popcorn made them lighter since the bubbles in the drink are lighter than the liquid. That's why the bubbles in a soda always rise to the top."

Just then Boris, her brother, came into the kitchen and asked what she was doing. Shantidas explained what she had done and asked Boris if he had any ideas about why the popcorn was "dancing."

"I think it's like a life vest. The vest makes you lighter and you float on top of the water. Then when you take off the vest, you sink."

"But I don't understand why adding something to the popcorn makes it lighter. It should make it heavier. And I don't understand why adding a heavy life vest makes you lighter, either."

"Yeah, but the gas doesn't weigh anything so it doesn't make the popcorn heavier. It just makes the popcorn float," said Boris. "I have to rethink the life vest thing."

"I think we need to watch it really carefully, Boris, and see what is happening every step of the way."

Afterward, they wondered if they could use things other than popcorn kernels and get the same results.

NATIONAL SCIENCE TEACHERS ASSOCIATION

PURPOSE

Perhaps some of you remember the California dancing raisin commercials of years past. Well, this is not that kind of dancing. The purpose of this story is to motivate your students to solve the mystery of why objects bob up and down in carbonated drinks. For young children, this is an experience in flotation; for older students, insight into the concepts of density and buoyancy.

RELATED CONCEPTS

- Buoyancy
- Systems
- Density

DON'T BE SURPRISED

Children think of floating or buoyancy in several ways. They consider the material involved, the shape of the object, the air, and the depth or other aspects of the liquid. They are likely to think that anything with holes in it will sink and that anything with air in it will float. Long objects will not float as well as short objects. They may tell you that large things float and the next minute that small things float and be entirely oblivious to the conflict in their reasoning. But the most telling idea of buoyancy by children is that adding air will make any "sinker" into a floater. This makes sense, because most children do not believe that air has any weight—after all, air bubbles always seem to float to the top of any liquid. They see it as a helium balloon added to an object.

CONTENT BACKGROUND

Buoyancy is fascinating to most of us because it defies the mind's belief that all things fall when released. We are amused by helium-filled or hot-air balloons, and we are lulled into feeling safe when we wear flotation devices out on the water.

Buoyancy is a force acting upon objects that are immersed in either a gas or a liquid. "Any object, wholly or partly immersed in a fluid, is buoyed up by a force equal to the weight of the fluid displaced by the object," said Archimedes of Syracuse, Sicily, a genius who lived more than 2,200 years ago. Sounds good, but what does it really mean for us?

Mostly it has to do with density, the ratio between mass and volume. If you compare a bowling ball and a volleyball, you know that the bowling ball is much heavier than the volleyball although they are both about the same size or volume. The bowling ball is said to be denser because it has more mass per unit of volume. You can easily predict what will happen if both of these are put into a pool. Students will say that because the volleyball is full of air, it floats. In a way this is true,

but it is not the air itself that makes the difference but that the air in the inflated volleyball adds little mass to the ball despite the amount of space it consumes.

Density is a property of matter. This means that despite how large or small a piece of material is, the density remains the same. In other words, if one sample of an object is quite large and another quite small, their densities are the same (since density, remember, is the *ratio* between mass and volume). There are exceptions to this, such as trees and other objects derived from living entities, where densities may vary slightly from one place to another. However, if you are considering pure substances like iron, aluminum, or any other element, density is considered to be a property that remains constant.

Now, back to Archimedes. He reasoned that a liquid exerts an upward force upon anything that is placed in it. He calculated that that force was equal to the mass of the water the object displaced or pushed aside. You can actually *feel* this force if you try to push a beach ball or a volleyball beneath the surface of the water. You can even feel the force if you try to push something as small as a Ping-Pong ball under water. These, of course, are examples using objects that float. What about those objects that sink?

Actually you can feel the force in a different way when you put something in the water that does *not* float. Each spring my wife and I rearrange the huge pots of water lilies that bloom in our fishpond. We do this while there is still water in the pond because the upward force of the water makes the pots easier to move. If the water is out of the pond, they feel like they are made of lead. We can lift them easily to the surface of the water but as soon as they leave the water, they seem to gain weight. They don't actually, but they feel like it because the upward force of the water is no longer helping us. You can measure this by attaching a spring scale to a rock or heavy object and submerging the rock in water. The rock will actually weigh less as shown on the dial of the spring scale. The mass of the rock has not changed, but the force of the water pushing up partially counteracts the downward force of the Earth we call weight.

So there are two forces acting on an object in air or water: the downward force of gravity and the upward force of the gas or liquid that was displaced by the object. If the upward force exceeds that of the downward force, the object will float. If the opposite is true, the object sinks. This is true of objects immersed in water or balloons immersed in the atmosphere. Archimedes calculated that the more water that the object displaced, the greater the upward force. This helps us to figure out why the popcorn kernels come to the top of the water column.

When the bubbles of carbon dioxide from the drink begin to form on the popcorn kernels, the volume of the popcorn-bubble system becomes larger. We should think of the popcorn and bubbles as a *system* since they interact with each other and are a *combined whole*. As in Archimedes' theory, together they displace more water and therefore the upward force on the popcorn-bubble system becomes large enough to push the popcorn (and its bubbles) to the surface. (It is important to note that the bubbles actually add mass as well as volume to the kernel-bubble system, but when you compare the mass of the bubble to the space they take up, it is minimal.) When

NATIONAL SCIENCE TEACHERS ASSOCIATION

the kernel reaches the surface, you see the bubbles burst, so the volume decreases. Since there is no longer the same upward force acting on the kernel system, it sinks back down to the bottom where the process begins all over again. In essence it *is* like putting a life jacket that has a lot of volume but little weight on the popcorn kernel. The volume has increased greatly but the mass has increased just a tiny bit.

Let me tell you a story that might help your understanding of buoyancy. In a third-grade class we were placing fruit in water and the children were predicting whether or not each piece of fruit would sink or float. Someone suggested peeling an orange that was floating and when we did, the orange without its peel sank to the bottom. One eight-year-old said, "I think that the peel is the orange's life preserver." How is that for a metaphor that signifies understanding?

If you are looking for formative assessment probes to use with your class on these topics, you can find four in *Uncovering Student Ideas in Science, Volume 2* in the probes titled "Comparing Cubes," "Floating Logs," "Floating High and Low," and "Solids and Holes" (Keeley, Eberle, and Tugel 2007). You may also find helpful articles to increase your knowledge from the various NSTA journals listed in the related publications and journal articles at the end of this chapter.

related ideas from the national science education standards (nrc 1996)

K–4: *Properties of Objects and Materials*
- Objects have many observable properties including size, weight, shape, color, temperature, and the ability to react with other substances. Those properties can be measured using tools such as rulers, balances, and thermometers.

5–8: *Properties of Objects and Materials*
- A substance has characteristic properties such as density, a boiling point, and solubility, all of which are independent of the amount of sample. A mixture of substances often can be separated into the original substances using one or more of the characteristic properties.

related ideas from benchmarks for science literacy (aaas 1993)

K–2: *The Structure of Matter*
- Objects can be described in terms of the materials they are made of (clay, cloth, paper, etc.) and their physical properties (color, size, shape, weight, texture, flexibility, etc.)

USING THE STORY WITH GRADES K–4

This story begs to have the students do the activity. If soda is not handy, I have found that putting half of an effervescent antacid tablet into a half tumbler of water will do just as well. The tablet soon dissolves and its released ingredients cause a chemical reaction that produces lots of bubbles and the popcorn will dance for a long time. You supply the music.

Ask your students to observe very carefully what is happening and to record their findings in their science notebooks. They can refer to these when you begin your chart on "What's happening?—Our best thinking." Ask students to tell what they think made the popcorn dance and then ask them to list questions they have about what happened.

If you've used the antacid tablets, these questions will probably center on the bubbles and what creates them. Since this is a bit too complex to go into at this age, try not to linger too long on this topic and just tell them that the chemicals in the tablet when mixed with water form gas bubbles. These questions don't usually come up when you use carbonated beverages because all children have noticed the bubbles in the drinks. Try to have them focus on what the bubbles did and how they affected how the popcorn behaved. Perhaps asking them to put the events in a sequence will help them see the relationship between the bubbles adhering to the corn and their rise and fall.

Questions usually arise also about what other things beside corn kernels might work. Have them feel the corn kernels and describe their results. Some may use the term *rough* or "have lots of edges or corners." Ask them if they can think of other things that are like that. Usually raisins are mentioned and beans such as lentils and pea seeds. It is important that they get a chance to test these out and make sure that the objects sink at first and then allow the bubbles to form on them. The surface of the objects is important. If they help you make a list of possible candidates, you can turn these into questions that can be investigated, such as: Will raisins also dance like popcorn? How does the number of bubbles attached to the corn affect how fast it rises? How do different types of soda affect how the corn behaves? This

sets the stage for some real inquiry about the elements involved. At this point you can hope they don't suggest your supplying vintage champagne.

As for the reasons for the phenomenon, try to make connections between activities the children have had when they have been in the water and the floating and sinking corn. They will probably suggest metal objects and will notice that if bubbles form on the rough pieces of metal, nothing happens. What is different between corn and metal? You can help them see that for their size, the pieces of metal are much heavier than the corn. That way you can start them on their way to considering two things at once, size and weight.

I like to have a life jacket available during the lessons so that I can put one on a child and the class can see that the life jacket weighs something and that they take up more space with the jacket on. With children this age I would not go into density more deeply than that. But, the experience will help them on their way to understanding the concept in later years. As I mentioned earlier, predicting the floating or sinking of various fruits can be an interesting activity with lots of predicting and many surprises. They will see that most pitted fruits (plums, peaches, cherries) sink while nonpitted fruits do not. Then the orange with and without the peel can raise some interesting questions about size, space, floating, and sinking.

USING THE STORY WITH GRADES 5–8

I believe that it is very important to allow the students to have a close-up opportunity to do this activity. Each student or at least every two students should have the setup in front of them. Observation of the phenomenon is very important. See the above section for ideas on what materials to use.

Students at this level are usually ready to look at density as a concept and to do some of the measurements necessary to substantiate the results. However, I am satisfied at this level if the students realize that there are only two ways in plain water that they can change a floater into a sinker or a sinker into a floater: change the volume of the materials involved or change the weight. Since density is a ratio, it is necessary that the students are mindful that both properties of a material must be considered at all times.

This is difficult for some students. If you choose to use the probes "Comparing Cubes," "Floating Logs," or "Floating High and Low," (Keeley, Eberle, and Tugel 2007), the student answers will enlighten you about their conceptions concerning floating, sinking, and density.

While understanding that the density of the liquid involved is also important, I have found that introducing this to students who are still struggling with density of the objects that sink or float can be distracting. Although the formula $D = M/V$ eventually may help students understand how density can be calculated (density equals mass divided by volume), it is usually helpful if the students have had a number of qualitative experiences before being subjected to the mathematical and quantitative experience.

Many members of your class may also believe that the depth of water may affect the sinking or floating of an object. This is easily tested.

There are several articles in *Science Scope*, the NSTA middle school journal, that may help you go even further in your quest to teach about density. These are

- "Looking at Density From Different Perspectives" (Peterson-Chin and Sterling 2004),
- "A Dastardly Density Deed" (Shaw 2003), and
- "Shampoo, Soy Sauce, and the Prince's Pendant" (Chandrasekhar and Litherland 2006). In fact, if you go to the NSTA website *(www.nsta.org)* and search for "density" in the middle school journal, *Science Scope*, you will find several more articles on this topic.

One last reminder: The concept of density seems to be a difficult one for all learners to understand completely and buoyancy adds to the confusion. It may not be until years later that a person will finally "get it," but the activities and investigations you give will provide the necessary steps that will eventually lead to understanding. Sometimes the understanding "lightbulb" goes off at unexpected times and you may not be there to witness it. Nonetheless you have had a part in throwing the switch.

related BOOKS and NSTa JOURNAL articles

Driver, R., A. Squires, P. Rushworth, and V. Wood-Robinson. 1994. *Making sense of secondary science: Research into children's ideas.* London and New York: Routledge Falmer.

Keeley, P. 2005. *Science curriculum topic study: Bridging the gap between standards and practice.* Thousand Oaks, CA: Corwin Press.

Keeley, P., F. Eberle, and C. Dorsey. 2008. *Uncovering student ideas in science: Another 25 formative assessment probes, volume 3.* Arlington, VA: NSTA Press.

Keeley, P., F. Eberle, and L. Farrin. 2005. *Uncovering student ideas in science: 25 formative assessment probes, volume 1.* Arlington, VA: NSTA Press.

Keeley, P., F. Eberle, and J. Tugel. 2007. *Uncovering student ideas in science: 25 more formative assessment probes, volume 2.* Arlington, VA: NSTA Press.

Konicek-Moran, R. 2008. *Everyday science mysteries.* Arlington, VA: NSTA Press.

Konicek-Moran, R. 2009. *More everyday science mysteries.* Arlington, VA: NSTA Press.

Shaw, M. 1998. Diving into density. *Science Scope* 22 (3): 24–26

references

American Association for the Advancement of Science (AAAS). 1993. *Benchmarks for science literacy.* New York: Oxford University Press.

Chandrasekhar, M., and R. Litherland. 2006. Shampoo, soy sauce, and the prince's pendant: Density for middle-level students. *Science Scope* 30 (2): 12–17.

Keeley, P., F. Eberle, and J. Tugel. 2007. *Uncovering student ideas in science: 25 more formative assessment probes, volume 2.* Arlington, VA: NSTA Press.

National Research Council (NRC). 1996. *National science education standards.* Washington, DC: National Academies Press.

Peterson-Chin, L., and D. Sterling. 2004. Looking at density from different perspectives. *Science Scope* 27 (7): 16–20.

Shaw, M. 2003. A dastardly density deed. *Science Scope* 27 (5): 18–21.

CHAPTER 14
COLOR THIEVES

Jenny liked to do projects for school. Well, actually what she really loved to do best was decorate the covers on her projects. She loved colors and shapes and would spend as much time on the covers as she did on the rest of the project.

This particular day, Jenny was just finishing a project for science. Balloons were the topic—helium and hot air balloons and what causes certain balloons to rise up and float away. The hot air balloons were her favorites, maybe because they were so colorfully decorated

with big flashy designs and shapes. Jenny lived in a valley where hot air balloons were in the air almost every morning and evening. You could hear the roar of the flame as the pilot made the balloon go higher.

The project was interesting and Jenny worked hard explaining what she had found out about how these big bags of hot air could float for long distances all over the countryside. But now came the fun part, creating the cover sheet and making it colorful and bright.

She had little trouble deciding on what she would draw.

"I'm going to draw a big hot air balloon with a star pattern made up of green, purple and blue diamonds on it," she told her mother. Then she set about drawing her patterns and coloring them in.

"I've got some beautiful see-through colored plastic covers," said Mom. "You can put your project in one of those and make it really special and colorful."

"Cool," said Jenny, and she continued to color in the reds, yellows, blues, purples, and greens.

It was spectacular! It was a masterpiece! Jenny was proud of both the project and the cover, but mostly the cover.

"Mom!" she shouted. "Where are those colored folders you told me about?"

"I put them on the dining room table," Mom called from the living room. "Take your pick. I think there are five or six different colors."

There were. Green, red, yellow, blue, green-blue, and colorless folders sat on the table. Which one to use? Jenny pondered. How about red? That should make all of the colors look brighter.

She slid the project cover under the red see-through folder and stepped closer to the table lamp for a good view. It looked…

"Gross!!" Jenny shouted. "The cover stole some of my colors!"

Her mother came in to see what the fuss was about.

"What do you mean, 'stole your colors'?"

"Look," said Jenny and held up the folder and project.

"You're right!" exclaimed Mom. "Some of the colors are… BLACK and others are gone! How can that be? I thought the red would make the colors all seem, well, prettier. Let's try the other covers."

And they did and the results were even more surprising. Later, Jenny slid the project into the clear folder and admired her work. But she still wondered how the other folders managed to steal her colors. And she wondered if she could ever make a cover that would not change even if it were put in a colored folder.

PURPOSE

This story poses a challenge to its readers to solve the mystery of light, color, and how we see color. It also asks the question, "What is color?" After investigating the phenomena of color and color filters, students should realize that light is made up of many colors in our visible spectrum and our eyes and brain contribute to the process of "seeing" color.

There is a secondary and broader purpose in this story as well: Help students understand that we see things, no matter how shiny or dull they are, by light that is reflected from the objects to our eyes. This is one of the most difficult concepts to teach. I hope that this story and the activities it generates will lead to at least a more enlightened view of how we see objects.

related concepts

- Energy spectrum
- Reflection
- Mixing colors
- Color
- Diffraction
- Primary colors

DON'T Be surprised

Most children and many adults believe that sight originates in the eye. It is said that beauty lies in the eye of the beholder, but that is *not* true of sight. We see objects because light reflects from objects into our eyes. So without light, we simply cannot see. Most of your students will believe that, given enough time for our eyes to adjust, we can see in total darkness. Thus, the idea of seeing because of reflected light is counterintuitive. In the DVD *A Private Universe* produced by the Harvard-Smithsonian Science Media Group, Karen, an eighth grader, sits in a completely dark room for 15 minutes and swears that she sees the yellow side of a block on the table in front of her. When the interviewer showed her that the yellow side of the block had been turned away from her, she still insisted that, given enough time, her eyes would eventually adjust. Despite the complete lack of light, she would be able to see at least the outline of the block.

Students also do not believe that light travels from place to place, but that light merely "fills" a space such as a room. Since light travels so fast, it is not hard to see how this misconception formed. Probes ("Can It Reflect Light?") and ("Apple in the Dark") from *Uncovering Student Ideas in Science, Volume 1* (Keeley, Eberle, and Farrin 2005) are aimed at finding students' ideas about light.

CONTENT BacKGrounD

Before we begin, I must emphasize that our perception of color is just that—we *perceive* color by the functions of our eyes, our brains, and what we have been taught. In other words, the light and color we "see" is a combination of learning and the capacity of certain cells in the eye, which in turn communicate with the brain. What we perceive seems "real" to us, but that perception may give us some false beliefs about the true nature of light. It can also explain why we all have resistant misconceptions about color and sight.

The behavior of light is very complex and I cannot possibly explain all of the intricacies in this volume. If you wish a more formal, detailed explanation about the various waves, dig into your copy of *Science Matters* and find the areas that are still confusing to you (Hazen and Trefil 1991). A very fine explanation covering many pages can be found in the teachers' section of the GEMS curriculum booklet *Color Analyzers,* from the vast number of units published by the Lawrence Hall of Science (Erickson and Willard 2005). You can also get a copy of Bill Robertson's *Light: Stop Faking It! Finally Understanding Science So You Can Teach It* (2003). This book has built-in activities that will help you understand light like you never have before. It is not necessary that you have a graduate degree in physics to teach this story but a little background will help you when you run up against your students' data and questions. It will help you ask the right questions or deliver the right comment to send your students back to their investigations with new insight. It will also help you help your students look without telling them what to see.

This story is concerned with the behavior of light and color. Light is the result of an electromagnetic disturbance, and for our purposes we will consider these disturbances as producing electromagnetic *waves.* This is very much like throwing a stone in a pond and seeing the waves or ripples moving outward from the point of contact between the stone and the water. We can compare these with sound waves caused by vibrating objects causing a disturbance in the air molecules around them. The source of the disturbance with light waves is the Sun and the various means for producing light that humans have come up with over the millennia include fire, electricity, battery-powered flashlights, and candles, to name a few.

Light waves have different *wavelengths* (the length between the crests or troughs of two adjacent waves). Humans have named the light of certain visible wavelengths. These are red, orange, yellow, green, blue, indigo, and violet (ROYGBIV). These waves are in our limited range of visible light that we have learned to call *white light.*

ROYGBIV (pronounced like a name: "Roy G. Biv") is an acronym to remember all of the light colors from the Sun in the order that they appear in a rainbow. Rainbows happen when white light is broken down into its component parts by another phenomenon (diffraction). The visible spectrum is a tiny part of the entire family of wavelengths that also includes many to which our senses are not privy. These include infrared, ultraviolet, radio waves, gamma rays, and x-rays.

Because of their various wavelengths and energy levels, visible light waves are prone to being separated by such things as water droplets, prisms, and a device know as a "diffraction grating" (more about this below). This bending and spreading out of the waves is called *diffraction.* In the visible spectrum, each wavelength bends differently so that they all separate into what we know as the color spectrum. In addition, whenever waves enter a medium of a different density, like water or glass, they tend to bend, some more than others and so they spread out. This is another example of diffraction.

Our eyes have millions of color-sensitive cells in the retina called cone cells because of their shape. There are also cells shaped like rods, but these only differentiate between

light and dark. Cone cells are activated only in bright light so we do not see color in dim light such as moonlight. It is believed that there are three types of cone cells, each of which has sensitivity to light of different wavelengths. These sensitivities are attuned to the wavelengths we call red, green, and blue. These are often called *primary colors* of light because when they are combined in equal intensities, we perceive white light. Please note that I said we *perceive* white light. This is important because, as I stated before, color is all about perception. Red, green, and blue light can also be combined in various other ways to produce almost any color. Your color TV set or computer monitor does this with the three kinds of pixels to produce the multicolor images you see on the screen.

"Wait!" you say. "Stop the presses! Misprint? Yellow, not green, is a primary color!" True, yellow is a primary color in *pigment* colors but not in *light* colors. We have to concentrate on the *light colors* to understand why things have the colors we see. This is an extremely important distinction. In writing this content section for you, I confess that after all these years, *I* finally understand why we see color! Basically it all boils down to concentrating on these primary *light colors*. Remember this vital point as we move along.

Since visible light is really made up of the various colors of the rainbow (ROYGBIV), when it strikes certain objects the objects absorb some of the colors and reflect others. The colors that are reflected give that object what we perceive as its color. For example, we see green leaves as green because leaves reflect the green wavelengths back to our eyes and then to our brain, which tells us, "Those leaves are green." We know this because way back in our childhood, someone taught us that when we see, that particular color, we call it "green." If, we were German we would call it *grün*, if we were Spanish, we would call it *verde*, and if French, *vert*. In other words, color names are a human construction.

All other colors in the white light are absorbed by the leaf and either warm the leaf up or help in the photosynthesis process. So that is why the leaf appears green—it reflects green light waves. By the same token, green paint is green because it reflects green light waves and absorbs all others. In other words, the colors of an object as you see it is not *in* the object itself but in the colors that the object selectively absorbs and reflects. White is not a color but the combined wavelengths of the visible spectrum. Truly white surfaces should reflect the entire visible light spectrum. This may not be true if you paint your walls with "Cirrus" or "Summer Cloud" or any other fancy name for an off-white color bought at the paint store.

Objects appear to be different colors when seen in different light environments. You may have taken a paint or fabric sample out of the fluorescent lighting in a store to look at it in the sunlight. What you see is the reflection of the elements of the light spectrum produced by the light source you are using. Not all lightbulbs produce the same spectrum and this will affect what the objects reflect. The new energy-saving bulbs have a different spectrum than the traditional incandescent bulbs, so their colors appear to be different. Things look different at dusk, as the Sun gets lower in the sky, than they do at noon.

Let's look for a moment at the difference between the mixing of colors as light and the mixing of pigments. Mixing of colors of light is called an *additive* process and mixing of pigments is a *subtractive* process. That needs some explanation!

First, we should look briefly at the additive process. It helps if you imagine everything dark and think that you are now going to add primary light colors to that darkness. Primary colors are defined as colors that when combined produce white *if they are colors of light* and produce black or gray *if they are pigments*. Thus, the three primary additive colors of light are red, green, and blue.

In the additive process, we combine the primary light colors R (red), B (blue), and G (green) to make W (white). Let's create a formula that says R + B + G = W. Now sometimes we mix less than all three. Let's say we mix R (red) + B (blue). That would appear as M (magenta). If we mix B (blue) + G (green), we get C (cyan), akin to aqua; and R (red) + G (green) = Y (yellow). This leads into a whole other set of color bases in paint, but we won't go there right now. Colors of light and pigment are challenging enough!

I held up a yellow notebook and suddenly realized it appeared yellow because it absorbed the B (blue) and reflected the R (red) and G (green) to my eyes. As we can see from above, R + G = Y! So the color of an object is not *in* the object but in the primary light color(s) it absorbs and the remainder of the spectrum it reflects to our eyes! In a formula it would look like:

$$(R + B + G) - B = R + G$$

$$R + G = Y$$

Written out, it would be: Red plus blue plus green (which combine to make white) minus blue equals red plus green, which equals yellow. So, that's why I saw yellow! I saw the combination of the reflected red and green that in light make yellow. Or it may be even a little more complicated than this, because it is possible that yellow light was reflected from the spectrum as well. My eye, however, was stimulated to see yellow either way. I could not distinguish the difference. It was all yellow to me. Thus perception of color is once again related to how our brains translate what we see.

I must be clear that the whole theory of color perception is still in the process of study. What I have tried to explain to you is close to the accepted theory at this point. This may be all too complicated for elementary school kids to understand but I hope it makes things clearer to you and it might well be appropriate for middle school.

Next, consider mixing pigments, the subtractive process. If you have a blue pigment, you see it as blue because only blue is reflected from its surface. If you mix this blue pigment with yellow, the mixture will seem green but *not* yellow or blue. Thus you have *subtracted* from your vision two colors that you could have seen separately, but cannot see combined. Less light is reflected because you have put together two colors that are going to absorb more light, thus *subtracting* the number of different light waves reflected to your eyes. The more pigments you add, the more light will be absorbed and the less reflected until so little light is reflected that you perceive it as gray or black. I'll bet you all have had some experience with primary colors in pigments. A favorite activity is to take white frosting from the can and give kids food coloring to make different color frostings to go on graham crackers. Not the healthiest activity, but once in a while it shouldn't hurt (except for diabetic or sugar-intolerant children).

This helps us understand a little more so we can talk about filters. What do colored filters do? One thing they do *not* do is change the color of light. Colored filters let certain colors through and do not let other colors through. For example, a red filter

allows red, yellow, orange, and pink through to varying extents (which blend in with a white background). On the other hand, brown, green, blue, and purple appear black because the light that they reflect cannot penetrate the red filter. Their wavelengths are completely absorbed, thus appearing black.

When you look at objects through a red filter, that filter only lets red or near-red colors get to your eyes. It absorbs green and blues. Why do I say *near*-red colors? Yellow pigments from crayons, markers, and other paints often reflect some red and green light as well as yellow. It is no wonder yellow objects seem so bright since they are reflecting more different colors. Can you guess why many emergency vehicles are painted yellow?

Orange objects also reflect some yellow and red as well as orange. Orange appears bright through a red filter. Do you think this is true if seen through a green filter? Give yourself points if you said no since the green filter would filter out yellow and red as well as the orange, since first, it absorbs red, and then you need red and green to make yellow. Red objects seen through a red filter will seem to disappear into the white background because the filter only allows red light from the background. So, the red object seems to fade into the background, sort of like camouflage.

Your students will be finding these things out as they make drawings and notes using different crayons and markers, then viewing them through red and green filters. There will be more details in the "Using the Story" sections. I suggest that you make yourself a pair of red filter glasses, get some colored markers, and try these things as you read this material.

I see this as an exciting chance to show that we see only that from which light is reflected. If light were not reflected from the things we see through the filter, the filter would not alter them! Perhaps this will convince some and perhaps not. But it certainly will not hinder their growth toward understanding light, color, and electromagnetic energy, if not now, maybe at another time in the future.

reLateD IDeas From the NaTIONaL SCIeNce eDUCaTION STaNDarDS (NrC 1996)

K–4: *Light, Heat, Electricity, and Magnetism*
- Light travels in a straight line until it strikes an object. Light can be reflected by a mirror, refracted by a lens, or absorbed by the object.

5–8: *Transfer of Energy*
- Light interacts with matter by transmission (including refraction), absorption, or scattering (including reflection). To see an object, light from that object—emitted by or scattered from it—must enter the eye.

- The Sun's energy arrives as light with a range of wavelengths, consisting of visible light, infrared and ultraviolet radiation.

related ideas from Benchmarks for science Literacy (aaas 1993)

6–8: Motion

- Light from the Sun is made up of a mixture of many different colors of light, even though to the eye the light looks almost white. Other things that give off or reflect light have a different mix of colors.
- Something can be "seen" when light waves emitted or reflected by it enter the eye—just as something can be "heard" when sound waves from it enter the ear.
- Human eyes respond to only a narrow range of wavelengths of electromagnetic radiation—visible light. Differences of wavelength within that range are perceived as differences in color.

Using the story with grades K–4

Although this is one of my very favorite stories, I admit that I was a bit hesitant to recommend it below grade 6. But then I read "Secret Message Science Goggles" by Christina DeVita and Sarah Ruppert in *Science and Children* (2007) and was convinced that it could be used at least as low as second grade and perhaps in earlier grades as well. Devita and Ruppert were not focused on the physics of the topic but tried to provide the students with a tool with which they could investigate the topic of color. I would suggest that you give your class the probe(s) "Can It Reflect Light" and "Apple in the Dark" from *Uncovering Student Ideas in Science, Volume 1* (Keeley, Eberle, and Farrin 2005). These probes will give you a head's up on what your students believe.

You might want to create two "Our Best Thinking" charts on "What We Know About Seeing" and "What We Know About Color." After the discussion, you can have the children make goggles with red filters out of cardboard (glue or tape transparent red plastic film over each eye hole). Have them describe and record their findings as they look around the room. They will be seeing the world through a filter that allows only red light to reach their eyes. Let them explore the world this way for a while and raise questions about what they observe on objects around the room, patterns on clothing, and pictures on the walls. You can write some secret messages, or put a red bird in a green cage, which will disappear or at least look ghostly when viewed through the red goggles.

Return to the charts and begin to develop investigations about color and see-ing by using the goggles or perhaps making others with blue or yellow filters. Students usually want to re-create the situation in the story and make a picture with many colors to be viewed through filters. This is a good idea since it puts the students in Jenny's position. They feel like they are "in" the story.

Your students will notice that certain colors will look black as seen through a red filter. Suppose they look at a green book cover or marker swatch. The red filter blocks out blue and yellow so that they do not penetrate the filter. This means that since there is no red in the green cover, nothing is transmitted through the filter and the cover looks black. Would the same be true if the cover were blue? Of course, since no color would penetrate the filter, the image of the cover would still appear black. Students will figure out what colors appear black and which they will be able to see and that if Jenny had avoided these colors she could have avoided the blackouts in her cover. They will also be able to see that by using different filters, they can hide words and other messages in designs and send secret codes by use of various filters.

Finally, the students are left with a challenge from the last line of the story. Is it possible to make a cover with colors that will not change if they are put in a colored folder? This can provide not only a great discussion but give the students an opportunity to try their ideas and get instant feedback. It will also give them a chance to finish the story.

USING THE STORY WITH GRADES 5–8

Students at this age also like to "live the story" with Jenny just to get the feel of the situation and see if it really is true. This means that you need to have a few see-through folders of different colors around for the students to try. Just like the younger children in the prior section, they can be encouraged to write secret mes-sages that can only be seen through a filter.

Students also respond very well to the probes mentioned in the prior section and get into a lively discourse about whether things reflect light and whether or not you can see in total darkness. I might add that most children have never experienced total darkness unless they have been in a cave or someplace similar, so their experience is usually *semi*-darkness. They will be adamant that in time their eyes will adjust. I have yet to visit a school where achieving total darkness is possible. If your school is lucky enough to have a photography darkroom, maybe that would work.

Your students will likely insist that shiny things like mirrors or windows will reflect light but not rocks or other dull objects. This is why "Color Thieves" is a story that might just provide them with enough disequilibrium to question their prior conceptions. First it will be necessary for you to show them that white light is made up of many colors. This means that you will have to have a sheet of diffraction grating so that students can view light sources and see the various spectra that make

up the light. Diffraction gratings can be purchased from online distributors such as Edmund Scientifics or Delta Educational. They are sheets of plastic with thousands of lines scribed into them so that light will be scattered and produce a spectrum. If the children bring old CDs from home they can tilt them and see a spectrum on them as well due to the diffraction of light on the surface of the CD. If you follow the ideas suggested in the GEMS unit *Color Analyzers* you can make up what they call color analyzers: index cards with three holes. One hole has a red filter, another has a green filter, and the third hole has the diffraction grating cut from a larger sheet. This saves money since the amount of filters and gratings used are small.

Using several types of lamps is helpful if the students are looking for differences in kinds of spectrums through the diffraction grating. Different hues may be missing or of varying brightness. This is another form of evidence that the colors we see are perceptions. Fluorescent lamps used to be rather narrow but now are manufactured to have a broader spectrum. If you have some older fluorescent lamps to compare to modern ones, this is an interesting activity.

Filters can be purchased at most art stores for very little money. The quality varies a great deal, which sometimes affects the results, but most of the time the main colors come through as expected. The folks at Lawrence Hall, the GEMS people, recommend the use of Crayola Classic brand markers for the truest colors. Take along a paper with color marks on it to help you test the filters you want to purchase.

You may want to return to the story and see that Jenny drew her cover using colors such as reds, greens, purples, blues, and yellows. Jenny's reds may have "dis appeared" into the background of the white paper; certainly the greens and purples and blues would have seemed black and the yellow might also have blended into the background. If this is the case, then students can write or draw on paper with different colors and then look at their papers through filters and find completely different messages or patterns. Certain color letters mixed in with other color letters might seem to say one thing without the filter and another through the filter. They will love to make secret messages.

Finally, the last sentence in the story does offer a challenge. I recommend a good discussion before letting the children try to create such a paper. Remember, differences of opinion are the key to good discourse and also let you in on imbedded assessment as you listen to the discourse. Here you might interject a few questions that will lead the children toward wondering if there isn't evidence here that shows that light has to be reflected from an object in order for them to see that object.

reLaTeD Books anD NSTa JournaL arTicLes

DeVita, C., and S. Ruppert. 2007. Secret message science goggles. *Science and Children* 44 (7): 30–35.

Driver, R., A. Squires, P. Rushworth, and V. Wood-Robinson. 1994. *Making sense of secondary science: Research into children's ideas.* London and New York: Routledge Falmer.

Keeley, P. 2005. *Science curriculum topic study: Bridging the gap between standards and practice.* Thousand Oaks, CA: Corwin Press.

Keeley, P., F. Eberle, and C. Dorsey. 2008. *Uncovering student ideas in science: Another 25 formative assessment probes, volume 3.* Arlington, VA: NSTA Press.

Keeley, P., F. Eberle, and L. Farrin. 2005. *Uncovering student ideas in science: 25 formative assessment probes, volume 1.* Arlington, VA: NSTA Press.

Keeley, P., F. Eberle, and J. Tugel. 2007. *Uncovering student ideas in science: 25 more formative assessment probes, volume 2.* Arlington, VA: NSTA Press.

references

American Association for the Advancement of Science (AAAS). 1993. *Benchmarks for science literacy.* New York: Oxford University Press.

DeVita, C., and S. Ruppert. 2007. Secret message science goggles. *Science and Children* 44 (7): 30–35.

Erickson, J., and C. Willard. 2005. *Color analyzers: Investigating light and color.* Berkeley, CA: GEMS, Lawrence Hall of Science, University of California.

Hazen, R., and J. Trefil. 1991. *Science matters: Achieving scientific literacy.* New York: Anchor Books.

Keeley, P., F. Eberle, and L. Farrin. 2005. *Uncovering student ideas in science: 25 formative assessment probes, volume 1.* Arlington, VA: NSTA Press.

National Research Council (NRC). 1996. *National science education standards.* Washington, DC: National Academies Press.

Robertson, B. 2003. *Light: Stop faking it! finally understanding science so you can teach it.* Arlington, VA: NSTA Press.

Schneps, M. A. 1996. *The private universe project.* Harvard Smithsonian Center for Astrophysics.

CHAPTER 15
A MIRROR BIG ENOUGH

Tenika needed a mirror for her room. She had a few problems to solve before she bought one, though. She had a very small room and finding a place for a full-length mirror was not easy. Naturally she wanted to see her image from head to toe, and she was tall for her age. There was only one wall that would hold a full-length mirror unless she wanted to rearrange all of her bedroom furniture, which she didn't. She had to learn a lot more about mirrors before she made her purchase. She also had a limited amount of money, so that created another problem.

At the furniture store Tenika looked all around and fell in love with a free-standing walnut mirror that would be just right. If she bought that one, she could put it anywhere in the room and the problem was solved. That was, until she looked at the price tag. Three hundred dollars! Well, that was that.

All of the other full-length mirrors that she liked were expensive too. There were a lot of cheaper and smaller mirrors for sale but she still had her heart set on seeing all of herself, not just part of her. All of the small mirrors were mounted on the wall just at her eye level so she could see her face from hair to chin clearly. But there was the problem of the size of her room. Could she get a smaller mirror and stand far enough away to see all of her? How far back did she have to move to see all of her in a small mirror? As she tried moving back from each mirror, she found that what she saw was not what she expected.

"What is going on here?" she wondered. "Are these mirrors weird, or what?"

She wandered around and tried looking in all of the mirrors. She found out a few things about how mirrors work that surprised and amazed her. Also, some of the mirrors were mounted too high and some were too low and that seemed to make a difference in what she could see.

Since the smallest mirrors were the cheapest, Tanika kept asking herself, "What is the smallest mirror I can buy so that I can still see myself, head to toe?" In the end, she was able to buy a mirror she could afford that worked for her.

NATIONAL SCIENCE TEACHERS ASSOCIATION

PURPOSE

Mirrors are part of our everyday lives. How many of us start our day in front of the bathroom mirror brushing our teeth or our hair? Our early ancestors probably did much of the same by looking into pools of water and seeing their reflections. And it does not matter how supple you think you are and how much experience you have had with yoga; it is still impossible to see the back of your head without the use of two mirrors. This story is designed to motivate students to explore how mirrors work and how mirrors reflect the light (first reflected from objects to the mirror and then to our eyes as images), and to discover in this particular case the famed rule that "the angle of incidence equals the angle of reflection." Think of the many times a mirror is used in your daily life and think also how much *you* understand how it works like it does. Mirrors are indeed the source of some of the most illusive everyday science mysteries.

RELATED CONCEPTS

- Light energy
- Vision
- Reflection
- Mathematics (angles)

DON'T BE SURPRISED

Children and adults alike tend to believe that mirrors and shiny things are the only objects that reflect light. Actually it is only because everything reflects light that we are able to see anything. If you give the probe "Can It Reflect Light?" from volume 1 of *Uncovering Student Ideas* (Keeley, Eberle, and Farrin 2005), you will find most of your students will probably not realize that all objects reflect light in different ways so that we *see* them as different objects. Although it is not absolutely necessary for students to believe that everything reflects light to their eyes in order to understand how mirrors work, it gives you as a teacher insight into the ways your students perceive the concepts of light and sight. In fact, it is one of the most difficult of preconceptions to change. I believe that the topic explored in the previous chapter "Color Thieves" stands the best chance of modifying this preconception, particularly for older students. But that is a different story altogether (literally!).

Adults also believe that they do not have to stand directly in front of a mirror in order to see their own image. Most believe that they can stand at the edge of a mirror and see their likeness. It is really strange that something we use everyday is still an enigma and the source of so many misconceptions.

CONTENT BACKGROUND

The image we see in a mirror is not real. It is a *virtual image,* or what we have learned to call a *mirror image,* inside the mirror or behind it. A mirror is a piece of glass that has aluminum or silver backing bonded to it. It is important for the metal to be present because when light energy reflected from an object in front of the mirror hits the metal backing, it excites the electrons in the metal. They respond by giving off light energy directly back in the same direction from which the light originated. Mirrors are very smooth and polished so that the light that is reflected back is barely distorted and gives a fairly accurate image of the object placed in front of it. Historically, mirrors were probably polished metals. Mirrors as we know them today were probably not available until the 18th or 19th century. As early as the 12th century, metal-backed mirrors were used in Europe; before that time, silver or bronze polished to high brilliance was used. These mirrors were still not as good as the mirrors of today.

I have mentioned that the image you see is not real. It cannot be touched and it has no mass, nor does it take up space. In essence, it is another dimension. It is really behind the surface of the mirror, as you perceive it. It is also twice the distance behind the mirror as you are in front of the mirror. Yet your image in the mirror is the same size. Think about that for a second.

Light is reflected from mirrors directly back toward the direction from which it came, if you are standing directly in front of the mirror. That is, if light strikes a mirror head on, the light is reflected directly back. If the light from the object strikes the mirror at an angle, the image is reflected back at that same angle but in the opposite direction. This is very much like a ball bouncing off a wall. If you throw the ball directly at the wall, it comes right back to you. But, if you throw it at an angle, it will bounce off the wall and go off at exactly the same angle in the opposite direction. The rule is that the angle of incidence (the angle that the ball hits the wall) will equal the angle of reflection (the angle the ball will move when it leaves the wall).

This is why you can see images of objects in a mirror even though you are viewing from a point to one side or the other. If you can see a person in a mirror, they can see you as well. You may have seen trucks or buses with a safety sign on the back that says, "If you can't see my mirrors, I can't see you." This means that if you can see the truck's mirrors, the reflection from you is visible in the truck's mirror as well.

You may have noticed that when you look at your side mirrors while driving or while sitting in the passenger seat, you do not see yourself but only the road behind you. You are at an angle outside the reflection angle of the mirror because it is set to see what is behind the car. The same is true of the inside rearview mirror, which is set to see out of the rear window. If you were to look at the rearview mirror through the rear window of the car you would be able to see the person in the driver's seat. Try it.

NATIONAL SCIENCE TEACHERS ASSOCIATION

Another conception common among children and adults is that if you move back from a mirror, you will see more of yourself. This preconception probably has its origins in the bathroom where we do most of our mirror gazing. Because most bathroom mirrors are mounted on the wall in front of a counter and cabinet, we are deprived of any reflection of objects below the level of the counter. As we move back from the counter, more of us can be reflected into the mirror because the counter no longer prevents it and we see more of ourselves, particularly that part below the waist. So, as long as your eyes are in the same horizontal plane as the mirror on the wall and the mirror is flat against the wall, you will see the same image whether you are close to or farther away from that mirror.

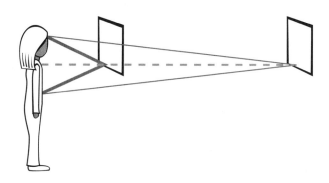

Now, let us imagine a mirror that is half the height of the girl in the picture. As she looks at the mirror, the angle of the reflected light from her feet will equal the angle that meets her eyes. Therefore, if the mirror is half the height of the person looking into it and the mirror is in the same horizontal plane as that person's eyes, she can see her whole body.

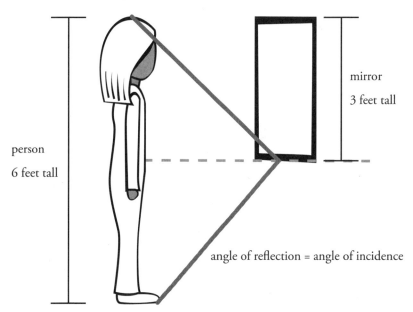

person
6 feet tall

mirror
3 feet tall

angle of reflection = angle of incidence

This will explain how Tenika solved her problem. She had to get a mirror at least one half her height, but considering that she would be growing, she had to estimate how tall she would be and buy a mirror half that size. She also realized that it made no difference how far she was from the mirror; she would see an image of herself that showed the same amount of her body.

To obtain some information on optical properties of light I refer you to *Science Matters* by Hazen and Trefil (1991, pp. 106–108).

related ideas from the national science education standards (nrc 1996)

K–4: Light, Heat, Electricity, and Magnetism

- Light travels in a straight line until it strikes an object. Light can be reflected by a mirror, refracted by a lens, or absorbed by the object.

5–8: Transfer of Energy

- Light interacts with matter by transmission (including refraction). To see an object, light from that object—either emitted by or scattered from it—must enter the eye.

related ideas from benchmarks for science literacy (aaas 1993)

3–5: Motion

- Light travels and tends to maintain its direction of motion until it interacts with an object or a material.
- Light can be absorbed, redirected, bounced back, or allowed to pass through. (*Note:* This is a new benchmark. It can be found in AAAS 2001, p.63.)

6–8: Motion

- Something can be "seen" when light waves emitted or reflected by it enter the eye.
- Light acts like a wave in many ways. Waves can explain how light behaves. (*Note:* This is a new benchmark. It can be found in AAAS 2001, p.65)

NATIONAL SCIENCE TEACHERS ASSOCIATION

USING THE STORY WITH GRADES K–4

Although the Standards and particularly the Benchmarks do not have much to say about this concept in the early years, the story can at least be a grabber to get the kids interested in trying to find out things about mirrors. Young children are marvels at trying new things with objects. With a little encouragement, you should have them telling you all sorts of things they "know" about mirrors. These statements, of course, can be put on the "Our Best Thinking" chart, changed to questions, and then tested. There is a great deal to be done with younger students and mirrors. To be sure, the young child may not have the vocabulary or the developmental acuity to understand all of the ideas behind the concept of reflection but their experiences with these objects are nonetheless valuable.

Kindergarteners and first and second graders love to play with mirrors and with guidance can learn a lot about the direction of the beams of light through such games as "mirrors and flashlights," where a child is asked to shine her light on her mirror and make the light shine on a specific object in the darkened room. For example, "Sally, make your mirror make the light shine on the clock." The child has to hold the light and the mirror in such a way that the light beam is reflected to that specific object. Then the child explains how she did it. In essence this exploration of mirrors and light sources is a form of inquiry especially if they are asked to predict why they are positioning their objects to get a desired result. They can draw these trials in their science notebooks and explain what happened and possibly try to explain why they think it did. These notes can be of great assistance to you in assessing where to go next.

They can play a mirror-acting game where two children face each other, and they pretend there is a mirror between them. One child acts as the leader and makes an action and the other has to respond or mimic the actions of the first child as though she was the mirror image. Then they switch roles. They can talk about what adaptations they had to make to move just like the leader. For example, "When you raised your right arm, I had to raise my left arm 'cause I'm in the mirror."

USING THE STORY WITH GRADES 5–8

With students from grades 3 or 4 through 8, I suggest starting the lesson by giving the probe "Mirror on the Wall" from *Understanding Student Ideas in Science, Volume 3* (Keeley, Eberle, and Dorsey 2008). This probe asks the students to choose from three options about a girl looking in a mirror and stepping back. It asks whether she will see the same amount of her image, less, or more. It addresses one the main preconceptions about seeing oneself in a mirror. It will provide you with a class profile of how students use ideas about light to explain how we see images in mirrors.

As usual, I would begin with asking the students what they "know" about how we see images in mirrors and writing those down on the "Our Best Thinking" chart as described above in the K–4 section. If you do not have access to the above probe, I suggest taking an idea from Eleanor Duckworth of Harvard Graduate

School of Education, who begins a class on science education using mirrors. Place a mirror on the wall and ask two students to show where they would stand so that they can see each other's reflections at the same time. Let the class discuss their predictions with reasons and then let the class experiment with their question on small mirrors placed around the room on the walls. With patience and some guidance from questions by you, it is possible that your students will realize that they have to stand so that the angles respective to the mirror are equal when they are both in view. In other words, they will realize that the angle of incidence will be equal to the angle of reflection (although probably not in that language).

It's helpful to put these findings into drawings that will be easier to explain. Be sure to use the science notebooks as you work your way through this story on mirrors. Make sure students keep all of their drawings and comments and especially tell them to note what *doesn't* work. With your help they can see how when their positions change, the angles change as well.

For other ideas for using mirrors, you can go to the NSTA archives and find the article "Circus of Light" in the February 2004 edition of *Science and Children*. Pay particular attention to the bouncing light section. I prefer when working on this concept reinforcement to have children sit on a floor about six feet from a wall so that they are parallel to the wall in a line. Mark a vertical line on the wall at about the midpoint of the line of children. They can roll the ball so that it hits the line and depending upon the angle at which the ball is rolled, it will roll to a child in the same position as the roller but on the opposite end of the line. Of course it depends upon how accurate the roller is in hitting the mark, but practice makes things go better and children love it. You can then substitute a mirror for the mark on the wall and in a darkened room have each child shine a flashlight on the mirror and the light will end up just as the ball did. This reinforces the idea of angle of reflection and incidence.

Now let's look at the problem inspired by the story. Students are going to try to find out how large a mirror is needed in order to see the whole body. By now they have realized that stepping back is no solution to the problem. The answer must reside in the height of the mirror. In my experience, students suggest using a full-length mirror, mounting it on the wall of the classroom, and using paper to cover the bottom part of the mirror. They must predict how much of the mirror would have to be showing so that they could see their whole body. They soon realize that the top of the mirror has to be at eye level to get the best results. Therefore, mounting the mirror does not work since students vary in height enough that the mirror has to be moved to match the eye level of each student.

So, the mirror can be held by several students and moved up or down to find the right spot. Teams of students can work together to take care of all of the tasks involved. Ask them to use their newly found knowledge of reflection to draw diagrams of their vision with arrows and then to predict where the angle that showed their feet would be on the mirror. The angle from their feet to their mirror is the key and that angle has to be equal to the angle that met the eyes. By moving the paper up and down the mirror, they finally can find the spot that just allows them

to see their whole body. Again, this varies with students of differing heights but they finally can obtain enough data to realize that the mirror has to be one half of any given student body length to satisfy the need. (See diagram in the background content section of this chapter.)

At this point you could distribute the original probe "Mirror on the Wall" that you used as a preinstruction probe. Although all students will probably know that the mirror has to be half the length of a body height, their written explanation will be of more value here in assessing how much they understand what they have discovered. A class discussion of the topic might help clarify the concept for those who are still having trouble understanding the mechanisms of reflection. They are now ready to finish the story with an explanation as well as a solution.

related Books and NSTA Journal articles

Driver, R., A. Squires, P. Rushworth, and V. Wood-Robinson. 1994. *Making sense of secondary science: Research into children's ideas.* London and New York: Routledge Falmer.

Hazen, R., and J. Trefil. 1991. *Science matters: Achieving scientific literacy.* New York: Anchor Books.

Keeley, P. 2005. *Science curriculum topic study: Bridging the gap between standards and practice.* Thousand Oaks, CA: Corwin Press.

Keeley, P., F. Eberle, and C. Dorsey. 2008. *Uncovering student ideas in science: Another 25 formative assessment probes, volume 3.* Arlington, VA: NSTA Press.

Keeley, P., F. Eberle, and J. Tugel. 2007. *Uncovering student ideas in science: 25 more formative assessment probes, volume 2.* Arlington, VA: NSTA Press.

references

American Association for the Advancement of Science (AAAS). 1993. *Benchmarks for science literacy.* New York: Oxford University Press.

American Association for the Advancement of Science (AAAS). 2001. *Atlas of science literacy.* Washington, DC: AAAS.

Hazen, R., and J. Trefil. 1991. *Science matters: Achieving scientific literacy.* New York: Anchor Books.

Keeley, P., F. Eberle, and C. Dorsey. 2008. *Uncovering student ideas in science: Another 25 formative assessment probes, volume 3.* Arlington, VA: NSTA Press.

Keeley, P., F. Eberle, and L. Farrin. 2005. *Uncovering student ideas in science: 25 formative assessment probes, volume 1.* Arlington, VA: NSTA Press.

Matkins, J. J., and J. McDonnough. Circus of light. *Science and Children* 41 (5): 50–54.

National Research Council (NRC). 1996. *National science education standards.* Washington, DC: National Academies Press.

CHAPTER 16
STUCK!

Jimmy was looking forward to his afternoon at the playground. The parents in the neighborhood had just built a whole new set of equipment. There was a new slide that was higher than the old one and a lot faster. He had been there yesterday and had gone down really fast. It was a real thrill ride! He couldn't wait to get to the playground and try it again.

"Put on your shorts today, Jimmy," called his mother. "It is really hot out. Your jeans will be too warm to be comfortable."

"Okay, Mom," answered Jimmy.

He took off his jeans, put on his shorts and got ready to go. They had to take his new little sister and she had to be changed and it took a long time to collect all of her things. Babies seemed to be a lot of bother, but as his mother said, he was one too, once. But now he was a big boy ready to get to the playground and meet his friends from school.

There it was, shiny, metal, high, and slippery! Jimmy looked up at it and thought it was as good as any roller coaster because it curved down and gave him a real fast ride. Sometimes it was even a little scary, but he liked that too.

He climbed the stairs to the top and sat down on the downward slope of the slide with a whole line of kids behind him urging him to hurry up so they could have their turns. Jimmy let go and waited for the speed to begin on his ride to the bottom. Instead, he could hear squeaking on the slide as he went down slowly, and his legs underneath got really hot. He even had to push himself along in some places!

When he got to the bottom, he was very disappointed and ran to get in line to try again.

"Maybe they forgot to wax it or something," he thought as he climbed up the rungs. He finally got to the top and sat down again.

"Now!" he thought. "Let's fly!"

But the same thing happened. What was the matter? The only thing different from yesterday was that he was wearing shorts instead of jeans. Could that make a difference? All of the other kids were flying down even though they looked hot in their jeans.

NATIONAL SCIENCE TEACHERS ASSOCIATION

PURPOSE

This story focuses on friction, both static and kinetic. Jimmy had trouble over-coming the *static friction* that needed a pushing force to get him started and then had trouble with his *kinetic friction*, his skin against the slide when he finally suc-ceeded in getting moving with the help of the force of gravity.

RELATED CONCEPTS

- Friction
- Kinetic friction
- Force
- Static friction
- Net force
- Interaction

DON'T BE SURPRISED

Your students will probably not consider friction to be a force. It would be surpris-ing if your students thought that friction was a force even in cases where there is no motion. They may also believe that there is no friction unless there is rubbing going on or that friction can occur with gases and liquids.

CONTENT BACKGROUND

Friction is a force, a fairly recent scientific theory. It is not one of the four *fun-damental* forces: gravity, strong and weak nuclear forces, and electromagnetism. It is derived from the electromagnetic force between charged particles such as molecules; atoms; and the subatomic particles, electrons and protons. When two surfaces—be they solid, gas, liquid or any combination of these—interact, there is a conversion of kinetic energy into thermal energy or heat. The interacting sur-faces are subject to chemical bonding and electrostatic forces. The roughness of the surfaces contributes to the amount of force, or *friction*.

Friction is often seen as the "enemy" of motion because it opposes it. The force of friction is always in the opposite direction of the force that acts on a body moving in one direction. This friction converts some kinetic motion into heat. It can cut down the efficiency of machines by losing this heat into the atmosphere. Physicists often work on problems where they use ideal situations, ignoring fric-tion. In this way they can use formulas to calculate acceleration and other types of motion without including the muddying and not always predictable force of friction on the interacting bodies they are studying.

Friction can certainly be a problem, but we would experience a different kind of life if friction were not present in our everyday world. Without friction we could not walk, run, drive, bicycle, or even use our computer mouse. Can you imagine a world without it? On the positive side, you could slide to any destination in a straight line after having given yourself a push off. On the dangerous side, you would have a hard time changing directions and slowing or stopping when you came to an intersection or a wall, tree, or even another person. We would all be like molecules bouncing off one another. Our cars and bicycles would not move because tires and roads could not push against each other. Our shoes wouldn't be able to push against the pavement, so we couldn't walk or run. Objects sitting on shelves would slide off at the slightest tremor. Anything in motion would remain that way and never stop. One exciting thing could happen—the illusive perpetual motion machine would finally be possible. That sounds wonderful, but the drawbacks, at least in my mind, outweigh the benefits!

Physicists talk about several types of friction, and here I will focus on two of them: *static friction* and sliding *kinetic friction*. When an object is placed on a flat surface, or at the top of an inclined surface, there are several forces acting upon it. First there is the force of *gravity* pulling down upon it toward the center of the Earth. We refer to this as weight. Second, there is the normal *force* that is the upward force that matches the downward force of its weight. This is Newton's third law that says for every force there is an opposite and equal force. Thirdly, there is the force of static friction between the interface of the object and the surface upon which it rests. This force resists motion just as does its inertia. *Inertia* is that property of matter that resists change in motion. Remember that according to Newton's first law of motion, an object keeps doing what it is doing until acted upon by an outside force. So the object is not about to move by itself. But when you do try to move it, there is not only the resistance of inertia, but there is also resistance because of the static (at rest) friction. We tend to assume that there is no friction unless there is motion. Scientists no longer believe this is true based on the current theory explaining that inter-molecular surface interaction is a cause of friction.

Once the object has enough force exerted upon it and it begins to move, overcoming both inertia and static friction, the friction of motion (kinetic friction) comes into play. The force needed to *keep* it moving is less than that which had to be applied to *get* it moving in the first place. This makes sense since now that it is in motion, the moving body has momentum and would require another force to stop it. This force is, of course, friction; not static friction, but kinetic friction. If you add the forward force caused by the push to the negative force of friction (opposing the movement), the *net force* would be the result. If the forward force is greater than the backward force, the net force would be in the direction of the positive force. In most cases, the net force *is* in favor of motion, so kinetic friction is less than the force of the push and momentum. In Jimmy's case, because he was wearing shorts and his skin provided more friction than the other kids' pants, the net force was in favor of friction, so he got stuck on the slide.

So we can see that friction is a force that acts between moving objects. We also can see that friction is our friend as well as our enemy. In the case of the story, Jimmy encounters both static and kinetic friction. At the top of the slide, he has trouble getting started because the static friction between his skin and the slide is too great

NATIONAL SCIENCE TEACHERS ASSOCIATION

for him to start moving easily. Then once he gets moving, his skin again rubs against the surface of the slide creating kinetic friction, and he is slowed down.

How can we measure friction? We often measure the resistance between two surfaces. These surfaces (say between the pavement and the rubber of the running shoe) are different, of course, and scientists assign each of these a value between 0 and 1, the higher number meaning a greater resistance. The ratio of these two numbers is called the *coefficient of friction*. Imagine that you are running on a grassy surface, and on one foot you are wearing a shoe with a slippery leather sole and on the other a rough, cleated running shoe. Which of the two would you think had the highest coefficient of friction? Go to any sports shoe department and examine the bottoms of running or sport shoes. They are designed to increase friction for obvious reasons.

We have all seen signs in public buildings telling us to use caution when floors have been washed. Moisture on tile floors reduces friction, and can be very slippery, causing loss of balance or worse. I have a smooth, slippery plastic seat on my lawn tractor and find myself in danger of falling off the seat when I turn corners. I have had to put a rubber mat on the seat for my own safety. That way my bottom can stick to the mat, and the mat sticks to the seat. A common item bought by those of us who travel in trailers is a plastic mat to put on shelves so that dishes and other utensils do not slide off the shelves while we drive from place to place. The mat has a rough surface on each side and is made of a material that forms a nice static connection to a shelf and to its contents.

While traveling through a construction zone the other day I was thinking about the new cement road blockers, their shape and material they are made of. They bulge out at the bottom and are more likely to come in contact with my tires should I be so unlucky as to scrape one. This would be to my advantage since my tires and the cement would provide a nice example of kinetic friction interaction, much more efficient and less damaging than if I hit a road guard made of metal at the level of my door. Now I appreciate that some engineer took friction into account when they were designed!

related ideas from the National Science Education Standards (NRC 1993)

K–4: Position and Motion of Objects
- An object's motion can be described by tracing and measuring its position over time.
- The position and motion of objects can be changed by pushing or pulling. The size of the change is related to the strength of the push or pull.

5–8: Motion and Forces
- Unbalanced forces will cause changes in the speed or direction of an object's motion.

related ideas from Benchmarks for Science Literacy (AAAS 1993)

K–2: Motion
- The way to change how something is moving is to give it a push or a pull.

3–5: Motion
- Changes in speed or direction of motion are caused by forces.

6–8: Motion
- An unbalanced force acting on an object changes its speed, direction of motion, or both.

USING THE STORY WITH GRADES K–4

Every child has encountered friction in one form or the other, although the name is not as evident as the effect it has had on his or her life. They can relate all kinds of pain and suffering visited upon them by that nasty force: carpet burns, mat burns in gym, skinned knees. If they have ever gone down a playground slide, this story will help them connect to the concept of friction.

You might ask them to list the friction episodes they have encountered, and then have them brainstorm ways in which something could have been changed so that those painful results might have been avoided or lessened. For example, if skinned knees resulted from a game of tag on a sidewalk, things might have been different if they had played on grass. Grass has a smoother surface than concrete, so they would have slid and not scraped. Smooth mats can prevent mat burns; protective clothing and other safety precautions can stop scrapes, and so on. This can segue into the story and what Jimmy could do to avoid his disappointing ride down the slide. Let's look at a list of possible responses from the children on how Jimmy might slide faster:

- Jimmy should wear smooth pants.
- Jimmy should slide down on a towel.
- Jimmy should slide down on a sheet of newspaper.
- Jimmy should slide down on waxed paper.
- Jimmy could wet the slide.
- Jimmy could wax the slide.

From this list you can change each statement into a testable question. For example, would something slide faster if it were to be placed on a towel? Various materials can be tried on the slide to see which ones provide a faster trip down. A different tack would be to find materials that would cause a slower ride. If a slide is not available on your playground, you can use a slippery board on an incline for testing. Then use a board with rougher surfaces.

Older children might be able to use spring scales to pull objects of different frictional coefficients along a flat surface. I have used small blocks with various grades of sandpaper glued to one side and a cup hook for attaching the spring scale screwed into the end. Place a heavy weight on the block to make the difference significant enough to measure. Be sure to have the children pull in a horizontal direction as a controlled variable. We have found that it is best to use an old board on which to try this activity because heavy sandpaper can scratch up the surface of a desk rather badly. Have the children predict the effect of each material they use and give reasons for their predictions. If you ask them to find out if it takes more force to start a block moving than to keep it moving, you can discuss the ideas of static and kinetic friction with them.

A further extension for older children would be to find ways to eliminate as much friction as possible with oil, grease, wax, water, and other forms of lubricants. Explain that we are dealing with something called *sliding friction*, which is different than *rolling friction* where only the small bit of surface touching the incline is a factor. Since the coefficient of rolling friction is usually much smaller than sliding friction, rolling objects will react differently on an incline than sliding objects. Toy cars will zip down an incline while a sliding block will go much slower. This type of discussion is fairly high level, so you should decide if this is appropriate for your age group.

If you would like to explore more about motion with your students and look a little more closely at Newton's Laws, I recommend an article for younger children called Science Shorts: "Knowing Newton" in *Science and Children* (Ohana 2008). The author illustrates how using toy cars in experimental situations helps kids understand motion and friction.

USING THE STORY WITH GRADES 5-8

Older students may be ready to discuss the empirical results of their investigations in the proper international units of newtons. (Guess who they are named after?) Disregarding friction, a newton is the amount of force necessary to accelerate a mass of one kilogram one meter per second. It is abbreviated as **N** (capitalized since it is named after a person). A kilogram is the international metric measure of weight. When we measure an object's *mass,* we are talking about the amount of matter and its resistance to change in motion. *Weight* is the gravitational mutual attraction between the object and the Earth. So there is a definite difference in the two speaking from a physics point of view. In the United States, outside of the scientific community, we commonly describe the amount of matter by its weight and use the term *pound.* A Newton is much more appropriate than the kilogram when describing mass since it measures the inertia of an object and its resistance to change. One kilogram weighs 9.8 newtons. If students want to do the conversion math, they will find out that one newton is equal to about a quarter of a pound.

For many reasons, the United States has not joined the rest of the world in accepting the metric system of measurement. Instead, we find that when we communicate with people from other lands, we have to do numerical conversion. Some schools even teach their children how to convert from one to the other rather than having them think in metric. This is odd, since in science, the metric system is accepted worldwide, yes, even in America! For this reason, we are happy to see science classes here use the metric system and measure forces in newtons.

The same activities described in the K–4 section can be done here as well. Students will want to test the static and kinetic friction of various surfaces and they can use spring scales calibrated in newtons if they are available. You may also want to use metric weights on the blocks, since measuring is easier with heavier objects. The data should show that once the initial static friction is overcome and the blocks are moving, the kinetic friction is lower. Once the sandpaper is glued onto the blocks, it is easy to substitute different kinds of cloth since the sandpaper will hold the swatches in place for testing. Some teachers will refer to weighing things in metric units as "massing." I personally think that since mass is a property of matter, the word *mass* should be left as a noun and not used as a verb. However, you and your colleagues may want to argue this one out.

In addition to the above activity, using various grit levels of sandpaper will show why rougher sandpaper uses friction to take larger amounts of wood off of a board and why smaller grit is used for fine work. They can try using various kinds of sandpaper on wood and will be able to feel the heat and compare the differences.

To engage the students in an extension of the use of friction into areas other than pure physical science, I would recommend reading and using the ideas suggested in the *Science Scope* article "Tread Lightly: The Truth about Science Friction" (Chessin 2009). In this article the author shows how animals have adapted to moving on different surfaces by having various ways of using friction. She also

has a great activity using an assortment of sneakers and measuring their resistance to motion due to friction.

related BOOKS and NSTA JOURNAL articles

Keeley, P. 2005. *Science curriculum topic study: Bridging the gap between standards and practice.* Thousand Oaks, CA: Corwin Press.

Keeley, P., F. Eberle, and C. Dorsey. 2008. *Uncovering student ideas in science, volume 3: Another 25 formative assessment probes.* Arlington, VA: NSTA Press.

Keeley, P., F. Eberle, and J. Tugel. 2007. *Uncovering student ideas in science, volume 2: 25 more formative assessment probes.* Arlington, VA: NSTA Press.

Keeley, P., and J. Tugel. 2009. *Uncovering student ideas in science, volume 4: 25 new formative assessment probes.* Arlington, VA: NSTA Press.

Konicek-Moran, R. 2008. *Everyday science mysteries: Stories for inquiry-based science teaching.* Arlington, VA: NSTA Press.

Konicek-Moran, R. 2009. *More everyday science mysteries: Stories for inquiry-based science teaching.* Arlington, VA: NSTA Press.

Konicek-Moran, R. 2010. *Even more everyday science mysteries: Stories for inquiry-based science teaching.* Arlington, VA: NSTA Press.

references

American Association for the Advancement of Science (AAAS). 1993. *Benchmarks for science literacy.* New York: Oxford University Press.

Chessin, D. 2009. Tread lightly: The truth about science friction. *Science Scope* 32 (6): 25–30.

Keeley, P., and J. Tugel. 2009. *Uncovering student ideas in science, volume 4: 25 new formative assessment probes.* Arlington, VA: NSTA Press.

National Research Council (NRC). 1996. *National science education standards.* Washington, DC: National Academies Press.

Ohana, C. 2008. Science Shorts: "Knowing Newton." *Science & Children* 45 (7): 64–66.

CHAPTER 17
ST. BERNARD PUPPY

Maya and Leo begged and begged for a puppy. Finally, after a lot of talking about who promised to feed it, walk it, and train it, Grandma agreed to add a new member to the family.

Maya, Leo, and Grandma went to the rescue pound to pick out their new pet. There were lots of older dogs there. Many of them were so friendly and handsome that the children were tempted to choose one of them. But they really wanted a puppy so that they could raise it from puppyhood to adult. Most of the dogs were of mixed breed, so they didn't know much about their parents or about what size they would become when they were grown.

Maya and Leo, luckily, fell in love with the same puppy and agreed that it was the "one" they had to have. It was brown and white and had short hair. Even though it had very large paws, the person who ran the shelter said that she didn't think that it would get too big. The puppy was a male, so they decided to call it Theo. Theo then went to his new home.

Theo was a very hungry puppy! It seemed as though he was hungry all of the time. He consumed large amounts of dog food and continued to grow and grow. Perhaps the lady at the shelter was wrong about it not being a big dog! Oh well, the dog was friendly and a lot of fun to play with, even if he did slobber all over them.

The children decided to keep track of his size and weight and began to keep a graph on the refrigerator door. At first, this was easy. One of the children got on the scale, recorded their weight, and then weighed themselves again with the puppy in their arms. The difference between the two weights equalled the puppy's weight.

That was all well and good until Theo got so big that neither of them could pick him up. He had become one big dog! In fact, Uncle Pedro came by one day and said, "I think you picked out a St. Bernard."

"Oh please," said Leo. "Don't tell Grandma! She might not let us keep a dog that big!"

Maya and Leo wanted to keep weighing Theo but soon ran out of ideas on how to lift him. He was too big by now to stand on the bathroom scale and when they got him to sit, he blocked out the dial so that they couldn't read the weight!

"I've got an idea," said Maya. "We'll get another scale and put his front paws on one scale and his rear paws on the other, then add up the weights."

"I don't know about that," said Leo. "What if one end is heavier than the other? Anyway, if you and I put each of our legs on different scales would the weight be accurate?"

"That's an easy one to test," said Maya. "I've seen people in the supermarket stand on one leg when they were weighing themselves. I think they were on a diet and were trying to lose weight on the scale!" She laughed at the notion of that.

"Well, I guess we can try some things and see what works," said Leo. "I've got some ideas."

PURPOSE

There are two purposes in this story. One is to allow students to test their ideas about the distribution of weight, and the other is to help them to realize that weight is the measurement of force that is acted upon objects (and beings) by means of gravity. Any attempt to extend the purpose of this story to understanding the difference between mass and weight is entirely up to the teacher or to the curriculum of the school system. I will give some information about this concept in the Content Background section, just in case.

RELATED CONCEPTS

- Pressure
- Gravity
- Force

DON'T BE SURPRISED

Strange as it may seem, some students are not aware that an object weighs as much as the sum of its parts. They probably also do not understand that the scale they use to weigh themselves is merely an intermediary between them and the Earth; that the attraction between the two is measured as weight on the scale. They may not realize that the weight of any object is determined by the amount of this attraction. Any person attempting to alter their posture on a scale, hoping to change the reading on that scale is not aware that their weight is unalterable except by changing the effects of the gravitational pull of the Earth.

CONTENT BACKGROUND

This is mostly a true story—the names of the children have been changed but not the name of the dog. Actually, we knew all along that we had bought a St. Bernard and were ready for the consequences. Theo lived with our family for several years and finally achieved a weight in excess of 180 pounds, according to the two-scale method. My two boys did try to graph the dog's weight and had the same problem that Leo and Maya had.

The weight of any object is equal to the sum of its parts. So placing the dog on two scales and adding the readings will provide a total weight. The same, of course, is true if you place one leg on one scale and the other leg on another. Even though your body weight is divided between the two scales, the total weight will be the sum of the two scales. You can try shifting your weight more to one side then more to the other; you will notice that the total sum never changes. You and the Earth are attracting each other through the mechanisms in the scale. Thus weight is a measurement of the force exerted on any body by the mutual attraction of that

body with whatever bears a gravitational pull upon it. On Earth, that force results from the action of *gravity* on that body.

Imagine that you are engaged in the mutual attraction with Earth's gravity. You step on a spring. This spring contracts due to this continued attraction between you and the Earth. If we *calibrate* the contraction of that spring by equating the different amounts of contraction to a set of standard units, we have an operational definition of weight. This calibrated spring with a platform to hold objects we want to measure is what we call a *scale*.

The units we know as pounds and ounces were not discovered; they were invented by people as standard units of measurement so that commerce could exist. When people began selling or trading commodities, they needed to have some way to consistently measure what they were selling. If you visit other countries and cultures, you will find different methods of measuring weights. Our supermarkets use standardized spring or hydraulic scales, while in some countries in Asia or Africa, shop owners use balances, some of which were designed thousands of years ago.

Technically, the weight of any object can vary as much as 0.5% on Earth depending on location or altitude. Location: Earth is not a perfect sphere; the velocity of Earth spinning has the effect of distorting the shape of the planet so that it has a greater circumference at the equator than it does pole to pole. Thus you would weigh less at the poles than on the equator because you are farther from the center of the Earth at the poles. Altitude: You would weigh a small amount less on top of Mt Everest (8,850 m or 29,000 ft.) than you would at sea level because you are farther from the center of the Earth.

Balance-based scales counteract these problems of weight differences on the Earth by using a lever balanced in the middle and measuring an unknown weight on one side against a known weight on the other side. The two weights are acted upon equally regardless of the location on Earth and so give accurate results. Commercial scales based on springs should be calibrated at the location where they are to be used, but this is not always done since some businesses think that the differences are so small and recalibration is bothersome. However, there are laws that govern the calibration of all scales used in commerce to protect the consumer.

A misconception often held by adults as well as by children is that astronauts in space are beyond the force of gravity and that is why they are considered "weightless." Actually at 250 miles above the planet, Earth's gravity is still 90% effective. Astronauts feel (and are) weightless because they and their space station or capsule are in free fall during its orbiting of Earth. This is the same as what you feel when you descend in a fast elevator, but at a greater level. If you were standing on a scale in an elevator you would register less weight than if you were standing still because the floor beneath you is falling away from you and the scale, therefore decreasing the effect of the gravitational pull. You can feel this lightness in your body as you descend. When the elevator stops suddenly, you feel heavier as you are pressed into the floor.

What are the differences between weight and mass? In everyday life, there is virtually no difference between weight and mass; but if we are to talk scientifically, they are quite different. *Weight* indicates the amount of gravitational force on an object and *mass* is a property of matter (the amount of material in that object). Weight requires a gravitational force to exist because weight is the measurement of the force of gravity on it, but mass exists as a basic property of all matter. On the Moon, an object would weigh less than on Earth because the gravitational pull of the Moon is less, but the amount of mass of that object would be the same at both places.

Mass is often described, particularly by Newton in his laws of motion, as a resistance to change in position or motion. Regardless of where the object is, it will still have the same resistance to changing that position or motion. It will be just as difficult to stop a moving boulder on the Moon as it would be on Earth. Likewise, it would be just as difficult to push a boulder on the Moon as it would be on Earth.

In short, equating mass and weight in standard situations causes no problems. But when you are dealing with physics and engineering, it is important to distinguish between the two since weight varies depending on the location of the object, but mass does not. Therefore, their relationship is proportional but not always equivalent. It is much too early for young children to spend time learning the difference, but by middle school, it may well be prescribed in curricula. However, with this story, there is no real need to enter into the distinction.

There may, however, be a reason to discuss *pressure* with your students, particularly when it comes to the part of the story that talks about changing weight by standing on one foot. Pressure is measured by a ratio of weight pressing down on a given area. For example, you might hear that something has a pressure of 10 pounds per square foot. If either the area involved or the weight of the object is changed, then the pressure is changed.

For example, if you think of a thumbtack, you realize that it is designed with the idea of pressure in mind. On the smooth round end, you press down over a larger area than the pointed end. If you pressed as hard on the tack without a head, you could watch it disappear painfully into your flesh. When you press down on the tack head's surface, you exert a force over an area that is larger (and painless), which is then translated to the tip of the tack. Let's say you press with a force of 10 pounds per square inch. As this force is carried through the tack to the pointed end, the same pressure is exerted, but now the surface of the point is much smaller, the ratio changes, and the pressure is concentrated in the point, which pierces the substance. The pressure placed on the smooth part of the tack is translated into a greater force as it is concentrated on a single point.

Thus, the person standing on two feet on a scale spreads his weight over both feet, but if he stands on one foot the pressure is concentrated on the one foot. However, the weight of the person is the same and even though the pressure is different, the total weight remains constant. The scale measures weight, not pressure and since standing on one foot does not change the amount of weight in the person, the weight will remain the same.

There is a lot of science in this story and many different educational roads that can be traveled. You as the teacher can question your students or, better yet, entice *them* to question the ramifications of weighing, balancing, and using pressure.

related ideas from the national science education standards (nrc 1996)

K–4: Abilities Necessary to Do Scientific Inquiry
- Use simple equipment and tools to gather data and extend the senses.

K–4: Properties of Objects and Materials
- Objects have many observable properties including size, weight, shape, color, and the ability to react with other substances. Those properties can be measured using tools, such as rulers, balances, and thermometers.

5–8: Abilities Necessary to Do Scientific Inquiry
- Use appropriate tools and techniques to gather, analyze, and interpret data.

related ideas from benchmarks for science literacy (aaas 1993)

K–2: Scientific Inquiry
- People can often learn about things around them by just observing these things carefully, but sometimes they can learn more by doing something to the things and noting what happens.

K–2: The Structure of Matter
- Objects can be described in terms of their properties.

3–5: Forces of Nature
- The Earth's gravity pulls any object on or near the Earth toward it without touching it.

6–8: Forces of Nature
- Every object exerts gravitational force on every other object.

USING THE STORY WITH GRADES K-4

First of all it is important to know what your students know about weighing things. You might ask them to tell about the times when they or other things were weighed. What things were weighed? Have they been weighed? How was it done? From these stories you can get an idea about what the students know about the process of comparing one object to another by weight.

Young children may not have encountered much about the concept and should be allowed to experience differences in weight. Have them choose things around the room that they can hold in their hands and then have them hold these things in opposite hands and guess which is heavier (also a good opportunity to distinguish between heavier and heaviest). You might even use the words, "Which hand has to work harder so that it does not get pulled down by the object?" This will set the stage for later understanding that weight is caused by the force of gravity. They need to push up to counter the downward pull. Ask them if they feel the difference in the way their bodies have to work to support different objects.

This is a good time to introduce your students to balances and the use of some sort of arbitrary standards of measurement. Many teachers use marbles or Centicubes or Lego cubes as standards. Students choose objects and match them up with numbers of the standards needed to bring the balance to level.

One teacher had the children collect acorns and use them as standards. When the children began to get different answers when weighing identical objects, the topic of needing a reliable standard unit came up. The children realized that the acorns were not all the same in all respects and therefore were not appropriate. They then sought objects that were all the same. This introduced them to the need for standardization in weighing and eventually all kinds of measurements.

Children also want to know if the position of the object to be weighed makes a difference. You can have them place rectangular blocks in various positions, such as upright or lying down, and they will find out that it makes no difference how an object is positioned. It weighs the same because regardless of position, the mass or amount of material remains the same.

As for using the story of the puppy, if there are any toys that can be disassembled, you may have the children weigh the parts separately (perhaps on two different balances) and then add the weights together and compare it with the whole object. This is similar to putting the puppy on two scales. If you have two bathroom scales, children can test the theory by putting different legs on different scales, and adding the weights together. With very young children who have not yet learned to add, they can count the number of standard objects that make the separated toy and compare that to the whole.

We have found that older children like to build mobiles out of different shapes and sizes of paper. By making these, they can see that the balance of various sizes and shapes can be managed in many ways. They can also try to find a method of determining and placing in order from lightest to heaviest, the relative weights of three or more objects using only the balance and the objects. Challenge them to do

so using the least number of steps. It is not as simple as it may seem and can elicit a great discussion among the students involved in the processes.

USING THE STORY WITH GRADES 5–8

Strange as it may seem, with middle schoolers, there may be more discussion about the story than with younger students. With the added years of experience, the number of ways of looking at phenomena may cause more different opinions among the students. As recommended with the younger students, it is to your advantage to find out what your students know about weight and in this case, gravity as a force.

If students have not already had experience with balances and scales, this is a great opportunity to have them build a balance from available materials such as paper cups, string, straws, pins and spring clothespins, and a soda can (Figure 17.1).

Building a balance and adjusting it so that it balances can be a very instructive tool showing how the balance works. Most schools give students balances and scales that are merely "black boxes" to the students because they have no idea how they work and how they can be adjusted to perform their functions. Since this story opens the door to weighing and balancing, it seems appropriate to allow the students to learn as much as possible about the forces involved. To get students involved with their balances, I suggest that you allow them to weigh many things with one gram Centicubes or an equivalent object with standard mass. The challenge of ordering three or more unknown objects using only the balance and the objects (as mentioned above) is also appropriate here.

Of course, your students will want to try the activities in the story. If you are adventurous and if the school rules allow, a dog can actually be brought in and weighed with bathroom scales. A parent may be willing to deliver the pet and then take it home. A small dog, which can be held and weighed by subtracting the weight of the dog from the weight of the dog and holder, would be best, but if the dog is too big to be picked up and has been to the vet lately, you may have a weight on the dog to begin with to compare with the two-scale approach.

Figure 17.1 Soda can balance

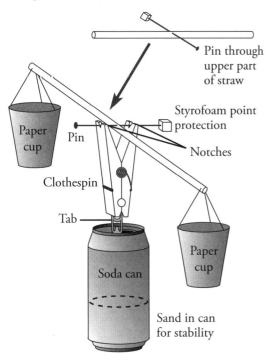

- Pin through upper part of straw
- Styrofoam point protection
- Notches
- Paper cup
- Pin
- Clothespin
- Tab
- Soda can
- Paper cup
- Sand in can for stability

When dealing with student weights, it can be a touchy situation. It would be good to ask for volunteers to try the two-foot approach or to pick a student who is not sensitive about his or her weight to conduct the investigation. While the student is shifting from one side to the other, another student can call out the weights and the class can do the math. It will then be evident that the sum of the two scales will add up to the total weight of the student and the dog.

NATIONAL SCIENCE TEACHERS ASSOCIATION

The other part of the story asks if standing on one foot can alter the weight of the person. I suggest that you give the probe "Standing on One Foot," in *Uncovering Student Ideas, Volume 4* by Keeley and Tugel (2009). This probe asks the same question that the story does but in a different format. Students are also asked in the probe to explain their thinking and to think of a rule that they could use to explain their answer. You should anticipate a lively discussion when the probe is discussed.

The activity can be carried out at this point with care taken as to which student is chosen. If you have an accurate kitchen scale, you might want to try the activities described in the section on younger students to see if your class has misconceptions of whether or not there is a difference in weight due to the placement of the object on the scale. Here your discussion with the class can focus on the fact that the amount of material never changes regardless of whether a block is placed upright or on its side. You might also be interested in giving them a piece of clay and challenging them to find a way to change the clay by molding it so that it weighs more or less. Some of the class will realize the futility of this, but I would be very surprised if some students did not spend some time changing the shape of the clay in anticipation of a weight change.

Putting these findings all together you can help the students to conclude that objects contain a finite amount of material and that this cannot be changed by physical manipulation. If your curriculum calls for a discussion on mass, inertia, and Newton's laws of motion, you may find this story to be a good lead-in to dealing with that topic. If that is the case, I direct you to Bill Robertson's book, *Force and Motion: Stop Faking It!* (2002). Robertson goes beyond where this story was designed to go and is full of great explanations written so that the novice can understand these somewhat difficult concepts. In addition you can find online an article by Robertson entitled "Science 101: Do balances and scales determine an object's weight or its mass?" from the March 2008 issue of *Science and Children*.

related Books and NSTA Journal articles

Driver, R., A. Squires, P. Rushworth, and V. Wood-Robinson. 1994. *Making sense of secondary science: Research into children's ideas.* London and New York: Routledge Falmer.

Keeley, P. 2005. *Science curriculum topic study: Bridging the gap between standards and practice.* Thousand Oaks, CA: Corwin Press.

Keeley, P., F. Eberle, and C. Dorsey. 2008. *Uncovering student ideas in science: Another 25 formative assessment probes, volume 3.* Arlington, VA: NSTA Press.

Keeley, P., F. Eberle, and L. Farrin. 2005. *Uncovering student ideas in science: 25 formative assessment probes, volume 1.* Arlington, VA: NSTA Press.

Keeley, P., F. Eberle, and J. Tugel. 2007. *Uncovering student ideas in science: 25 more formative assessment probes, volume 2.* Arlington, VA: NSTA Press.

Konicek-Moran, R. 2008. *Everyday science mysteries*. Arlington, VA: NSTA Press.

Konicek-Moran, R. 2009. *More everyday science mysteries*. Arlington, VA: NSTA Press.

Nelson, G. 2004. What is gravity? *Science and Children* 42 (1) 22–23.

references

American Association for the Advancement of Science (AAAS).1993. *Benchmarks for science literacy*. New York: Oxford University Press.

Keeley, P., and J. Tugel. 2009. *Uncovering student ideas in science: 25 new formative assessment probes, volume 4*. Arlington, VA: NSTA Press.

National Research Council (NRC). 1996. *National science education standards*. Washington, DC: National Academies Press.

Robertson, W. 2002. *Force and motion: Stop faking it!* Arlington, VA: NSTA Press.

Robertson, W. 2008. Science 101: Do balances and scales determine an object's weight or its mass? *Science and Children* 46 (1): 68–71.

CHAPTER 18
ICED TEA

Caroline wiped the water from the outside of her glass of Kool Aid. The weather was hot and humid. The weather person said it was the hottest July on record. Caroline believed it. She was only nine years old, but she couldn't remember any summer that had been so uncomfortable. The ice cubes clinked in her glass and touched her nose as she drank the deliciously cool liquid.

Lisa, her older sister, drifted out onto the porch with a tray of glasses and a pitcher of iced tea.

"I'm out on the porch!" Lisa shouted over her shoulder as she kicked the screen door shut with her left foot. That meant that the rest of the family would join them soon. The glasses rattled on the tray as she regained her balance. Lisa walked over to the table and set the tray and its contents down.

Caroline didn't move. She didn't care for tea. She had a sweet tooth and tea, even with sugar in it, didn't quite make it. Lisa was always teasing her to give up her Kool Aid, and she didn't waste any time today.

"Hey, Carrie," she said, "give up that sugar water and have a grown-up drink. It's better for you anyway."

"I'll have a grown-up drink when I'm grown up," replied Caroline. "Right now I'm still a kid."

"What's the matter, my iced tea is not sweet enough for you?"

"I can make it as sweet as I want but I still won't like it," snapped Caroline.

"How sweet can you make it?" asked Lisa.

"I can put a whole bowl of sugar in it and then I'll have tea sugar water. So what's the difference?"

Lisa ignored her question. Instead, she retorted, "I'll bet you can't dissolve a whole bowl of sugar in a glass of this iced tea. In fact, I bet you can't even dissolve a quarter of a cup before the family gets out here."

"Bet I can," replied Caroline defiantly. "What's the bet?"

"My chores against yours for all the rest of this week."

"You're on!" said Caroline confidently.

Caroline poured herself a large glass of iced tea, ice cold right from the pitcher. She grabbed the sugar bowl and a spoon as well. Slowly she dipped the spoon into the bowl and moved a heaping spoonful to the glass of iced tea and let the sugar fall into the tea. It fell like snow, clearly visible as it trailed down to the bottom of the glass. She did this twice more until she had three teaspoonfuls of sugar in the glass of tea.

"It needs to be stirred," observed Caroline and she reached for the long handled teaspoon on the table. She stirred the mixture and the white stuff that no longer looked like sugar whirled up and around as she kept the liquid in motion.

She stopped stirring and watched. The cloudy, swirling substance slowly became calm and finally piled up in a sloppy mess at the bottom.

"Told you!" said Lisa, smirking.

"I'm not done yet!" said Caroline, stirring madly at the iced tea. Why won't it dissolve? she thought. Several more attempts at stirring did not produce any visible results. Well, maybe a *little*. Caroline made a move toward the sugar bowl with her spoon.

"Right!" said Lisa, sarcastically. "If it won't dissolve three teaspoons, try more."

Caroline stopped and thought. As much as she hated to admit it, her big sister had her. She decided to taste the tea. It was a little sweet, but not very sweet—not sweet enough anyway. What was the matter here? She had tasted sweetened iced tea before, yet hers was not nearly that sweet, and the sugar wouldn't dissolve. How could she get the iced tea to accept the sugar and sweeten it? There had to be a way. And why *wouldn't* the sugar dissolve?

Just at that point her thoughts were interrupted by the arrival of her family and the roll of paper towels and a bottle of spray cleaner that fell into her lap.

"I was supposed to do the kitchen windows today little sister," said Lisa. "Do a good job—remember, no streaks!"

NATIONAL SCIENCE TEACHERS ASSOCIATION

PURPOSE

Dissolving things in the universal solvent water is an everyday experience for almost all of us. We don't have a lot of trouble dissolving honey in our hot tea, but when it comes to sweetening cold iced tea, it is quite a task, if not almost impossible. Obviously, water is not really a "universal solvent" as it is sometimes called; otherwise we couldn't find anything to keep it in. But it does dissolve more substances than any other liquid in common use. This is also a wonderful opportunity for you to show the students the effect of temperature on dissolving substances in liquid and to make the distinction between dissolving and melting. For older students, learning about the molecular structure of water might be appropriate.

RELATED CONCEPTS

- Molecules
- Solute
- Melting
- Solid
- Solvent
- Solution
- Chemical bonds
- Liquid

DON'T BE SURPRISED

One of the biggest misconceptions among children and even some adults is the distinction between dissolving and melting. Children will often say that the sugar put into a drink "melted." Melting, of course, is a change in state caused by bringing a substance to its melting point by adding heat energy. Dissolving is the combination of two or more substances into a solution. Common language and even some dictionary definitions do not help the situation since the two words are often inferred to have the same meaning. However, in science they are two completely different concepts.

CONTENT BACKGROUND

Lisa was pretty certain she would win that bet. Why? Probably because she had experienced trying to sweeten cold tea with sugar. Did you notice that she put a time limit on the bet? Eventually, with enough stirring, the sugar would probably have dissolved, but it would have taken a very long time and more patience than either Caroline or your students would have. Iced tea is usually sweetened while the tea water is still hot, which speeds up the dissolving, or it is sweetened afterward using a liquid syrup made of sugar dissolved in hot water. The liquid solution of sugar and water dissolves much faster than solid sugar in water. How is this different, then, from melting?

Raising a substance to its melting point by adding heat energy causes it to melt. Ice cream melts in warm weather, as anyone will attest if they have ever tried to finish an ice cream cone before it dribbled all over the front of his or her clothes. This is a physical change—the melted ice cream is still ice cream but in a different state. Every substance has a melting point. We don't realize this because most things we recognize as solids have melting points well above the normal temperatures we experience in our world. Perhaps some of you made lead soldiers and remembered how much heat had to be put into the solid metal in order to get it to melt so you could put it into the molds.

Solid (frozen) water, on the other hand, melts at room temperature. This shows that water is naturally in its melted state in our world except for times when the air temperature drops below its melting point. In other words, it changes to ice when the temperature around it reaches water's freezing point: 32°F or 0°C.

Water, which is used to make iced tea, is called a *solvent*, and the tea as well as the sugar are called the *solutes*. So, the dissolver is the solvent and the thing that is dissolved into the solvent is called the solute. Water dissolves more substances than any other substance on Earth. That is why it is called the "universal solvent" although, as I mentioned above, that is an exaggeration. It's a good thing, too, since it would dissolve our body's cells and everything around us since there is so much water in the world! We can't do without it for more than a day or two and it makes up more than half of every living thing.

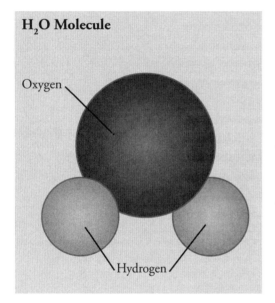

H₂O Molecule

Oxygen

Hydrogen

Water is also unique in its properties (a quality of a substance which is predictable, such as the boiling or freezing point), so scientists use it as a standard for many functions. For instance, in calculating density, everything is compared to the density of water, which is 1 gram for each cubic centimeter. And, the calorie measurement in heat is based upon how much of the heat is needed to raise one cubic centimeter of water one degree Celsius.

So why is water such a good solvent? The answer lies in the shape of its molecule, which is like a tiny boomerang, and its electrical polarity. The oxygen atom is at the top or point of the boomerang and the hydrogens are at the ends of the arms. There are two hydrogens attached to one oxygen, thus the famous symbol or formula for water as H_2O. The molecule has a negative end and a positive end, thus it is called a *polar* molecule. This means that it attracts other molecules of its own kind as well as other polar molecules—of which there are plenty. The negative end attracts the positive ends of other molecules and the positive attracts the negative ends.

When another polar substance such as salt or sugar is put into water, their molecules break apart because the elements (which are now charged ions) are surrounded by the water molecules and are unable to stay attached to each other. For example, when a crystal of sugar is dropped into the water or tea, a molecule of sugar leaves the crystal and breaks apart because of the attraction of the polar molecules in the water. The elements of the crystal are immediately

surrounded by the water molecules in the tea and become part of what we call a *solution*. These molecules cannot be filtered out and will not fall out due to gravity once they are in solution. If however, you should boil away all of the water, you would be left with the molecules that were dissolved as a residue on the bottom of the pan.

Any solution can be reversed and the component parts separated based on the properties of the items in the solution; for instance, water will boil away at 212°F or 100°C, but the sugar won't, which is why there is a residue. However, a filter cannot separate the various components of a solution. So there is really no chemical reaction, no change of state (in other words, no melting) and a new substance is not formed, yet the solute molecules are within the solution and are, in essence, part of the whole. The water still tastes sweet. In the process of going into solution, the solute is distributed homogeneously throughout the solution. This means that if you took a sample anywhere in the solution, the ratio of solute to solution would be the same.

Now, since the water molecules are hitting the sugar crystals at a rate commensurate with the temperature of the water, warmer water would make the water molecules more active and therefore the number of water molecules hitting the sugar crystal at any one time would be much greater. This would speed up the process of dissolving, which is why dissolving sugar in hot water is much faster than trying to dissolve it in cold tea. In fact, higher temperatures generally speed up any reaction between two or more reactants.

At some point, for reasons too complicated to explain here, a solvent can absorb no more solute. This is called the *saturation point*. However, any definition of saturation includes the qualification "at a given temperature." If the temperature is raised, the amount of solute that can go into solution increases. If the solution is then cooled, it is oversaturated and we say that the solution is *super-saturated* at that temperature.

When we think of Caroline adding more and more sugar, we know that at the ice-cold temperature of the tea, it was limited in how much sugar it could take into solution. She may have been at a saturation point or, depending upon the amount of sugar and the temperature of the tea, the sugar might have dissolved a bit more with much, much more stirring. Whatever the situation, Caroline got stuck with doing the windows and Lisa won an easy bet.

related ideas from the national science education standards (nrc 1996)

K–4: Properties of Objects and Materials

- Objects have many observable properties, including size, weight, shape, color, temperature, and the ability to react with other substances. These properties can be measured using tools such as rulers, balances, and thermometers.
- Materials can exist in different states—solid, liquid, and gas. Some common materials such as water can be changed from one state to another by heating or cooling.

5–8: Properties and Changes of Properties in Matter

- A substance has characteristic properties, such as density, a boiling point, and solubility, all of which are independent of the amount of the sample. A mixture of substances often can be separated into the original substances using one or more of the characteristic properties.

related ideas in benchmarks for science literacy (aaas 1993)

K–2: The Structure of Matter

- Things can be done to materials to change some of their properties, but not all materials respond the same way to what is done to them.

3–5: The Structure of Matter

- Heating and cooling cause changes in the properties of materials. Many kinds of changes occur faster under hotter conditions.
- Materials may be composed of parts that are too small to be seen without magnification.

6–8: The Structure of Matter

- All matter is made up of atoms, which are far too small to see directly through a microscope. The atoms of any element are alike but are different from atoms of other elements. Atoms may stick together in well-defined molecules or may be packed together in large arrays. Different arrangements of atoms into groups compose all substances.
- Atoms and molecules are perpetually in motion. Increased temperature means greater average energy of motion, so most substances expand when heated.
- The temperature and acidity of a solution influence reaction rates. Many substances dissolve in water, which may greatly facilitate reactions between them.

national science teachers association

USING THE STORY WITH GRADES K–4

You may want to use the probe "Is It Melting?" from *Uncovering Student Ideas in Science, Volume 1* (Keeley, Eberle, and Farrin 2005), as a pre- or formative assessment along the way. This will help you discover what your students are thinking about the difference between dissolving and melting.

After reading the story to the children, allow them to discuss the various aspects of mixing sugar in materials and ask them to tell you what they "know" about what happens when you add something like sugar or salt to a liquid. Write these on the "Best Thinking So Far" chart for discussion. Many children will say that the sugar or salt disappears. After talking about safety procedures, which would include the rule that they should not taste anything unless an adult says it is okay, ask them if they can think of a way to see if the sugar really disappears into a liquid. Have students put sugar into paper cups filled with warm water at their desks and observe what happens to the sugar. You can say that it is okay to taste the liquid and allow them to take a sip of the solution. They will taste the sugar so that you can ask them if the sugar really disappeared. The same thing can be done by adding a bit of lemon juice to the solution and asking them to taste that to see if the lemon juice disappeared. When they say they can taste both the sugar and the lemon, you can introduce the term *solution* and then continue to refer to solutions as you proceed through the lessons and the inquiries. You might also introduce the term *dissolve* here and tell them that the sugar and lemon dissolved in the water.

Some children may say that the sugar melted in the water. You can tell them that melting happens when you add heat to a solid and that it becomes a liquid. Showing them an ice cube and a sugar cube and allowing the ice cube to melt will be an example of melting. The sugar cube, of course, will not melt at room temperature. Putting the sugar cube into water will be an example of dissolving and the difference can be stressed. You might then make a chart that has two columns, "Melting" and "Dissolving," and ask the children to place events they have experienced in the proper column. Then let them discuss the columns and agree or disagree with the things that have been written. Ask them to use their knowledge of what constitutes melting and dissolving to decide if the event belongs in one column or another. Having them discuss as a class is very important here since entering into a discourse on the topic allows students to listen and respond to one another using evidence from their experiences.

Of course, reproducing the events of the story is in order and if your students do not suggest temperature as a variable, you may have to entice them to try that. Using syrup or making syrup is another way to look at Caroline's problem. Caroline could have won the bet had she made her sugar into syrup and added that to the iced tea. Next time she will know better—after students give her a clue!

You may also find the article by Peggy Ashbrook "Mixing and Making Changes" from *Science and Children* (2006) helpful since it looks at these concepts from an early childhood level.

USING THE STORY WITH GRADES 5-8

After listening to the story, a lively discussion should ensue since the narrative involves a bet and a challenge. The "Our Best Thinking" chart could include suggestions for Caroline to dissolve sugar in the tea.

Experience tells us that most suggestions will involve heat. However, sometimes students suggest grinding the sugar up into smaller particles or using powdered sugar. These students may realize that the smaller the particle, the more surface area is in contact with the water and the less the particles have to be broken down into the molecular level. Some will suggest making syrup out of the sugar and a little water, their experience telling them that liquids dissolve in liquids more easily than solids in liquids. In syrup, the sugar molecules have already been broken down into smaller molecular sizes and will mix with the water more quickly.

There are obviously investigations to be done here. All of the above suggestions can be changed into questions and therefore into investigations. One caution about investigations of this sort is in order: Students need to define what they mean by "dissolve." How will they decide when the substance has dissolved? Two different groups may have different criteria and thereby not reach a consensus. I call this making an *operational definition*. They will also have to develop a *procedural definition*, which is a description of how they will add the solute to the solvent and in what amounts.

Many predictions are to be expected, such as

- The hotter the water, the more sugar can be dissolved.
- The hotter the water, the faster sugar will dissolve.
- Some liquids will dissolve more sugar than others.
- Some liquids will dissolve sugar faster than others.
- Syrup will dissolve more sugar in water than solid sugar.
- Syrup will dissolve sugar faster than solid sugar.
- Powdered sugar will dissolve faster than sugar crystals.
- Powdered sugar will dissolve more than sugar crystals.

In the end, your students should be able to keep data tables in their science notebooks and also graph the results. The students should find out that temperature does make a difference in dissolving amounts and rates; that there is a saturation point for all solutions; that particle size does affect amount and speed of dissolving; and that the sugar can be reclaimed from the solution by evaporating the water either by heat or by natural evaporation. Another activity that might come up is making rock candy by supersaturating some sugar solution and then hanging a string seeded with some sugar crystals into the solution while it cools. The giant crystals that grow on the string will provide more evidence of the presence of sugar in the solution.

Finally, to see a graphic and very understandable explanation of how things dissolve, visit the Northlands Community College Biology Animations website: *www.northland.cc.mn.us/biology/Biology1111/animations/dissolve.html.*

NATIONAL SCIENCE TEACHERS ASSOCIATION

Driver, R., A. Squires, P. Rushworth, and V. Wood-Robinson, 1994. *Making sense of secondary science: Research into children's ideas.* London and New York: Routledge Falmer.

Keeley, P. 2005. *Science curriculum topic study: Bridging the gap between standards and practice.* Thousand Oaks, CA: Corwin Press.

Keeley, P. 2008. *Science formative assessment: 75 practical strategies for linking assessment, instruction, and learning,* Thousand Oaks, CA: Corwin Press.

Keeley, P., F. Eberle, and C. Dorsey. 2008. *Uncovering student ideas in science: Another 25 formative assessment probes, volume 3.* Arlington, VA: NSTA Press.

Keeley, P., F. Eberle, and L. Farrin. 2005. *Uncovering student ideas in science: 25 formative assessment probes, volume 1.* Arlington, VA: NSTA Press.

Keeley, P., F. Eberle, and J. Tugel. 2007. *Uncovering student ideas in science: 25 more formative assessment probes, volume 2.* Arlington, VA: NSTA Press.

references

American Association for the Advancement of Science (AAAS). 1993. *Benchmarks for science literacy.* New York: Oxford University Press.

Ashbrook, P. 2006. Mixing and making changes. *Science and Children* 43 (5): 28–31.

Keeley, P., F. Eberle, and L. Farrin. 2005. *Uncovering student ideas in science: 25 formative assessment probes, volume 1.* Arlington, VA: NSTA Press.

National Research Council (NRC). 1996. *National science education standards.* Washington, DC: National Academies Press.

Northland Community College, Minnesota. Animations website. *www.northland. cc.mn.us/biology/Biology1111/animations/dissolve.html*

CHAPTER 19
PASTA IN A HURRY

It was almost time to leave for the movie and no one had thought about putting something on the stove for dinner. Actually it was the kids' night to cook, but they had been playing games on the computer and had forgotten the time.

Suddenly, the clock struck five times. Cavan looked up and remembered not only that she and her brother, Daniel, were supposed to make dinner that night but the movie started at 6:00 p.m. Oh boy! They were in trouble and might have to skip the movie if they didn't do their job in time. There had to be time to eat and wash the dishes before they could leave. And this was a movie they had begged their parents into taking them to for weeks.

"I got it!" said Daniel, after his sister had reminded him. "We'll throw some pasta in water and open a jar of sauce. That'll be fast and get us out of this jam. Throw in a salad and we'll be eating in ten minutes."

"Sounds great," said Cavan. "Let's go. You get the water boiling for the angel hair and I'll make the salad. Angel hair is really thin so it will cook faster!"

"That sounds like a plan," said Daniel and he filled the pot with hot water to save even more time. In a few minutes, the pot was bubbling in a rolling boil and was ready for the pasta. Daniel put the pasta in and waited for the water to boil again. He wondered why putting in pasta stopped the boiling, but there was no time to worry about that now. Finally, it did boil again and Daniel turned up the heat even more.

Whoa!! The pot of pasta and water foamed up to the top of the pot. Daniel complained to Cavan that it was hard to keep the heat up high when the pasta was in it because it boiled over and made a mess.

"Turn the heat down to medium or low," said Cavan, "And it won't boil over."

"But, we're in a hurry aren't we, so I have to make the water as hot as I can!" cried Daniel.

"It's as hot as it is going to get," said Cavan. "Boiling is boiling, and I think I remember Mom telling me that once water is boiling, it doesn't get any hotter—but don't ask me why."

"No offense to Mom, but that doesn't make sense to me," said Daniel. "If I'm adding more heat to the pot, the water has to get hotter! Common sense—duh!"

In the meantime, the water boiled and the pasta cooked until Daniel looked again at the pot.

"Darn, look at the water level, it's gone down, and it's not covering the pasta. I'll have to add more water and that will slow things down," complained Daniel.

"Maybe not," teased Cavan, "You put so much extra heat in there it might not slow down the boiling at all."

But it did and cooking the pasta took a little longer than Daniel had hoped.

"I know, I should have put more salt into the water so it would boil at a higher temperature."

"What does salt have to do with it?" asked Cavan.

"I'm not sure but I know that salt makes ice melt so I think it may do something to the temperature that water boils at," said Daniel.

"I don't know about all of this," said Cavan, "and the pasta looks almost done so let's let it go for tonight. We can find out later about all this heat and salt and stuff."

The meal was fine and the movie was even better than expected, but there were still some questions lingering in their heads about boiling and salt and all that other stuff.

NATIONAL SCIENCE TEACHERS ASSOCIATION

PURPOSE

This story should give students an opportunity to discover that every liquid has its own unique boiling point and that heat applied to any liquid that has reached its boiling point will not result in an increase in temperature but will be used to change the state from liquid to gas, resulting in evaporation. It also touches the point that adding substances that dissolve and ionize (break down into charged particles) to water changes the freezing and boiling points of the water.

RELATED CONCEPTS

- Energy
- Change in state
- Heat
- Boiling and boiling points
- Temperature
- Properties of matter

DON'T BE SURPRISED

The idea of a substance like water having a boiling point that will go no higher even if more heat is added is counterintuitive. As Daniel says, putting in more heat has to make it hotter. That makes sense to all of us if we look at it from our experience with lots of things in our world. In a way, Daniel is correct that heat is going into the water at a high rate but that heat is being used in a way that causes him trouble as time goes on. It speeds up evaporation—more on this in the content section. On the other side of the coin, kids know that putting salt on ice makes it melt faster, so the idea of it changing the boiling temperature isn't so far-fetched, or is it? Anyway, Daniel, Cavan, and your students have a few problems to solve about boiling points, salt, and other stuff. That "other stuff" will probably include the fact that the children, and perhaps most of the adults you know, do not realize that the bubbles you see in boiling water are bubbles of water changed to a gas and are not oxygen or any other gas.

Another misunderstanding about boiling is that some students may believe that boiling is synonymous with cooking something, regardless of the temperature. A student might say, "As long as water is boiling, shouldn't it be hot enough to cook pasta?" This may be the result of our sloppy language about boiling. We know that in a vacuum we can cause water to boil at room temperature or lower. *This* boiling water won't even feel hot. It will cook nothing; soak it, yes, cook it, no!

CONTENT BACKGROUND

To put it simply (perhaps too simply), the boiling point of any liquid is the temperature at which the liquid changes its state from liquid to vapor. It may make

more sense to define it in a different way: The *boiling point* of a liquid is reached when the temperature causes the internal atmospheric pressure to equal or exceed that of the atmospheric pressure surrounding it. This means that the molecules in the liquid must have enough energy to equal or exceed the pressure surrounding the liquid, turning it into a gas. We see it as bubbles, which are, for instance in water, bubbles of water in a gaseous form that rise everywhere in the container being heated and escape from the surface of the liquid into the air as water vapor. At this point the temperature rises no more because the heat is being used to transform the liquid to gas and not to raise the temperature. The amount of heat needed to change liquid to gas is substantial.

Physical chemists and engineers often refer to vaporized water as steam. The vapor cloud seen above a teakettle or a pot is often *called* steam but it is not, since true steam is an invisible gas. What is visible is a cloud or a mist of the vapor condensing back into water droplets. In fact, if you look closely at a boiling teakettle, you will notice a space between the spout and the cloud where the steam is escaping the kettle but has not yet cooled enough to show a visible cloud.

We have direct evidence of the importance of atmospheric pressure in the boiling definition when we try to cook at higher altitudes, say in Denver or other places in altitudes of above 5,000 feet (1,500 meters). Because of the reduced atmospheric pressure at these heights, water boils at a lower temperature since the internal atmospheric pressure does not have to rise to the same temperature in order to boil, as it does at sea level. Sea-level boiling point is usually listed as 212°F (100°C). Water will boil at 203°F (95°C) at an altitude of 5,000 feet (1,500 meters) and at 196°F (91°C) at 7,500 feet (2,300 meters). Even though the water is boiling, it is boiling at a lower temperature; possibly so low that *cooking* the food in the water is almost impossible. This again brings up the point that some people believe that if water is boiling, it is providing enough heat to cook. The very word "boiling" conjures up in most people's minds, HOT!! This is because we think of boiling as being a sea-level phenomenon. We know that if water boils at sea level, it is dangerously hot. You would not think of plunging a hand into boiling water at sea level. Yet, in areas of very low atmospheric pressure, water may boil at so low a temperature, you would be able to submerge your hand in the water without risk of burning. We count on the water temperature being at near 100°C and so do most recipes, which give an estimated time for cooking eggs, pasta, noodles, and beans, for example. If the water is boiling at a lower temperature, the lack of heat will naturally call for an increase in the cooking time.

Some experts will tell you that beans will not cook to an edible consistency above a mile high without the use of a pressure cooker. This is a pot with a lid that increases the pressure above whatever you are cooking so that the boiling temperature is higher and therefore cooks faster. Since boiling depends on the atmospheric pressure, it is possible to boil water at room temperature or below if it is done in a vacuum. For a quick and simple look at changes of phase, I recommend reading up on it in *Science Matters* (Hazen and Trefil 1991, p. 99).

As for adding salt to the water to make it boil faster, that too would have probably been futile in a practical sense. Daniel was used to seeing his parents add salt to water when cooking grains but that would have been mostly for seasoning purposes. Some folks believe that they are raising the boiling temperature of the water, but in order to do so it would take about 2 oz. (58 g) of salt to raise 34 oz. of water (one liter) 1.8°F (1°C). This amount of salt would be much too extreme for our tastes.

The scientific explanation for raising the temperature (thus the boiling point) through the application of salt is that the salt dilutes the water molecules with sodium and chlorine ions between the water molecules so their energy level is decreased. This means fewer collisions of molecules, less of a release of water vapor molecules, and therefore less pressure. Thus, a higher temperature would be needed to exceed atmospheric pressure and a higher boiling temperature would be achieved.

So you can see that Daniel is doomed to having his pasta cook at the normal rate without the use of a pressure cooker and the copious amount of salt he would have to use to hurry the process. Daniel even cost himself time by using high heat after reaching boiling temperature and causing increased evaporation of his pasta water (when it boiled over).

The above content explanation is for your benefit and perhaps not totally appropriate at this time for the students. The basic ideas to be achieved would be that boiling liquid reaches a temperature that will go no higher once boiling is achieved, that huge amounts of salt are necessary to raise the boiling point of water, and that heating water makes it evaporate faster.

Related Ideas From the National Science Education Standards (NRC 1996)

K–4: Properties of Objects and Materials
• Materials can exist in different states—solid, liquid, and gas. Some common materials, such as water, can be changed from one state to another by heating or cooling.

5–8: Properties and Changes in Properties of Matter
• A substance has characteristic properties, such as density, a boiling point, and solubility, all of which are independent of the amount of the sample. A mixture of substances often can be separated into the original substances using one or more of the characteristic properties.

related Ideas From Benchmarks For Science Literacy (aaas 1993)

3–5: *The Structure of Matter*

- Heating and cooling cause changes in the properties of materials. Many kinds of changes occur faster under hotter conditions.

6–8: *The Structure of Matter*

- Atoms and molecules are perpetually in motion. Increased temperature means greater average energy of motion, so most substances expand when heated. In solids, the atoms are closely locked in position and can only vibrate. In liquids, the atoms or molecules have higher energy, are more loosely connected and can slide past one another; some molecules may get enough energy to escape into a gas. In gases, the atoms or molecules have still more energy and are free of one another except during occasional collisions.

USING THE STORY WITH Grades K–4

I assume it is obvious that young children should not be boiling water unattended because of the dangers involved. They can be asked to contribute to the "Best Thinking" chart what they "know" about boiling water. You can change these into questions, initiate the investigation, and manipulate the water and other items that the children want to explore. This does not mean that children cannot help to design an investigation. They may not be answering all the questions that Cavan and Daniel have raised, but they will have an opportunity to find out how their knowledge about boiling matches the reality of the research they create based on their own questions. For instance, it is common for very young children to want you to compare the amount of water in a pot that has been boiling for 20 minutes with the amount with which you began. Students should be encouraged to record all data in their science notebooks for further discussion.

With older children, Cavan and Daniel's questions can be addressed with the insistence that there are variables to be controlled. Again, there is no need for them to handle boiling water. A demonstration of the temperature reaching a high and then stabilizing will be just as effective done by you as if they were to do it at their own work stations. You might want to start out with a formative assessment probe to find out what your students know about boiling liquids.

Actually, the second volume of the *Uncovering Student Ideas in Science* (Keeley, Eberle, and Tugel 2007) provides you with three different probes that you can use. "Turning the Dial" is aimed at finding out what students think about boiling

points of water, whether they realize that boiling points are characteristics of all matter and that they remain constant regardless of how much heat is added. "Boiling Time and Temperature" elicits children's ideas about what happens to the temperature of boiling water after heat has been applied over a long time. "What's in the Bubbles?" asks the question, "Do you know that the bubbles in boiling liquid are made up of that liquid changing state to become a gas?" Each of these can be used at different times during instruction and again at the end of the unit.

When the children have decided how to set up the investigation, you may ask a student or group of students to read the thermometer and write the temperature at regular intervals on a chart or chalkboard. If you are able to borrow or if you have a probe thermometer, it will be easier to read than a regular thermometer. Be sure to measure the amount of water you start with and note it on the chart. This allows students to record all information in their own science notebooks.

As the boiling progresses, the children may notice that the amount of water is decreasing. If not, you can ask them if they think there will be as much water after the pot has boiled for 10 minutes as there was to begin with. Answers will vary but it will be necessary to let the water cool a bit and compare the before boiling amount to the after boiling amount. Do not be concerned if the temperature rises slightly after a long period of time if you are using tap water, since the impurities in the water will become more concentrated as the water evaporates and this may raise the boiling point slightly but not usually significantly. This could lead into a question about adding salt to the water to change its boiling point.

USING THE STORY WITH GRADES 5–8

You will have to use your own discretion and your school's regulations about what you allow your students to do safely in your labs. The lack of temperature change in water once it has reached boiling point will be a surprise to many students. It will bear out Cavan's statement. You may ask for predictions from your students before the investigation begins, of course asking them to give a reason for them. These should be kept in their science notebooks for future reference along with the design of the investigation and the data that results. If possible in the demonstration setup or individual setups, use a clamp or other device to suspend the thermometer or probe so that the temperature of the water is being taken, not the temperature of the container.

A spirited discussion should follow as you help them see that boiling point is a standard property of all pure matter that does not change any more than other properties. The idea of the purity of matter may raise the question brought up by Daniel about adding the salt to raise the boiling point, thus changing water from a pure substance to a "contaminated" substance.

This salt investigation will have to be designed and the amounts and increments of salt added considered by the class. My experience is that additions of five grams of salt each time the water begins to boil again will show an increase in

temperature. I would like to add the caveat that you or your students put the salt added to a small amount of water in **carefully** and **slowly** so that eruptions do not occur as they sometimes do when things are added to boiling water in large amounts. Also, it should be the temperature of the water that should be measured and not of the beaker or pan, so if possible suspend the thermometer so that it does not touch the container as mentioned above. I personally would use this in demonstration form with student observers and data readers. I would also suggest that you consider using the probes mentioned in the K–4 section.

You will find that the temperature differences will go up slowly and the question as to whether a small amount of salt added to the water would make the pasta cook any faster will be answered. It usually turns out that in order to make much of a difference, the amount of salt needed, perhaps 25 g, would make the resulting meal very salty and not worth the small amount of time saved. There is also the point of saturation. Boiling salt water can dissolve only so much salt and if the salt added does not dissolve, it will no longer have an effect on the boiling point. Student observers may notice that after a certain amount of salt has been added, new additions will merely lie on the bottom and will not go into solution.

Students will probably have a great deal of difficulty in believing that the bubbles in the boiling liquid are water vapor. There is little you can do except to ask them to explain the decrease in volume of water in the pot as boiling continues. Invisible gases are a problem for many students and adults as well. It may be that the majority of students will understand this concept only when they are in high school and have had more experience with molecular theory. Perhaps showing students that the phase change is reversible by holding a cool plate over the boiling pot will show them that it is water in vapor form that is escaping and that it can be condensed back again into water.

I have had considerable failure in convincing *adults* about the nature of the bubbles. Their past experiences have convinced them that it is the oxygen in the water that is bubbling out. Never mind that the water seems to disappear. Certainly there is oxygen dissolved in the water, but the elimination of this amount of gas would not explain the loss of an entire pot of water if allowed to boil until gone. The misconception is well ingrained. Another possible source of confusion is that when asked what is in the space between molecules in any bit of matter, most adults will answer that it is "air." The idea of nothing but empty space between molecules is beyond their belief. This may contribute to their mistaken idea of oxygen or air bubbling out of the boiling liquid. What seems like perfect logic to us is a mystery to many students of science.

The students should now be able to finish the story about "boiling and salt and, all of that other stuff."

Related Books and NSTA Journal Articles

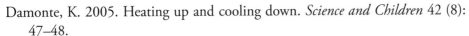

Damonte, K. 2005. Heating up and cooling down. *Science and Children* 42 (8): 47–48.

Driver, R., A. Squires, P. Rushworth, and V. Wood-Robinson, 1994. *Making sense of secondary science: Research into children's ideas.* London and New York: Routledge Falmer.

Keeley, P. 2005. *Science curriculum topic study: Bridging the gap between standards and practice.* Thousand Oaks, CA: Corwin Press.

Keeley, P., F. Eberle, and C. Dorsey. 2008. *Uncovering student ideas in science: Another 25 formative assessment probes, volume 3.* Arlington, VA: NSTA Press.

Keeley, P., F. Eberle, and L. Farrin. 2005. *Uncovering student ideas in science: 25 formative assessment probes, volume 1.* Arlington, VA: NSTA Press.

Keeley, P., F. Eberle, and J. Tugel. 2007. *Uncovering student ideas in science: 25 more formative assessment probes, volume 2.* Arlington, VA: NSTA Press.

Link, L., and E. Christmann. 2004. A different phase change. *Science Scope* 28 (3): 52–54.

May, K., and M. Kurbin. 2003. To heat or not to heat. *Science Scope* 26 (5): 38.

Pusvis, D. 2006. Fun with phase changes. *Science and Children* 29 (5): 23–25.

Robertson, W. 2002. *Energy: Stop faking it! Finally understanding science so you can teach it.* Arlington, VA: NSTA Press.

References

American Association for the Advancement of Science (AAAS). 1993. *Benchmarks for science literacy.* New York: Oxford University Press.

Hazen, R., and J. Trefil. 1991. *Science matters: Achieving scientific literacy.* New York: Anchor Books.

Keeley, P., F. Eberle, and J. Tugel. 2007. *Uncovering student ideas in science: 25 more formative assessment probes* (vol. 2). Arlington, VA: NSTA Press.

National Research Council (NRC). 1996. *National science education standards.* Washington, DC: National Academies Press.

CHAPTER 20
THE MAGNET DERBY

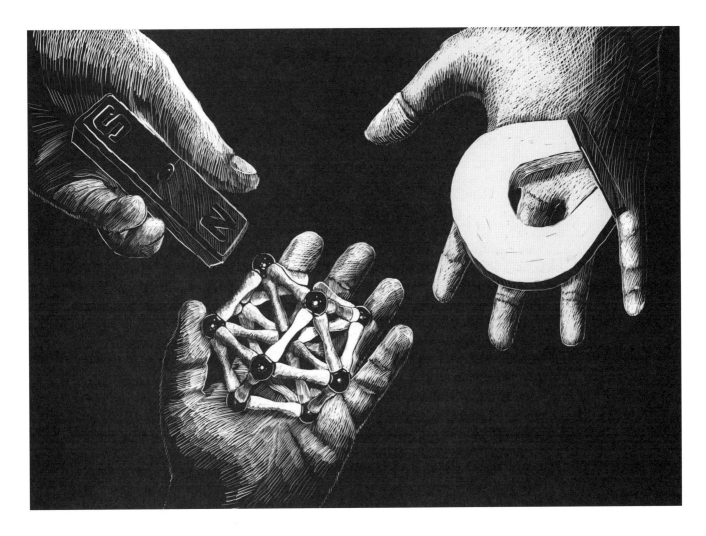

There are lots of magnets of all colors, sizes, and shapes. Some are bar magnets, some are cylinders, and others are shaped like horseshoes. Sally's teacher, Ms. Ramirez, had a whole box of them in the science cabinet.

To say that Sally liked to play with magnets was an understatement. She *loved* to play with magnets.

In fact, Sally had her own collection of magnets that was bigger than the teacher's. She could never seem to get enough so when she and her dad were in the mall at the dollar store, she went in and found a group of magnets that looked more like broken pieces of metal attached to a metal cabinet. Sally tried to take one off of the cabinet and found that she could not budge it. This was the strongest magnet she had ever seen and she had to have it.

"Please Dad, this will beat all of the other magnets I have and the ones at school too, I know it!"

Sally's dad rather liked that she was fond of science things and had visions of her becoming an engineer someday.

"Okay, if you can get it off of the cabinet, you can have it," said her dad.

Sally pulled and pulled but it wouldn't come straight off. Then she had an idea. The cabinet was smooth, so she thought she could slide it off the side, which she did without trouble.

"Pretty clever young lady," said her dad and together they went to the cash register.

"What makes this magnet so strong?" Sally asked the cashier.

"I'm not sure," she said, "but I think it is made of some different kinds of metals put together. They really are strong, aren't they? You should have seen us trying to get them apart when they arrived from the factory."

"Wait 'til I get this magnet to school, Dad. I'll really have the strongest magnet in the class."

Sally was disappointed that the next day was Sunday and there was no school, but on Monday morning, she ran to the bus with the magnet tucked into her pocket ready to take on all challengers. Of course, she went to Ms. Ramirez first and told her that she had a magnet that was stronger than all of the magnets in the room.

Ms. Ramirez decided she would have a little fun with Sally and also set up a neat science problem at the same time.

"Oh yeah?" asked Ms. Ramirez. "How do you think you can prove that to me and the rest of the class? We have a lot of magnets here and I'll bet some of the other kids have their favorites too. What do you say to a "Magnet Derby?""

"Sounds great to me," said Sally. "I'll go get the paper clips."

"Not so fast, Sally, I've got a different idea. Up 'til now we have always measured the strength of magnets by how many paper clips they pick up. Let's think of some different ways to measure strength so that we can have some data that is more than just numbers of clips. Anyway I'm not sure that the paper clip count is all that accurate. Remember how sometimes we got different numbers out of the same magnet? Maybe there are different ways to test strength. Let's get the class involved."

And so they did. Sally put her magnet up against all others after the class came up with several different ways of testing the strengths. They all had a lot of data at the end so that the decision was pretty certain whose magnet won the derby.

PURPOSE

Magnetism is a force that acts over a distance. Children play with magnetic toys all of the time. Any family that has a refrigerator knows that the number of magnets on the door defines the size of the appliance. This story should give students an opportunity to test some of their conceptions about magnets, namely what they will attract, their strengths, their interactions with each other, and how they are used in everyday life. It also allows for a great deal of investigation, testing of hypotheses, and drawing of conclusions.

related CONCEPTS

- Force
- Repulsion
- Poles
- Attraction
- Properties of matter

DON'T BE SURPRISED

Your students will probably expect that magnets will attract all metals. They may also believe that the strength of the magnet is determined by its size or shape. If they have been involved with measuring magnet strength before, they will assume that the number of objects they can pick up and hold judges all magnets. They will be challenged to find other ways of testing magnetic strength and to develop data-collecting skills they may not have used before. They may believe that magnetism can travel through all sorts of materials. They may talk of things "sticking" to magnets rather than being attracted or pulled toward them. They may think that poles exist only at the ends of a magnet or that circular magnets have no poles. Finally, the relationship between magnets and the Earth's magnetic field will probably not occur to them. They may imagine that the magnet's needle, the north-seeking pole, is actually the north pole of the magnet.

CONTENT BACKGROUND

Magnetism is a force to be reckoned with. It is capable of doing work; it can push and pull certain objects or change their position; it can cause them to move and cause them to stop. The interesting part of the magnetic force is that it can operate through a distance—it doesn't have to touch anything. So this puts it in the same force category as gravity and electricity. In this story I am going to limit the field to permanent magnets and leave the area of electromagnets to another time. So what do we know about magnetism and magnets?

- Magnetism is a force.

- Magnetic force is created around every magnet in the form of a magnetic field.
- Magnets always have two opposite poles.
- Earth is a magnet.
- Magnetism and electricity are indelibly related.
- Like poles of magnets repel each other.
- Unlike poles of magnets attract each other.
- The forces of the magnet are strongest at the poles.
- Magnetism is a force that acts through a distance.
- Magnetic force can penetrate certain materials.

In 1861, a Scottish physicist named James Clark Maxwell said that electricity and magnetism were two aspects of the same force. He basically said that you cannot have one without the other and proved this with four mathematical equations that stand even today. He stated that every time a magnetic field changes, an electrical field is created and that every time an electric charge moves, a magnetic field is created. This means that from the magnets that adorn your refrigerator to the static electricity that gives you a bad hair day, magnetism and electricity are both involved. If you wish to delve more deeply into Maxwell's equations and this area of magnetism and electricity, I suggest you dig out your copy of *Science Matters* and read the chapter on electricity and magnetism (Hazen and Trefil 1991). I, however, shall now go on to focus on magnets as they relate to the story.

Magnetism has affected human life probably since the first human noticed the magnetic qualities of the natural magnets called lodestones. Somewhere along the line humans realized that certain metals were attracted to the lodestones and that when they were allowed to move freely, they oriented themselves in a certain direction. Later these directions were named *north* and *south*. By the same token, the end of the magnet that points in the direction we call north is called the north pole of the magnet. (Actually it was originally called the north-seeking pole and then later shortened to just north.) Its opposite was obviously named south.

Now you may well ask, if similar poles repel each other how can the north pole of a magnet or compass point to the north? Shouldn't it be repelled? Great questions, and the answers lie in the semantics of naming, maps, and directions. By convention it has been agreed that the end of the magnet that points to the pole that is in the northern hemisphere will be called north. If we think of the Earth as a magnet, then the pole that is at the top of the globe must be the south magnetic pole or else it would not attract the north pole of the compass. However, since it is in the hemisphere that we call the northern hemisphere, the pole in that hemisphere is called the north magnetic pole. It is just the opposite in the southern hemisphere. As you can see, it can seem very confusing and it's probably best not to try to introduce your students to this semantic conflict of terms. It is sufficient to concentrate on the fact that the north end of the magnet points toward the magnetic pole in the northern hemisphere and vice versa in the southern hemisphere.

In order to simplify things we paint a big *N* on one pole of the magnet and a big *S* on the other and call them north and south poles. To me, this is just another

NATIONAL SCIENCE TEACHERS ASSOCIATION

example of the fact that scientific information and nomenclature is a result of human construction. However, one interesting fact is that the poles on the Earth move around a lot, and over the years have migrated hundreds of miles. So the pole is not really at the "tip" or top of the globe we know as Earth.

Magnets can be made of nickel, cobalt, or iron. Lodestones are strictly made of iron. Magnets today are often made of combinations of the three metals. It is possible to make a temporary magnet by stroking a piece of pure iron, nickel, or cobalt with a magnet, but it will eventually lose its magnetic properties. Putting the proper metal(s) in a strong magnetic field makes permanent magnets. These do not lose their properties over time.

What kinds of things are attracted to magnets? If there is iron in something, it will be attracted to a magnet. This supposedly even includes paper if there is printing on it using ink with iron in it. Steel, which is made with iron, is attracted and, of course, the other magnetic metals such as nickel and cobalt and their alloys. And there are some rare minerals and elements, which are not likely to find their way either into our lives or our classrooms, that are attracted to magnets.

There are ceramic materials that have been infused with metals that are drawn to magnets; melding iron oxide and strontium carbonate forms one kind of ceramic magnet. All kinds of novelty displays use the flexible magnets which are made by putting ferrite magnet powder and polymers together and melding them into permanent magnets.

Magnets come in so many sizes and shapes it is difficult to predict their strength just by looking at them. There are horseshoe magnets, bar magnets, cylinder magnets, button magnets, ring magnets, and many variations of those. But they all behave alike in that they all have two poles and attract the same kinds of materials; and they all exhibit the attraction and repulsion phenomenon at the poles.

I mentioned that all magnets have two opposite poles, regardless of size. If you break a bar magnet in half, you will have two magnets, both with a north and south pole. Break it as many times as you wish and you will have smaller magnets but each will still have two poles. Even the atom is a tiny magnet with two poles. This is described by Maxwell's second equation, which says that there are no isolated poles.

Magnets are a source of fun and certainly a source of mystery, as they have been for centuries. In your class magnets should continue to stimulate your students to more and more investigations as they try to finish this story and in the meantime learn more about magnets.

related ideas from the national science education standards (nrc 1996)

K–4: *Light, Heat, Electricity, and Magnetism*
- Magnets attract and repel each other and certain kinds of other materials.

5–8: *Motions and Forces*
- The motion of an object can be described by its position, direction of motion, and speed. That motion can be measured and represented on a graph.

related ideas in benchmarks for science literacy (aaas 1993)

K–2: *Forces of Nature*
- Magnets can be used to make some things move without being touched.

3–5: *Forces of Nature*
- Without touching them, a magnet pulls on all things made of iron and either pushes or pulls on other magnets.
- Without touching them, material that has been electrically charged pulls on all other materials and may either push or pull other charged materials.

6–8: *Forces of Nature*
- Electric currents and magnets can exert a force on each other.

Using the story with grades K–4

Students react to this story with a competitive verve. They are ready to grab their favorite magnet and put it to the test. Again, it is important to help them define what they mean by "strongest." Since they are accustomed to using magnets to pick up things, the number of objects is usually the tack they take in defining *strongest*. Accept this and tell them that maybe they can find other ways to define strongest later on.

At the risk of dampening some of their competitive spirits, I suggest that you begin, as usual, with the "Best Thinking" chart and find out what they know about magnets. The chart will probably include some of the following:

- Magnets pick up things.
- Magnets only pick up metal things.
- Magnets can make things move.
- Magnets can pick up nails and pins.
- The ends of magnets either like each other or don't like each other.
- Magnets are stronger at their ends than in the middle.
- I have magnets in some of my toys.
- Magnets work under water.

Changing the first part of each statement, can change these to questions in search of evidence:

- Do magnets pick up all metal things?
- Are magnets stronger at their ends than in the middle?
  Can you stop a magnet from picking up things?

Their research and data as a class can be kept on another chart, but it is important for them to be ready to put all of their own personal results into their science notebooks.

Now the investigations can begin. I like to hold back some new magnets that they haven't seen so that there is an element of surprise when they design the derby later on. It is a good idea to have metal coins, aluminum foil, brass paper fasteners, paper clips, plastic bottle caps, metal bottle caps, Popsicle sticks, Legos, and lots of other objects for them to try. They will be especially surprised that some of the metal objects will not react to the magnet. You can have them sort those objects into "Don't Get Picked Up" and "Do Get Picked Up" piles. Then they can try to predict if something will be attracted to a magnet. They can use the objects that are attracted to test some of the other questions, such as on which part of the magnet the strength is greatest. After they have had a chance to really explore their magnets, they will be more ready to think about designing a magnet derby.

You may want to go to the NSTA archives and look at Peggy Ashbrook's article in *Science and Children* "More Than Messing Around with Magnets" (2005). Also useful is the article in *Science and Children* by Judith Kur and Marsha Heitzmann titled "Attracting Student Wonderings" (2008). Both articles have interesting additions to the use of magnets in K–4 classrooms.

You might give the students a hint about looking for other methods of measuring strength of magnets, such as, "You saw the paper clip move toward the magnet before it was picked up. Can you use movement of the paper clip to measure strength?" Perhaps this will allow some of your students to connect the fact that distance between magnet and object can be a measure of strength. If a paper clip is placed on lined graph paper and a magnet is brought near the clip, the number of spaces required to attract the clip to the magnet can be quantified. Object and distance can be graphed with a histogram where each magnet is measured by the number of squares required to move the clip. Students may weigh different objects and compare magnets' abilities to move them or lift them.

As a final diversion, the age-old puppet stage with cut-out characters weighted down with paper clips, may allow the students to put on puppet plays by moving the characters around the stage using magnets from below.

USING THE STORY WITH GRADES 5–8

As surprising as it seems, the sophisticated middle schoolers like to play with magnets as much as the younger kids. However, we expect a bit more ingenuity from them. They should have the opportunity to put their past experience to use in new and exciting ways. Many of the ideas suggested in the last section can be modified to fit the age of the grade 5–8 students. Finding ways to measure and compare magnet strengths uses creativity and a no-holds-barred use of their minds. But once they have been able to put magnets in order from weakest to strongest, they should have an opportunity to ask questions that are seldom addressed. Unless you wish to delve into the area of electromagnets, I suggest that you ask your students to limit their investigations to the realm of permanent magnets.

Some questions to have them explore are:

- How do you limit a magnetic field?
- What kinds of materials shield a magnet's field?
- Do magnets work in a vacuum?
- Are magnets' strengths affected by a medium such as water?
- Are both poles of a particular magnet of equal strength?
- Where on a bar magnet does the polar superiority begin or end?
- Do stronger magnets also have stronger middle sections?
- Do ceramic and flexible magnets have N and S poles?

You might put questions such as these into a box and have students pick them at random and conduct investigations, then contrast and compare data with other students.

Another area that can interest your students is to take this topic into the technology realm. You might challenge them to create a levitation train such as the ones used in Germany and Japan, using only magnetic strips and everyday objects. You can make the stipulations for construction specific or leave them vague. I prefer to make certain specifications such as the materials must cost less than $5 and the "train" should travel in a straight path for a minimum of one meter without leaving the "track" after one push. You and the students can determine a rubric of minimum standards so that teams of students can work on the train to meet the standards.

All in all, magnets are mysterious and fun. Studying them can lead to developing all or most of the skills and knowledge specified in the Standards and Benchmarks quoted in the prior section.

related Books and NSTa Journal articles

Driver, R., A. Squires, P. Rushworth, and V. Wood-Robinson. 1994. *Making sense of secondary science: Research into children's ideas.* London and New York: Routledge-Falmer.

Keeley, P. 2005. *Science curriculum topic study: Bridging the gap between standards and practice.* Thousand Oaks, CA: Corwin Press.

Keeley, P., F. Eberle, and C. Dorsey. 2008. *Uncovering student ideas in science: Another 25 formative assessment probes, volume 3.* Arlington, VA: NSTA Press.

Keeley, P., F. Eberle, and L. Farrin. 2005. *Uncovering student ideas in science: 25 formative assessment probes, volume 1.* Arlington, VA: NSTA Press.

Keeley, P., F. Eberle, and J. Tugel. 2007. *Uncovering student ideas in science: 25 more formative assessment probes, volume 2.* Arlington, VA: NSTA Press.

references

American Association for the Advancement of Science (AAAS). 1993. *Benchmarks for science literacy.* New York: Oxford University Press.

Ashbrook, P. 2005. More than messing around with magnets. *Science and Children* 43 (2): 21–23.

Hazen, R., and J. Trefil. 1991. *Science matters: Achieving scientific literacy.* New York: Anchor Books.

Kur, J., and M. Heitzmann. 2008. Attracting student wonderings. *Science and Children* 45 (5): 24–27.

National Research Council (NRC). 1996. *National science education standards.* Washington, DC: National Academies Press.

THE COOKIE DILEMMA

Mom was baking cookies—chocolate chip cookies—and Cerisa and her sister Barbara could hardly wait for the cookies to come out of the oven. At the moment they were only a promise, since Mom was busy mixing all of the ingredients. There was flour, baking soda, sugar, butter, eggs, and chocolate chips. Mom always mixed the dry ingredients first and then added the eggs and butter at the end. But the phone rang and it was for Mom. She left the bowl with the dry ingredients on the counter and talked to her friend for a while. It seemed like an hour to Cerisa and Barbara, but that is the way time passes when you are hungry for nice warm cookies!

When she came back to the cookie bowl she said, "Oh goodness, I lost my place and don't know if I put in the baking soda or not. If I didn't put it in or put in double the amount, it will probably ruin the cookies. I guess I'll have to start over again!"

She got out an identical bowl and began again. This time she made sure she added the baking soda first and then checked it off the recipe. After the dry ingredients were mixed, she was ready for the butter and eggs.

Wouldn't you know it, the front door bell rang and of course it was someone for Mom. While she was at the door, Dad came in and noticed the bowls on the counter. He thought, "I'll just push these bowls over here so I can use the counter space to make myself a sandwich."

When Mom came back, she looked at the bowls and said, "Did you move these?" to the girls.

"Nope, Dad moved them because he needed counter space," said Cerisa. "Which one is which?"

"Oh rats," said Mom, "I can't tell the difference! And I am not about to start over again! What a waste!"

Cerisa and Barbara both saw their visions of cookies going down the drain but were not about to give up. Cerisa picked up the bowls and turned to her mom.

"Mom, we have been doing something in school called *Mystery Powders* and if you give us some time I think we can tell you what ingredients are in the bowls. I'll need some stuff from the cupboard, though."

Mom was, of course, delighted to have them solve this mystery and helped them find the materials they needed to test the contents of the bowls. And, within a few minutes they came up with the answer to the problem and now were able to get two batches of cookies when they had their answers.

"Amazing!" said Dad as he munched on his cookie a half hour later. "How did you do that?"

NATIONAL SCIENCE TEACHERS ASSOCIATION

PURPOSE

This story is based a bit on the ESS (Elementary Science Study) activity "Mystery Powders." The problem with the original activity was that the students were introduced to the tests for various ingredients without a motivating hook. Alecia Peck wrote a similar story to motivate her third grade class in western Massachusetts. It was of course, finished with a cookie treat for all. The new modification then became part of the third-grade curriculum for the school district. There are two purposes: Have children engage in problem solving and use their collective knowledge to identify certain chemical compounds in a mystery mix.

RELATED CONCEPTS

- Chemical reactions
- Problem solving
- Designing scientific investigations

DON'T BE SURPRISED

Some of your students will not have had experience in testing for various food substances such as starch, baking soda, baking powder, sugar, salt, and flour. Some may not be aware of how to design an investigation and control for variables. During the discussion following the reading of the story, you will probably become aware of any deficits.

CONTENT BACKGROUND

You will mostly be testing for chemical reactions that occur when two or more substances are combined and react with one another to form new substances. These new substances have different properties than any of the original reactants alone. Thus, mixing vinegar and baking soda will result in a combination of the two with carbon dioxide as a by-product, which will appear as a fizzing gas. Since, neither of the two substances are gases, the appearance of a gas is a definite clue that a chemical reaction has taken place.

Changes can occur in matter in at least two different common and observable ways; physical changes and chemical changes. Changes in state, shape, or color are usually considered to be physical changes. Melting or freezing, molding into a different shape and becoming part of a mixture are all considered to be physical changes. Physical changes do not change the chemical properties of the substances involved. Evaporation, condensation, melting, freezing, and going from a solid to a gas (sublimation) are all examples of physical changes. Carving a piece of wood or hammering a piece of soft metal are also examples of physical change. Putting two substances together that mix but do not chemically combine is another

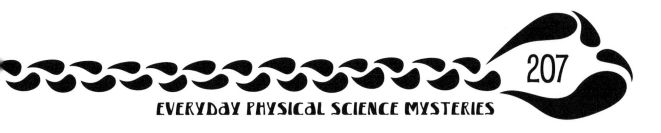

example. Mixing salt or sugar into water results in the sugar or salt dissolving in the water but the salt, the sugar, and the water are not changed in their chemical makeup. The water can evaporat, another physical change, leaving behind the sugar or salt as a residue, thus proving that the substance has not really combined with the substance in which it is dissolved. This and the others mentioned above are examples of mixtures, all of which encompass physical changes.

Chemical changes, on the other hand, do involve changes in the reactants at a molecular level and involve the formation of new compounds. Rusting is a common example of a chemical reaction that we have all witnessed. Oxygen reacts with iron to form a new compound, iron oxide, commonly called rust. Usually this happens in a moist environment and is aided by any additional elements in the moisture that create movement of charged atoms or molecules in the system. Charged atoms are called ions. These have either a positive or negative electrical charge due to an excess or deficiency of electrons. In a chemical reaction the product has different properties than any of the reactants involved. These chemical reactions either give off heat or light, or require heat or light to initiate them.

Two of the most common chemical reactions will be used in this story. First, iodine, in the form of potassium iodide, when added to starch (flour) will result in a blue or blue-black color change. Vinegar (acetic acid), when added to baking soda (sodium bicarbonate), will undergo a chemical reaction that results in the release of carbon dioxide gas, usually observed as fizzing or bubbling. Caramelizing sugar involves heating sugar until its temperature is above 100°C (210°F) which causes the oxidation or combination of oxygen with the sugar. The tantalizing odor you smell is the release of those gaseous compounds. Crème brulé, that tasty French custard dessert, has a crusty sugar coating on top usually accomplished by adding sugar to the top of the custard and heating it with a portable torch. Finally, looking with the aid of a magnifying glass for the salt crystals in the form of little cubes usually identifies it easily. To be even more certain, salt will dissolve in water whereas flour will not. Baking soda will also dissolve in water, but will be the only one to react to vinegar as well. Sugar will dissolve in water, but will also respond to the fire test whereas salt will not.

related ideas from the National Science Education Standards (NRC 1996)

K–4: Properties of Objects and Materials
- Objects have many observable properties including size, weight, shape, color, temperature, and the ability to react with other substances.

National Science Teachers Association

5–8: *Properties of Objects and Materials*

- Substances react chemically in characteristic ways with other substances to form new substances (compounds) with different characteristic properties. In chemical reactions, the total mass is conserved.

related ideas from benchmarks for science literacy (aaas 1993)

K–2: *The Structure of Matter*

- Objects can be described in terms of the materials they are made of (e.g., clay, cloth, paper) and their physical properties (e.g., color, size, shape, weight, texture, flexibility).
- Things can be done to materials to change some of their properties but not all materials respond the same way to what is done to them.

3–5: *The Structure of Matter*

- When a new material is made by combining two or more materials, it has properties that are different from the original materials.
- No matter how parts of an object are assembled, the weight of the whole object made is always the same as the sum of the parts and when a thing is broken into parts, the parts have the same total weight as the original object.

6–8: *The Structure of Matter*

- Because most elements tend to combine with others, few elements are found in their pure form.
- An especially important kind of reaction between substances involved the combination of oxygen with something else, as in burning or rusting.
- No matter how substances within a closed system interact with one another, or how they combine or break apart, the total mass of the system remains the same. The idea of atoms explains the conservation of matter. If the number of atoms stays the same no matter how they are arranged, then their mass stays the same.
- The idea of atoms explains chemical reactions. When substances interact to form new substances, the atoms that make up the molecules of the original substances combine in new ways.

USING THE STORY WITH GRADES K–4

This story was first tested with third graders to fit within a unit on chemical and physical changes in matter. As mentioned before, the teachers were concerned that the students were merely following a specified worksheet and not seeing any relevance to their lives. So we wrote a story to which they could relate. After the story, they were shown two bowls of white powders and told that they contained the ingredients mentioned in the story. One bowl had all of the required dry ingredients, flour, sugar, baking soda, and salt. The other was missing the baking soda. They were promised a cookie party if they were able to tell their teacher what was contained in each of the bowls.

The children met with the teacher to discuss the problem and to reach consensus on a solution that would reward them with a batch of chocolate chip cookies. There seemed to be little confusion, and in about 35 minutes they had agreed upon a plan. They decided to test for everything in each bowl. They agreed that they would take a sample from each bowl and label it so that five teams of students would each receive a sample to test for the various materials.

When asked if they knew how to test for baking soda, many had had experience with making rockets or volcanoes using vinegar and baking soda and knew about the fizzing reaction. They remembered the smell of burning sugar. These children knew what salt looked like under magnification and knew that it would dissolve in water. They didn't know of a test for starch, so the teacher presented them with a demonstration of starch and iodine. She also demonstrated the safety factors involved in testing for each substance. All children wore safety glasses, and only did the burning tests with the help of the teacher. She set up a burner and supervised the placing of powders on an aluminum foil tray so that the students could observe the reaction with heat.

The next thing to do was to set up the experimental design for each test. The fact that the substances were mixed did not cause a problem since when putting the powders in a foil tube and heating, the flour gave off a burnt toast smell and the sugar gave off the distinctive burnt sugar smell, sweet and caramel-like. The students tried all tests and found that in the sample from one bowl, the vinegar test did not work but all other tests did. In the other bowl, all tests were positive. They concluded, therefore, that one bowl contained all the ingredients, and that the other lacked baking soda.

The one problem occurred when the teacher asked them how they would record their results. They did not see why it was necessary to form a table of ingredients and their response to each test. The teacher allowed each group to use their own method of keeping data. With some groups, there was no problem. With other groups they were pressed to remember the results of their tests. The teacher could have insisted that they use the table used in the ESS "Mystery Powders" booklet, but decided to let them see the need for a way to record data. She concluded that they did not see the problem until they were involved enough to be aware of the need to revisit data. In subsequent situations, they were careful to

NATIONAL SCIENCE TEACHERS ASSOCIATION

work this out. It was only because of experiencing a problem that they were aware of a need.

The cookies were delicious and helped to conclude an experience that amazed the teachers who witnessed the process. Cookies were served while students had a group discussion to discuss the process and what the students had learned.

USING THE STORY WITH GRADES 5-8

The process used with middle school children should not be too different than that with grades K–4. One teacher chose to add several different new tests that included testing for pH. Testing for acids and bases will give your students another way of categorizing matter. Acids are usually sour and bases are usually bitter, but taste is not a good way to test things. It can be quite dangerous! Instead we use indicators such as litmus or an easily made indicator extracted from red cabbage. I usually put some red cabbage in a blender with some water and blend thoroughly. I filter it through a coffee filter, producing a pinkish liquid. This liquid will change color when combined with an acid or base. It will become red with strong acids and turn greenish yellow with strong bases. Examples of acids found in a home are citrus juices, vinegar, and tomatoes. Soaps, detergents, hydrogen peroxide, and antacids are examples of bases.

What are acids and bases? Simplified, when acids or bases are in aqueous solutions, they break apart into (H+) ions and (OH-) ions. If there is a preponderance of (H+) ions in a solution, it is an acid and the opposite is true for bases. As you can probably guess, it they are put in a solution together, they come together and form water, a neutral substance. Thus, if you have an acid stomach and add an antacid (base), they are neutralized in your stomach and you get relief, at least temporarily. There will probably be a "burp" as your stomach gets rid of the gas.

The only chemical from the story that will give you a definite pH reading is the vinegar. However, receiving pH readings of neutral are still data. Since sugar and salt dissolve in water, you would not expect them to alter a pH reading. The same is true of cornstarch and flour. If your students get caught up in the use of the cabbage juice, you can help them to try detergents, antacids, citrus juices, and if you feel safe in demonstrating it, drain-cleaning compounds, which, although highly toxic, give strong basic reactions. Students should never touch the latter, and of course safety glasses should be worn throughout the activities.

If you would like to have additional information and ideas on teaching about chemical and physical change, you can connect to NSTA's website (*www.nsta.org*) and members can download articles from past journals. Two interesting articles are "Using Easy Bake Ovens to Teach Chemistry" by Herald (2004), and "Enhancing Student Understanding of Physical and Chemical Changes," by McIntosh, White, and Suter (2009). I was excited particularly in how inexpensive and safe little ovens can be used in the classroom.

related books and NSTa journal articles

Keeley, P. 2005. *Science curriculum topic study: Bridging the gap between standards and practice.* Thousand Oaks, CA: Corwin Press.

Keeley, P., F. Eberle, and C. Dorsey. 2008. *Uncovering student ideas in science, volume 3: Another 25 formative assessment probes.* Arlington, VA: NSTA Press.

Keeley, P., F. Eberle, and J. Tugel. 2007. *Uncovering student ideas in science, volume 2: 25 more formative assessment probes.* Arlington, VA: NSTA Press.

Keeley, P., and J. Tugel. 2009. *Uncovering student ideas in science, volume 4: 25 new formative assessment probes.* Arlington, VA: NSTA Press.

Konicek-Moran, R. 2008. *Everyday science mysteries: Stories for inquiry-based science teaching.* Arlington, VA: NSTA Press.

Konicek-Moran, R. 2009. *More everyday science mysteries: Stories for inquiry-based science teaching.* Arlington, VA: NSTA Press.

Konicek-Moran, R. 2010. *Even more everyday science mysteries: Stories for inquiry-based science teaching.* Arlington, VA: NSTA Press.

references

American Association for the Advancement of Science (AAAS). 1993. *Benchmarks for science literacy.* New York: Oxford University Press.

Elementary Science Study (ESS). 1957. *Mystery powders.* Newton, MA: Education Development Corporation.

Herald, C. 2004. Using Easy-Bake ovens to teach chemistry. *Science Scope* 27 (5): 24–29.

Keeley, P., and J. Tugel. 2009. *Uncovering student ideas in science, volume 4: 25 new formative assessment probes.* Arlington, VA: NSTA Press.

Konicek-Moran, R. 2008. *Everyday science mysteries: Stories for inquiry-based science teaching.* Arlington, VA: NSTA Press.

Konicek-Moran, R. 2009. *More everyday science mysteries: Stories for inquiry-based science teaching.* Arlington, VA: NSTA Press.

McIntosh, J., S. White, and R. Suter. 2009. Enhancing student understanding of physical and chemical changes. *Science Scope* 54–58.

National Research Council (NRC). 1996. *National science education standards.* Washington, DC: National Academies Press.

NATIONAL SCIENCE TEACHERS ASSOCIATION

CHAPTER 22
SWEET TALK

You may remember Caroline and Lisa, the sisters in the story "Iced Tea" in *More Everyday Mysteries*. Let's go back to their porch and listen to another conversation they had about adding sugar to iced tea. It provides a look at another everyday science mystery and at two words that are very confusing to a lot of people.

Caroline was stirring her iced tea madly.

"What are you doing?" Lisa asked. She was a lot older than Caroline, but she always stopped to check in with her little sister. She sat on the porch swing with some nail polish and began to paint her nails.

"I'm trying to make this sugar melt!" Caroline answered. "It's a lot harder with iced tea than when you put sugar in hot tea!"

"Actually you aren't *melting* anything," said Lisa, "You are *dissolving* the sugar— or at least you're trying to." Lisa loved her science classes in the high school.

"Melting, dissolving … what's the difference?"

"If you knew the difference you probably wouldn't be doing what you are doing!" said Lisa. "What kinds of things do you know that melt?"

"Ice cream, ice cubes, candy in my mouth, sugar in hot tea, chocolate, and… well, lots of things!"

"Well, that list is *almost* right." Lisa answered. She worked on her nails for a few moments. "Well, then, what kinds of things do you know that dissolve?" she asked, after a while.

"Aren't they the same?" asked Caroline, looking glumly at the bits of sugar swirling at the bottom of her glass.

"Nope. Okay, I'll give you a hint. I think you are clever enough to know which things in your life dissolve and which things melt."

"Better try me and see," said Caroline. "Maybe it takes more than being clever."

"Think of the difference between putting sugar into iced tea and watching your ice cream cone dribble all over the front of you. The hint is what is *missing* in one case but *present* in the other?"

"If I can figure that riddle out, can I get my iced tea sweet?" asked Caroline.

"I think so but, then again, maybe not. Want to bet on it?" asked Lisa. And she gave her sister a sly smile.

PURPOSE

This story's purpose is to acquaint students with the very different physical processes of melting and dissolving, which will help further their understanding of various changes of states.

RELATED CONCEPTS

- Melting
- Temperature
- Mixtures
- Solute
- Dissolving
- Change of state
- Solvent

DON'T BE SURPRISED

Melting and dissolving are two of the most often misunderstood concepts in both child and adult populations. Many children believe that when a substance dissolves in a solvent it does not exist any longer. They think it disappears. Even though they can still *taste* sugar dissolved in a drink, since they can no longer see it, it no longer exists for them. In fact, if asked if the sugar added to a liquid increases the total weight, many will say that it does not. This lack of understanding of conservation of mass is most common among elementary age students.

CONTENT BACKGROUND

Dissolving

When a substance is put into a solvent, such as water, it *dissolves* and becomes part of a homogeneous mixture, involving a *solute* and a *solvent*. The solute is the substance being dissolved and the solvent is the substance into which the solute is mixed. The result is a mixture and is a physical change that can be reversed so that the solute can be recovered again to its original crystallized form. For example, when sugar or salt are added to water, the water helps to break the solute particles down into very small molecules, which then distribute themselves equally throughout the solvent into what we call a *homogeneous* mixture. This means that if you were to sample the mixture from anywhere in the container, the ratio of sugar molecules to water molecules would be the same. Mixtures can also be *heterogeneous*. Concrete is an example of a mixture that is not homogeneous, given that gravel and sand are usually not equally dispersed throughout the mixture.

Mixtures can also involve the dissolution of gases in liquids (carbonated drinks), gases in gases (water vapor in air), and solids in solids (amalgams). In my (and probably your grandparents') day, dentists used to make fillings out of a

mixture of mercury and silver. Over time, the mercury would leach out, leaving a solid, hard filling of silver. As the mercury left the amalgam, there was only one place for it to go—into our bodies. However, we now know that mercury is very harmful in the human body and is no longer legally used for anything with which we may come in contact.

Various liquids dissolve solids at various rates. Temperature is a factor in that higher temperatures in the solvent almost always result in faster dissolution. If you used the story "Iced Tea" (Chapter 18 in this book), you will remember that Caroline believed that she could dissolve as much sugar in the cold iced tea as she wished. Her sister Lisa knew that this was unlikely and challenged Caroline to prove her statement. Caroline was surprised and humbled when she realized that she couldn't dissolve much sugar in the iced tea because the cold solvent was able to accommodate only a small amount of sugar before it became saturated and could dissolve no more. Temperature affects some solutes, but not all. Salt, for example, is not affected to the same extent.

Also affecting the rate of dissolution is the particle size of the solute. This is an investigable question testable using sugar cubes for example and comparing their rate of dissolving with granulated sugar, granulated sugar crushed in a mortar and pestle or confectioners sugar.

Melting

Melting is an entirely different process. Melting is a physical change that involves a transfer of heat and the changing of any substance from a solid to a liquid state. Heat from the environment is necessary to change any substance from a solid to a liquid, and then to a gas. It is very easy to see the change in state in the melting of an ice cream or ice cubes.

Water, the best-known exemplar of thermodynamic change of states, can go from solid (ice) to liquid (water) to gas (water vapor) under the influence of temperature change. Some substances need extremely high or low temperatures in order to change states. In rare cases, materials such as dry ice (solid carbon dioxide) go directly to the gaseous form in a process called *sublimation*. If you have ever had occasion to watch dry ice at room temperature, you notice the white clouds appear as the solid goes to the gaseous form without going to the liquid form first. A very few metals, such as mercury, are liquid at room temperature.

So you can see that melting and dissolving are two very different things. Students who think that melting happens when sucking on sugar candy or a lollipop do not understand the difference between the concepts. With help, they can see that dissolving that lollipop is the same as dissolving sugar in water except that they are dissolving the sugar from the candy in saliva. The same thing happens when they chew gum. The sugar flavoring in the gum is dissolved in the saliva and swallowed.

Every child has had the opportunity to see ice cream melt and know that they have to eat quickly or lose their treat, often all over their shirts. They may find that it is difficult to differentiate between placing ice cubes in liquid and saying that the ice cube is melting in the liquid and placing a sugar cube in water and saying

NATIONAL SCIENCE TEACHERS ASSOCIATION

it is dissolving. However, since the ice cube is a frozen liquid, the difference in temperature that occurs in the outside liquid is a direct clue that something other then dissolving is happening.

related Ideas From the National Science Education Standards (Nrc 1996)

K–4: Properties of Objects and Materials

- Objects have many observable properties including size, weight, shape, color, temperature, and the ability to react with other substances.
- Objects are made of one or more materials, such as paper, wood, and metal. Objects can be described by the properties of the materials from which they are made, and those properties can be used to separate or sort a group of objects or materials.
- Materials can exist in different states—solid, liquid, and gas. Some common materials such as water can be changed from one state to another by heating or cooling.

5–8: Properties and Changes of Properties in Matter

- A substance has characteristic properties, such as density, a boiling point, and solubility, all of which are independent of the amount of the sample. A mixture of substances often can be separated into the original substances using one or more of the characteristic properties.

related Ideas From Benchmarks For Science Literacy (aaas 1993)

K–2: The Structure of Matter

- Things can be done to materials to change some of their properties, but not all materials respond the same way to what is done to them.

K–2: The Earth

- Water can be a liquid or a solid and can be made to go back and forth from one form to the other. If water is turned into ice and then the ice is allowed to melt, the amount of water is the same as it was before freezing.

3–5: The Structure of Matter

- Heating and cooling cause changes in the properties of materials.

- Atoms and molecules are perpetually in motion. In liquids, the atoms or molecules have higher energy, are more loosely connected, and can slide past one another.

USING THE STORY WITH GRADES K–4

A probe from *Uncovering Student Ideas in Science, Volume 1* (Keeley, Eberle, and Farrin 2005) called "Is It Melting?" asks students to choose from among a variety of options, those that are melting and those that are dissolving. Giving this probe to students and discussing their ideas before using the story may be a very helpful formative assessment. I cannot emphasize enough that these probes are not tests to be used to evaluate students but are assessments useful in helping you to plan your "next steps," in your teaching strategy. It helps you to see how many of your students hold the idea that the two processes are synonymous, and it may give you a glimpse of your work in trying to move them toward the current scientific view.

Asking children to participate in an ice cube melting contest is a good way to introduce the concept of melting. Give each child an ice cube in a cup and tell them to make it melt doing anything except touch it. This activity can be a type of embedded formative assessment because watching what your students do gives you information about their understanding of the process.

Recently, I tried another tactic to see if students were aware of what happened to ice cubes when they are placed in water. Each child was given a beaker of water and then an ice cube colored green with food coloring (colored ice cubes can be made by placing a bit of food coloring in the bottom of each compartment of an ice cube tray, then adding water and mixing the solution until it is homogeneous in color). When the colored ice cube is placed in the water, the melting green water is visible as it descends to the bottom of the container (remember, cold substances sink, warm substances rise).

Given a little time, the green ice water warms a bit and begins to circulate around the beaker, mixing in. If a sample of the water is set aside and allowed to evaporate, the green color will remain behind, showing that it is a mixture—the food coloring was dissolved in the water and can still be separated. So, both melting and dissolving take place. Students can start to distinguish between the two processes by comparing them. It really is quite fun and dramatic as the dissolved food coloring drops down to the bottom of the vessel (to the cool water level) as it melts, then swirls around the beaker as the convection currents distribute the food coloring all through the fluid after temperature equilibrium is reached.

Placing a piece of candy in a container of cool water will show that the candy dissolves and that no discernable heat was necessary to cause it to go into solution.

If you find that your children need some more information about the different properties of matter, I can recommend an article in *Science and Children* entitled "What's the Matter With Teaching Children About Matter?" (Palmeri et al. 2008).

USING THE STORY WITH GRADES 5–8

Students at this age also find the probe mentioned in the K–4 section a challenge to their thinking and their responses can provide you with valuable information about their understanding of the subject. If your students seem fairly confident about knowing the difference between melting and dissolving, it may help them to prepare an activity for younger students that makes the difference obvious. I think that we have all had the opportunity to realize that the person who is preparing the teaching activity learns more from the process than expected.

Your students may like to try to dissolve different dry ingredients such as cocoa, instant coffee, or sugar, in cold water. After that, they can try to dissolve these same ingredients in warm water.

Since a great many of your students may already have a good handle on the difference between melting and dissolving, you could try a very reliable activity that will cause them to think and rethink their conceptions—putting salt onto ice cubes. The salt dissolving in the water on top of the ice cubes (there's always a little bit of water there) will cause the cube to melt very quickly as compared to unsalted cubes. Salt dissolved in water lowers the freezing point temperature. A control should also be used so that the students can compare the two cubes. They may relate this to using salt on the highways to melt ice but perhaps have never had the opportunity to control the process and watch it unfold, firsthand. A good way to start this activity is to ask them what they think will happen if they place a teaspoon of salt on an ice cube. Have them record predictions and reasoning both in their science notebooks and publicly on the board or on a sheet of chart paper. This activity is aimed mainly at starting a discussion about both dissolving and melting, since the salt dissolves in the water but the ice cube melts. Questions may arise about the amount of salt, they may wonder if more salt will cause the cube to melt any faster. Doing this with several cubes and different amounts of salt will result in a cube "race" that will stimulate discussion.

Have them write an ending to the story with an explanation by Caroline about whether the sugar in the iced tea is dissolved or melted. Here is an embedded assessment for your use and an opportunity for the students to do some thinking about their thinking and engage in a bit of scientific literacy.

RELATED BOOKS AND NSTA JOURNAL ARTICLES

Keeley, P. 2005. *Science curriculum topic study: Bridging the gap between standards and practice.* Thousand Oaks, CA: Corwin Press.

Keeley, P., F. Eberle, and C. Dorsey. 2008. *Uncovering student ideas in science, volume 3: Another 25 formative assessment probes.* Arlington, VA: NSTA Press.

Keeley, P., F. Eberle, and L. Farrin. 2005. *Uncovering student ideas in science, volume 1: 25 formative assessment probes.* Arlington, VA: NSTA Press.

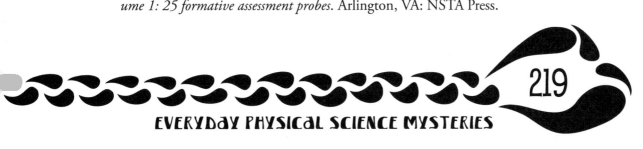

Keeley, P., F. Eberle, and J. Tugel. 2007. *Uncovering student ideas in science, volume 2: 25 more formative assessment probes*. Arlington, VA: NSTA Press.

Keeley, P., and J. Tugel. 2009. *Uncovering student ideas in science, volume 4: 25 new formative assessment probes*. Arlington, VA: NSTA Press.

Konicek-Moran, R. 2008. *Everyday science mysteries: Stories for inquiry-based science teaching*. Arlington, VA: NSTA Press.

Konicek-Moran, R. 2009. *More everyday science mysteries: Stories for inquiry-based science teaching*. Arlington, VA: NSTA Press.

Konicek-Moran, R. 2010. *Even more everyday science mysteries: Stories for inquiry-based science teaching*. Arlington, VA: NSTA Press.

references

Keeley, P., F. Eberle, and L. Farrin. 2005. Is it melting? In *Uncovering student ideas in science, volume 1: 25 formative assessment probes*, 73–77. Arlington, VA: NSTA Press.

Konicek-Moran, R. 2009. Iced tea. In *More everyday science mysteries*, 169–177. Arlington, VA: NSTA Press.

Palmeri, A., A. Cole, S. DeLisle, S. Erickson, and J. Janes. 2008. What's the matter with teaching children about matter? *Science & Children* 46 (4): 20–23.

CHAPTER 23
THE SLIPPERY GLASS

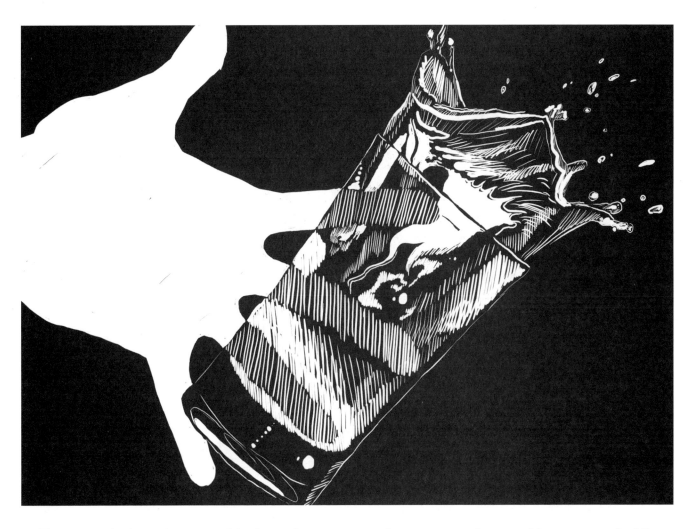

J oyce picked up her ice-cold glass of grape juice hoping that a cold drink would cool her off on this hot and humid day. She grasped it firmly, but suddenly it slipped through her fingers and smashed into pieces on the floor. Joyce was both embarrassed and puzzled.

"Grape juice makes a terrible mess even if it falls on a bare floor. Gosh, I'm glad I didn't do this on the rug," she thought.

"I had a good grip on that glass but it just acted like it was greased or something," she said to herself as she look around to see who had been a witness to her accident. Luckily, all the rest of her family was out.

After she had cleaned up the mess, she decided to try again since she was still hot and thirsty.

Joyce got a clean glass, put some ice cubes in it and poured in the grape juice. She immediately picked up the glass and took a long cool drink. No problem this time. The glass wasn't slippery at all and she set it down on the table.

Cirrus, the family dog, went to the door and looked at Joyce as if to say, "How about letting me out for a quick run?" Joyce didn't want to clean up another mess so she took the dog out for a walk and then returned to the porch in about 10 minutes.

Joyce reached for her glass and WHOOPS!! It almost happened again. Once again, the glass was wet and slippery. Luckily, Joyce had picked up the glass very carefully and there was no repeat of the first accident, but it was certainly a mystery as to where the slipperiness had come from.

First, she checked to see if the glass was leaking. It didn't seem like it had any cracks. Then she noticed a ring of water on the table. It had to have dripped down off the glass onto the table, and she remembered that she had been told to use a coaster or paper towel when she placed a glass on the good tables. And now she knew why.

"Boy, this is my day for getting in trouble!" she thought. When she wiped up the water ring with a paper towel, she noticed that the paper towel wasn't colored blue like grape juice. So at least she was sure that the glass wasn't leaking, or else the liquid in the ring would have been juice.

"I know," she said to herself. "The juice must have splashed out of the top of the glass and run down the side. Maybe I wasn't careful about putting it down. But that still doesn't explain why the water ring isn't colored. This is getting to be annoying!"

"Maybe it's the glass," she thought. She got a metal tumbler from the cupboard and put some juice and ice in it to see what would happen. She waited for a few minutes and … guess what? Right, the metal tumbler had water on the outside too! Joyce wracked her brain to figure this one out and could only think that maybe it was the juice. So she tried it again with another glass with plain water and ice. She sat back and waited.

Guess what happened?

PURPOSE

I think that most of us have experienced this phenomenon. I wonder how many people can remember when they realized that the water that formed on their glasses of cold liquid came from the atmosphere or what convinced them that this "unlikely" source of water was indeed a plausible explanation. The purpose of the story is to provide an opportunity to explore this phenomenon and to learn more about what makes it happen through developing and testing questions. It is similar to "The Little Tent That Cried," *in Everyday Science Mysteries* (Konicek-Moran 2008) but is more of an everyday experience than the camping story. Many of the same concepts apply but the situation can be reproduced and the questions can be answered either at home or in the classroom with little difficulty or equipment.

RELATED CONCEPTS

- Evaporation
- Condensation
- Humidity
- Cycles

DON'T BE SURPRISED

Most children have a difficult time believing that air has mass and takes up space, so the concept of water vapor floating in the air is just as problematic. Walking around in air seems effortless—how can there be stuff in it? Unless the children can relate the idea of the discomfort they feel on a relatively humid day to the relationship of the temperature of the air to the amount of water vapor in it, they will be confused when we try to tell them that the water on the glass comes from the air around it.

When we breathe on a mirror or see our breath on chilly days, we are aware of the clouds we are able to form. When we see the fog on the bathroom mirror after taking a shower, we usually don't give it a second thought, but turn on the exhaust fan or wipe the mirror off so that we can see our image. When questioned, the children all admit to having experienced these phenomena but may not relate them to each other. While the water cycle may be an often mentioned concept, making it an explanation of a sweaty glass or drink can be a stretch for many children as well as adults. They are likely to see the water cycle as the simple evaporation-condensation-cloud-rain-evaporation cycle, since that is how it is so often depicted in texts and pictures. But it is, of course, much more common in any number of examples. If condensation and evaporation in our lives were a musical composition, it would be called "Theme and Variations on the Water Cycle." This is why the everyday science mysteries are sometimes so difficult to see. Because they are so widespread and familiar, they are ignored.

CONTENT BACKGROUND

How does a liquid attain a gaseous state and how does a gas return to a liquid state? First, it might be good to address the idea of how water gets into the air in the first place. We are all familiar with water in its liquid form. We drink it, bathe in it, swim in it, and cook with it. What we can't see with the naked eye is that this water is made up of molecules, and these molecules are in a relationship with one another so that they can roll over one another and therefore pour out of the vessel in which they are contained. These molecules are also in constant motion and can, if they have enough energy, escape the container into the atmosphere, or *evaporate*. In doing so, they enter the atmosphere as a gas where they are free to roam and bounce off of the other molecules in the atmosphere. If they touch something cooler than themselves, they give up that extra energy that allowed them to become a gas, and they return to a liquid state, often on a glass of ice-cold drink, a mirror, a window, or on grass as dew.

Why does a water molecule give up its energy to a surface that is cooler? Heat energy tends to flow from a warmer to a cooler environment. This has been observed without exception in the natural world for so long that it has become the backbone of the second law of thermodynamics. This also explains how the water vapor returns to the liquid state. Any change of state involves an energy shift. Put another way, if there is a change of state, energy has moved from one substance to another. When an ice cube or ice cream melts, it is because heat energy has flowed into the colder material and caused it to melt. Energy has not been lost or created, it has merely moved from one place to another.

So, you can see that a lot of this story is about energy transfer and changes in state. It is also about the water cycle. The fact that the water cycle is involved in a single room in a single house does not exclude the larger water cycle concept of the atmosphere. The atmosphere in the room where Joyce is doing everyday science is most likely connected to the atmosphere outside the room. The high relative humidity in the room is probably directly related to the relative humidity in the out of doors. I say "probably" because there may be water boiling in the kitchen that could provide the house with extra amounts of water vapor. However, let us imagine that Joyce is on a screened porch and that the relative humidity in the sur-rounding atmosphere is very high. The story states that it is a hot and humid day.

We need to look at the idea of humidity here. At any specified temperature, only so much water vapor can exist within a given volume of air. The higher the temperature, the more water vapor can exist within that volume of air because as the temperature rises, the space between the molecules of air increases, mak-ing more room for the water vapor molecules to coexist with the air molecules. Since it is a hot day in the story, there is a lot of potential for a great deal of water vapor in the air. This is when scientists and weather people say the relative humid-ity is high. We often call such days "muggy." The term *relative humidity* is used to denote, at a given temperature, what percentage of water vapor the air is now

accommodating. For example, if the air contains half of what it is capable of, the relative humidity would be 50%.

You may notice that I am not using the common term *holding* when I speak of water vapor in the air. The molecules of water are much lighter than the nitrogen and oxygen molecules in the air and can coexist nicely on their own by moving among the air molecules. So, air molecules certainly do not "hold" the water vapor molecules. In fact, the term *holding* often leads to misconceptions about relative humidity and how air accommodates other gases.

How does this make us feel? What is our comfort zone? It has been determined that we are most comfortable when the relative humidity is around 45%. We cool our bodies by perspiring. When this perspiration can escape our bodies by evaporation, energy is lost as the perspiration changes to a gaseous form and our bodies feel cooler. Our bodies perceive heat loss in comfort rather than actual temperature. In high relative humidity circumstances, our perspiration does not evaporate as well as in low relative humidity cases. Therefore, less heat is lost and we feel uncomfortably warm. On the other hand, in desert climates where relative humidity is usually very low, our perspiration evaporates quickly leaving us feeling relatively comfortable. In fact, I distinctly remember being in a desert during the hottest time of day and noticing no perspiration at all because it was evaporating so quickly.

So, no matter what liquid Joyce puts in the glass or if she uses a metal, stone, or any other kind of vessel on a hot and humid day, she is going to have to deal with the condensation on her tumbler. As long as the surface of the vessel is cooler than the temperature of its surrounding air, the heat energy will be transferred to the vessel, and the water vapor in the air will be converted back to water. The exception is containers made with double walls, which act as insulators so the phenomenon does not occur.

I must take exception to the statement in the *Benchmarks* (AAAS 1993, p. 150) about water "disappearing." I believe that using that language with children, especially in the K–2 age group, can be misleading. Although the word *disappear* is technically correct in that the water is no longer visible, I prefer to use other phrases such as the water "seems to disappear." Also, I believe that the statements describing the water cycle are limited and do not mention that the vapor does not have to ascend to great heights to condense into water. As the story shows and our experience tells us, the water cycle can occur in a small area like a room equally as well as in the general Earth system.

related ideas from the national science education standards (NrC 1996)

K–4: *Properties of Objects and Materials*

- Materials can exist in different states: solid, liquid, and gas. Some common materials such as water can be changed from one state to another by heating or cooling.

5–8: *Structure of the Earth System*

- Water, which covers the majority of the Earth's surface, circulates through the crust, oceans, and the atmosphere in what is known as the "water cycle." Water evaporates from the Earth's surface, rises and cools as it moves to higher elevations, condenses as rain or snow, and falls to the surface where it collects in lakes, oceans, soil, and in rocks underground.

related ideas from Benchmarks for Science Literacy (aaas 1993)

K–2: *The Earth*

- Water left in an open container disappears, but water in a closed container does not disappear.

3–5: *The Earth*

- When liquid water disappears, it turns into a gas (vapor) in the air and can reappear as a liquid when cooled, as a solid if cooled below the freezing point of water. Clouds and fog are made of tiny droplets of water.

6–8: *The Earth*

- The cycling of water in and out of the atmosphere plays an important role in determining climatic patterns. Water evaporates from the surface of the Earth, rises and cools, condenses into rain or snow, and falls again to the surface. The water falling on land collects in rivers and lakes, soil, and porous layers of rock, and much of it flows back into the oceans.

USING THE STORY WITH GRADES K-4

Our experience with this story tells us that a great way to start is with a demonstration. Place two glasses in front of the class, one filled with room temperature, colored water and the other with colored ice water. If you can use opaque vessels so that the children cannot see the contents, this is even better. Ask the students to observe the two systems carefully for the next 5 to 10 minutes. Depending on the relative humidity in the classroom, time will vary. They will of course notice that one glass will begin to sweat and the other will not. This *discrepant event* will be the catalyst for a discussion. You may allow them now to ask you questions of the yes or no type, which you will answer until they have determined the difference in the two systems. This is very much like a "20 questions" game, which many have played before. They may ask you if the glass is cracked, you would answer, no, and so on.

After they have exhausted their questions and have realized that the difference between the two glasses is that one is cold and the other is not, you may want to refer back to or even reread the story. You may ask them which glass they think is like Joyce's glass. Most will choose the glass of ice water. Try to make them focus on the fact that the difference between the two glasses is that one is cold and the other is not. Some students may say that the moisture comes from the air and others will not believe this. The Standards do not recommend this concept for K–2 students, but there are ample opportunities for the students to engage in finding answers to their questions through inquiry. This is even truer for the grades 3–5 students. Depending on the questions asked during the 20 questions segment, you may put these on a large sheet of paper and use these to motivate the children's inquiry activities. Some questions may be

- Are the glasses the same thickness?
- Are the glasses made of the same material?
- Does one glass have something different in it?
- Would the thickness of the glass make any difference?
- Would the stuff the glass is made of make any difference?
- If I breathe on the glass, will it get wet?

With help, the students can develop methods of inquiring into the questions, which may lead them closer to the idea that the water appearing on the glass came from the air. The following section on using the story with grades 5–8 may also be helpful in leading your class into more inquiry about this phenomenon.

If you have a copy of the probe "Wet Jeans," from *Uncovering Student Ideas in Science, Volume 1* by Keeley, Eberle, and Farrin (2005), you may wish to give this probe to your older students. It asks them to choose among seven different opinions as to what happened to the water in some wet jeans that were put out on the clothes line to dry. This will give you an idea of where your students lie in their understanding of evaporation and its relationship with the atmosphere. It will also generate a discussion among the students who may not choose the same answer.

Having this happen is great, since talking and discussing the phenomenon will more likely lead to conceptual change or validation of current scientific beliefs.

USING THE STORY WITH GRADES 5–8

The story itself will probably not evoke as much mystery for older students since many have had the phenomenon explained to them by adults already. This does not, however, mean that they understand it. You may want to give the probe "Wet Jeans" (Keeley, Eberle, and Farrin 2005) mentioned in the previous section. Students are asked to explain in writing why they picked the choice they did, which is where you can find out what they really understand about evaporation and condensation.

Students may be interested in finding out the answers to some of the mysteries implicated in the story. Following is a list of possible investigations they can undertake:

- Does more water form on metal than on glass tumblers?
- Does water form more quickly on metal than on glass?
- Does the water form more on some days than others?
- Is there a relationship between the temperature of the drink and the time it takes for condensation?
- Is that relationship the same on different days?
- Does this happen in a refrigerator?

Many teachers prefer to allow the entire class to discuss the questions listed previously and predict what they expect to happen. Any predictions should be backed up by some sort of evidence and not be just a guess. Your role in this is to make sure that each prediction is based on some sort of previous experience or knowledge. For example, if student A believes that more water will form on a metal container than on a glass one, that student should be able to explain why she believes this. She may say that since metal conducts heat better than glass, the water will condense on metal more. As you move into the actual investigations, be sure to remind students about controls and variables so that they control everything in the test except the one variable for which they are testing.

One way to check the amount of water formed on a vessel is to use a sensitive kitchen scale or the most sensitive scale you can find. Students may need to have a lesson on "taring," which is the weighing of the system, recording those data, recording the weight of the system after a certain time segment, and then subtracting the weight of the original system. Some scales automatically do this with the push of a button but others may not, and it is a good skill to know, especially when measuring differences. It also comes in handy if they are weighing different objects on a particular plate or towel. The weight of the towel or plate must always be subtracted from the total weight to give the weight of the object itself.

NATIONAL SCIENCE TEACHERS ASSOCIATION

If your students or you decide to explore the relationship between temperature and condensation, you will be entering the area of meteorology or weather. Specifically, you will be dealing with *dew point*, which is the temperature at which, under standard pressure, the moisture in the air condenses. The temperature of the water in the container can be used to give a rough estimate of this indicator. If the temperature of the water in a glass is 50°F (10°C) and water begins to condense on the glass, you know that the dew point is at least the temperature of the water. Actually it may be higher or lower, which will require a set up of glasses at various temperatures. A good way to do this is to start with a metal can that contains water at room temperature. With a thermometer in the can, add ice one cube at a time and stir with a stirring rod (*not* with the thermometer, which might break). Watch the outside of the can and when the first drop of moisture appears, read the temperature and record it, and that should approximate the dew point temperature in the room. Do this several times and average the data. This activity may actually arise spontaneously as the students try to answer the question "Is there a relationship between the temperature of the drink and when water begins to condense?"

Dew point temperatures rarely exceed 80°F (26.6°C) and at that point you can virtually feel the moisture in the air as you breathe.

This may also lead you into the topic of the *heat index*. When you look at some weather forecasts, you may see that the temperature is given and added to that is the phrase "feels like ...." You may remember that our bodies cool off by perspiring and when the relative humidity is high, that perspiration evaporates with difficulty. Therefore you do not feel as comfortable as you are when the relative humidity is low and your perspiration can evaporate and do its job better. Some meteorologists have tried to calculate the discomfort we feel in high relative humidity situations. It is based on how you "feel" at certain temperature/relative humidity combinations. Basically we all know that if it is hot and humid we "feel" warmer. This index is based on our perceptions and is therefore considered controversial within the scientific community. But it is worth a discussion, especially if you have been in Florida or Phoenix, Arizona, in the summertime.

related Books and NSTa Journal articles

Driver, R., A. Squires, P. Rushworth, and V. Wood-Robinson. 1994. *Making sense of secondary science: Research into children's ideas.* London and New York: Routledge Falmer.

Hand, R. 2006. Evaporating is cool. *Science Scope* 29 (7): 12–13.

Keeley, P. 2005. *Science curriculum topic study: Bridging the gap between standards and practice.* Thousand Oaks, CA: Corwin Press.

Keeley, P., F. Eberle, and L. Farrin. 2005. *Uncovering student ideas in science: 25 formative assessment probes, volume 1.* Arlington, VA: NSTA Press.

references

American Association for the Advancement of Science (AAAS).1993. *Benchmarks for science literacy.* New York: Oxford University Press.

Keeley, P., F. Eberle, and L. Farrin. 2005. *Uncovering student ideas in science: 25 formative assessment probes, volume 1.* Arlington, VA: NSTA Press.

National Research Council (NRC). 1996. *National science education standards.* Washington, DC: National Academies Press.

Project WET, Curriculum and activities guide. 1995. *The amazing journey.* Bozeman, MT: Water conservation Council for Environmental Education. *www. montana.edu/wwwwet/journey.html*

NATIONAL SCIENCE TEACHERS ASSOCIATION

CHAPTER 24
FLORIDA CARS

mber was riding along with her brother Jake in their mother's car. They were going to see if Jake could find a used car he could afford. That meant visiting a lot of car dealers along the road. Amber enjoyed listening to her brother and the salesmen dicker about prices. She knew it was a big game but she still liked to hear the guys go at it.

"This one is a little more expensive," said the dealer about a nice little red job sitting on the lot. "First, it's red, and second, and most important, it's a Florida car. It just came on the truck yesterday. Guaranteed Florida! Low mileage too, but most important, it's a Florida car!"

"Owned by a little old lady who only drove it to church on Sunday too, I'll bet," said Jake, not expecting an answer.

"I wonder what's so important about Florida," thought Amber. "I wonder if they make better cars in Florida than they do here in Detroit."

"Go ahead, look her over, and see if you can find one speck of rust on her!" said the dealer with confidence. "I'll even put her on the lift for you so you can look underneath."

"Can I see the transportation documents so that I can be sure it came up from Florida?" said Jake. "Not that I don't trust you, but it will put my mind at ease to be sure it came from Florida."

Sure enough, the car had been picked up in Homestead, in south Florida—even better than he expected.

"I'll have to think it over," said Jake. "I'll be back tomorrow or the next day."

"Don't wait too long young fella. It won't be here long," the salesman replied.

As they drove on to the next lot, Amber asked Jake, "What's so special about a Florida car?"

"Well, for one thing we don't have to worry about a lot of rust on the car," said Jake.

"Why is that?" asked Amber.

"Think about it, sis," said Jake. "Down there it never snows and they don't have to put salt on the road so there's no rust."

"Does rust always need salt to make it happen?" asked Amber.

"Sure it does. Don't you know anything about rust?" said Jake, sarcastically.

"Actually, I do know some things about it, I think. It's something that seems to happen to everything I leave out in the weather."

"Well, sure, it happens a lot to bicycles and metal stuff that we leave out, but salt makes it happen faster and better!" said Jake confidently.

"Always?" asked Amber.

"I never believe in 'always,'" said Jake. "There are always exceptions to a rule!"

"Always?" said Amber.

"Okay, don't get smart, little sister. You know what I mean."

"Well, I think I'll just go ahead and test that idea about salt 'cause I'm not so sure salt is 'always' needed for things to rust. Maybe other things cause rust to form faster and maybe other things stop it from happening."

"Knock yourself out, sis, and then let me know if a Florida car is a sure bet," answered Jake.

PURPOSE

Rust is a well-known curse that ruins our metal belongings. Once again, one of the most common of everyday phenomena is probably one of the least understood. This story is an attempt to get our students and their teachers involved in some tests to see what they can learn about rust through observation and study. I have to credit my friend, Phil Scott, from Leeds University in the United Kingdom for the ideas for much of this inquiry-based lesson. He asked kids to put bare nails in the place where they thought they would get most rusty. Not only did that set the stage for some neat investigations, their actions told him a great deal about what his students' preconceptions about rust were.

RELATED CONCEPTS

- Oxidation
- Chemical change
- Conservation of matter
- Chemical reactions
- Changes in matter

DON'T BE SURPRISED

We have tried rust activities many times with children of different ages. Our experience tells us that they may believe the following about rust:

- Rust is alive and can cause disease.
- Rust exists only on the surface but eats up the middle of objects.
- Rust only happens when it is cold.
- Rust forms faster in warm surroundings.
- Rust absolutely needs salt to happen.
- Rust happens to things submerged in carbonated drinks.
- Rust eats up the material on which it forms.
- Rust is really only another form of the metal on which it forms.

It turns out that most of these misconceptions can be tested. Besides that, they lead to more questions, which is an integral part of the nature of science.

CONTENT BACKGROUND

Almost all children have had an experience with rust. What they do not usually understand is that rust is a new compound. A *compound* is formed by the interaction of two or more substances.

Rusting is a chemical reaction between iron and oxygen. It is called an *oxidation reaction* because it is a chemical change that features the transfer of electrons from the iron molecules to the oxygen molecules—thus the metal is "oxidized." This transfer results in a new compound, iron oxide, commonly known as rust. The chemical equation for this change is $4Fe + 3O_2 \rightarrow 2Fe_2O_3$, which means that four atoms of iron (Fe) plus three atoms of oxygen (O_2) results in two atoms of iron oxide or rust (Fe_2O_3). This is what chemists call a *balanced equation*, which means that there are the same number of atoms on the left side and on the right side of the equation. In other words, in the chemical reaction, all of the ingredients are accounted for. Since all of the atoms involved remain the same—although rearranged—the total mass remains constant. Nothing is lost and nothing is gained. This is what we mean by the *conservation of matter*.

This is easily shown by putting iron in a moist sealed jar, weighing the whole thing (iron and jar), and then allowing rust to form before weighing it again. The weight will remain constant in this closed environment, showing that all of the matter involved in forming the new compound has been conserved. See "Nails in a Jar" in *Uncovering Student Ideas in Science, Volume 4* (Keeley and Tugel 2009) for a probe that elicits from students their ideas about what will happen to the weight of a closed system in which rusting occurs. Many adults, as well as children, expect the rusty nail to have either gained or lost weight. You are measuring the amount of oxygen and iron in the jar each time you weigh the jar since the materials in the jar are trapped in this closed system and the weight does not change.

When you are dealing with an *open* system, the results are different. If you refer to the probe "Rusty Nails" in *Uncovering Student Ideas in Science, Volume 1* (Keeley, Eberle, and Farrin 2005) you will see that if the system is open to the air, the nails will actually *gain* a small amount of weight since first you are weighing only the nails and not the combination of the entire closed system. As the nails combine with the oxygen in the surrounding atmosphere the new compound is heavier due to the addition of the oxygen to the iron in the nails. This may seem contradictory, but if you think about it carefully, you can understand why this difference occurs. Stated in another way—in the closed system, you are measuring iron *and* oxygen both times you weigh, while in the open system, you are weighing *only* the iron in the first weighing and in the second, the iron *and* the oxygen available from the entire atmosphere is involved in the chemical reaction.

Iron and oxygen react with each other very readily in nature, and this is why it is rare to find pure iron anywhere in nature. In fact, it is rare to find any metal in a pure form because oxygen combines with metals so easily. When iron, air, and water are present, the carbon dioxide in the air combines with the water to form a weak carbonic acid that begins to eat away at the iron and dissolve it. The water starts to break apart and free up the oxygen since water is composed of oxygen and hydrogen. The oxygen and hydrogen get electrons from the iron, which gives oxygen a negative charge and allows it to combine with the iron. In the process, charged atoms or *ions* are formed, which travel via the liquid to other parts of the object. The liquid is important since it provides a medium in which charged ions travel and rust spreads. This liquid is called an *electrolyte*.

Regular water is not the best electrolyte, but it is still good enough to create rust. Electrolytes with more ions are better. Acids and salts provide this difference, thus salt water is usually a better conductor of ions. In northern areas of the country, where ice and snow are prevalent in the winter seasons, salt is spread on roads to help melt the ice and provide traction for vehicles. This provides the salt water that acts as a great electrolyte for the formation of rust on autos. Thus, in Florida where little or no snow falls, the need for salt is eliminated and thus Florida cars tend to be more rust free.

related ideas from the national science education standards (nrc 1996)

K–4: Properties of Objects and Materials

- Objects have many observable properties including size, weight, shape, color, temperature, and the ability to react with other substances.

5–8: Properties of Objects and Materials

- Substances react chemically in characteristic ways with other substances to form new substances (compounds) with different characteristic properties. In chemical reactions, the total mass is conserved.

related ideas from benchmarks for science literacy (aaas 1993)

K–2: The Structure of Matter

- Objects can be described in terms of the materials they are made of (e.g., clay, cloth, paper) and their physical properties (e.g., color, size, shape, weight, texture, flexibility).
- Things can be done to materials to change some of their properties but not all materials respond the same way to what is done to them.

3–5: The Structure of Matter

- When a new material is made by combining two or more materials, it has properties that are different from the original materials.
- No matter how parts of an object are assembled, the weight of the whole object made is always the same as the sum of the parts, and when a thing is broken into parts, the parts have the same total weight as the original object.

6–8: *The Structure of Matter*

- Because most elements tend to combine with others, few elements are found in their pure form.
- An especially important kind of reaction between substances involves the combination of oxygen with something else, as in burning or rusting.
- No matter how substances within a closed system interact with one another, or how they combine or break apart, the total mass of the system remains the same. The idea of atoms explains the conservation of matter. If the number of atoms stays the same no matter how they are arranged, then their mass stays the same.
- The idea of atoms explains chemical reactions. When substances interact to form new substances, the atoms that make up the molecules of the original substances combine in new ways.

USING THE STORY WITH GRADES K–4

Even the youngest student has had some experience with rust. With very young children, we hope to encourage them to notice that things change over time and that these changes are normal. Children have had their toys rust or corrode in some way if they have been neglected and left out in the weather. They may even have heard their parents or older siblings talk about rust and salted roads. It is usually a good idea to begin with a chart of their current beliefs about rust. Those who have been warned that stepping on a rusty nail could cause nasty illness may believe that rust is alive and that rust is a germ. Other preconceptions are listed in the Don't Be Surprised section on page 233.

From the chart, you can elicit from students where a group of nails could be placed to make them get rusty. Show them a bag of nails that you have placed in alcohol or vinegar for a day or overnight to remove any protective oil. Ask, "Where shall we put them to make them get rusty?" Even the youngest children will suggest that water is necessary. Some students will suggest putting the nails outside; others will vote for inside with water nearby or putting them in water. Make sure they have a reason for putting the nails in any given place. Have enough nails to follow the suggestions and then have the children put them in the various environments. It usually does not take much time for the rust to begin to form, and the students can watch as the process continues. They can record what they see in their science notebooks, observing which ones begin to rust first, and then which seem to rust the most.

USING THE STORY WITH GRADES 5–8

(*Note*: I see no reason why the following cannot be done with students as young as fourth grade.)

Give each student (or pair of students, if you wish) two nails soaked all day or overnight in vinegar or alcohol to remove their protective covering. Tell the students to take the nails home for a week and put them where they think each nail will get the rustiest. Ask them to place the nails in a spot and then allow them to move the nails if they get a better idea or if nothing happens. Tell them that they should bring the nails back in one week taped to a card with the following information on it about each nail:

- Where did you put your nail?
- Why did you put it there?
- What kinds of things do nails need to get rusty?
- What do you think rust is?

When they return with their nails, have them display them on a table or in a place where all of the students can view them by doing a walk around. If you record the data, you will have a summary of what your students' ideas are about rust. This is, of course, a formative assessment of their thinking and will give you an idea of what kinds of misconceptions and conceptions your students have brought to this activity. In effect, it is a different kind of assessment probe, one where their actions have a direct connection to their thinking.

This is what we have learned from trying this activity. Some students will

- place their nails in a carbonated beverage (they have been told that it will disintegrate teeth, so why not nails?);
- place their nails in bleach;
- place their nails in salt water;
- place their nails on a paper towel wetted with water;
- place their nails in a refrigerator because of the need for cold;
- place their nails on a heater because of the need for warmth;
- place their nails in a bathroom because of the humidity; or
- place their nails on a gutter downspout, outdoors in the weather.

There will undoubtedly be other variations and a discussion where each student relates his or her experience should be most enlightening. We have found that because of this discussion and the results they have seen, they will want to redo the investigations or will want to change a variable in some way to answer a new question. Your job is to help them make sure that they are controlling variables and making each setup the same except for the variable they are testing. If the students describe their new investigations before the whole class, all of the members will have an opportunity to critique the setups and with your aid, help one another in a constructive manner.

Warning! This could go on for some time particularly if other questions come up such as the following:

- What would happen if you use copper, brass, or galvanized metal?
- What happens if you use other kinds of metal objects such as aluminum or steel wool?

- What kinds of ways can you prevent rust from happening?

In the meantime, I suggest that you give the probe "Nails in a Jar" found in *Uncovering Student Ideas in Science, Volume 4* (Keeley and Tugel 2009). Because this probe limits the nail rusting to a closed system, the students will have to think about their beliefs concerning the conservation of matter in that system. This probe asks students to consider nails and water in a closed jar and to predict whether the rusting will cause any change in weight after the nails have rusted or in other words, after a chemical reaction. After you have gathered the results of the probe, they will need to discuss their answers and argue the points. This naturally leads to a trial of the question in the probe and an answer that will surprise some and validate others. This will be a good time for you to elaborate about the conservation of matter in chemical reactions and perhaps to help them review the difference between chemical change, where new compounds are formed, and physical change, involving merely a change of state or shape.

There may be some questions about the nature of the new substance, rust, and whether it is really a new substance. You can help them test the substance and find differences between the original nail and the brown flaky substance called rust. For one thing, the nail was responsive to a magnet. Will the rust be responsive? "Try it and see," will be your response. If students present nails in water and the rust is suspended in the water, suggest that they might evaporate the water in a large dish. The rust will be left behind since it is not in solution. Then they will have the rust to test for its various properties.

In the end, I believe that your students will agree that a Florida car is less likely to have rust than a northern car. Of course, you could encourage your students to interview auto dealers to talk about rust and how they prevent it. Don't forget to have them ask about Florida cars!

related books and NSTA journal articles

Driver, R., A. Squires, P. Rushworth, and V. Wood-Robinson. 1994. *Making sense of secondary science: Research into children's ideas.* London and New York: Routledge Falmer.

Keeley, P. 2005. *Science curriculum topic study: Bridging the gap between standards and practice.* Thousand Oaks, CA: Corwin Press.

Keeley, P., F. Eberle, and C. Dorsey. 2008. *Uncovering student ideas in science: Another 25 formative assessment probes, volume 3.* Arlington, VA: NSTA Press.

Keeley, P., F. Eberle, and J. Tugel. 2007. *Uncovering student ideas in science: 25 more formative assessment probes, vol. 2.* Arlington, VA: NSTA Press.

Konicek-Moran, R. 2008. *Everyday science mysteries.* Arlington, VA: NSTA Press.

Konicek-Moran, R. 2009. *More everyday science mysteries.* Arlington, VA: NSTA Press.

references

American Association for the Advancement of Science (AAAS). 1993. *Benchmarks for science literacy.* New York: Oxford University Press.

Keeley, P., F. Eberle, and L. Farrin. 2005. *Uncovering student ideas in science: 25 formative assessment probes, volume 1.* Arlington, VA: NSTA Press.

Keeley, P., and J. Tugel. 2009. *Uncovering student ideas in science: 25 new formative assessment probes, volume 4.* Arlington, VA: NSTA Press.

National Research Council (NRC). 1996. *National science education standards.* Washington, DC: National Academies Press.

CHAPTER 25

THE NEIGHBORHOOD TELEPHONE SYSTEM

Laurie lived next door to Maria. They were best friends and had been since kindergarten. Now, in the fourth grade, they seemed to spend more time together than ever. Every evening after supper they would be on the phone, yakking away about all sorts of things.

"Hey, you have been on the phone for an hour!" said Maria's dad. "I'd like to use the phone too."

"Right!" said her mom. "I'm expecting a call from Auntie Felicia tonight."

"But I'm taking to Laurie," begged Maria. Suddenly Maria had an idea. "Hey, why don't you and Laurie's parents get us our own phones; cell phones might be really nice? Then we wouldn't be on your phone all the time."

"Do you have any idea how much the monthly bills are?" said her dad. "For Pete's sake, you live right next door. You can practically talk to each other from your bedroom windows…." Suddenly he stopped. "That's it!" he cried. "You can talk to each other from your bedroom windows."

"Daaaad," Maria laughed, "everybody in the neighborhood would hear us shouting at each other from our windows!"

"No, no, no!" exclaimed Maria's dad. "You can use TCTS. Completely private and really, really, cool. And the price is perfect!"

"Okay, I give up, what is TCTS?" asked Maria.

"No mystery. It's a simple device, two tin cans connected by a string. Now can you guess what TCTS stands for?" asked her dad.

This all sounded interesting so Maria talked to Laurie the next day and they decided to give this idea a try. With a little help from Maria's mom and dad, they used two empty tomato cans connected by a long string knotted on the inside of the cans, so that it would not come out of the hole punched in the can. It looked like this.

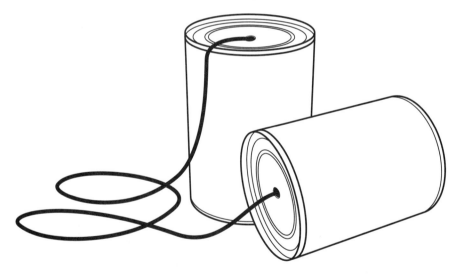

In no time at all they had the telephone system set up between the windows of their rooms and were ready to try it out. Laurie held her can up to her ear and Marie talked softly into the can on her side, hoping that her voice would

travel along the string to Laurie. Nothing! Their mothers were waiting below and shouted up, "you have to have the string between the cans pulled tightly."

The girls pulled the string tight and soon they were talking to each other across the distance although the words were not always clear.

"Why does the string have to be tight?" shouted Laurie.

"Good question. Think about it a while and we'll talk," said Laurie's mom.

"What's so magic about the string?" asked Maria.

"Another good question!" said Maria's mom. "Another question to think about."

"How can we make it clearer? Sometimes I can barely make out your words," asked Laurie.

"How about using bigger cans?" asked Maria. "Or maybe a plastic or paper cup instead?"

"Or, using bigger string, maybe?" replied Laurie.

"Or use something other than a string. Maybe a wire?" added Maria's mom. "Maybe the sound will travel better through a wire."

"Looks like we have some experimenting to do," said the Maria.

Purpose

This story has a two-pronged purpose. One has to do with learning something about sound (science) and the other has to do with learning about using science to modify the things in the world to solve human problems (technology).

Few adults have not had the opportunity to use a "tin can" telephone (TCT) during his or her childhood. The goal of transmitting sound across a distance has been around for a long time. It is even rumored that Alexander Graham Bell, the inventor of the telephone, played and experimented with one as he was closing in on his invention that would change the world. Obviously Bell was trying to eliminate the string but the principles of vibration and transmission of sound waves were still the guiding principles. Bell found a way to transmit the vibrations electrically, eliminating the need for direct contact between the speakers. This story uses the TCT as a focus for inquiry into the transmission of sound waves along a medium and also provides an opportunity for kids to try their hand at improving a simple device so that it works better. Students will experiment with various parts of the TCT changing variables and trying to find the best combination for optimum transmission of their voices.

In this electronic age, it is probably difficult for children to imagine a time before cell phones, television, blackberries, palm pilots, and portable media systems. Yet, it is often exciting for children to backtrack and experience the earlier days before modern communication and information technology became a way of life. School curricula are full of demonstrations of sound transmission through solid and liquid media but here in the TCT story is an opportunity to investigate an old toy and find out what makes it tick. There is plenty of room for the science and technology aspects of the standards to be applied. Building a better mousetrap is usually exciting for students and here is one that gives instant feedback, and makes changing variables easy and fun. If you play with one before you take the idea to your students you will find that several variables make a difference in sound transmission. It will also help you to be prepared with different materials for students to use in their experimentation. You will also notice the inclusion of the technology standards in this background material so that you can see what types of technology standards as well as science standards can be met.

Related Concepts

- Waves
- Sound transmission
- Energy
- Technological design
- Sound
- Vibration
- Energy transmission

DON'T BE SURPRISED

Children may reject the use of nonmetallic objects to design the telephone since they usually think of sound coming from vibrating metals such as cymbals or strings. Children also think of sound as a substance that moves from the sender to the receiver. On the other hand, those who believe in sound emanating from vibrating objects may immediately connect the string or wire connecting the "cans" as picking up vibrations and transmitting sound.

CONTENT BACKGROUND

Sound waves, like all waves, are energy waves. All waves transmit energy. Sound waves emanate from vibrating objects. They travel through air or any other medium but can be distorted by other sounds or anything that can disrupt the medium through which the waves travel. Vibrations in the originator of the sound such as vocal cords, drum skins, objects falling on pavement, clapping hands, or a multitude of banging or clanging can generate sound waves, which then travel through gas, liquid, or solid but not through a vacuum. This is because they need to excite molecules in the medium so that they transfer the energy of the original sound to nearby molecules, which then transfer them on to others in the form of a sound wave. These waves are compression waves and might be visualized as lines on a bar code, pushing against each other in a uniform pattern so that the sound travels from one end to the other. You may remember a science teacher from your past placing an alarm clock in a vacuum jar, and removing the air from within it. If the clock was ringing, the sound stopped when the air was removed. There were no molecules of any sort to be excited by the energy generated by the alarm. This of course brings up the old philosophical quandary, "If a tree falls in a forest where no one is present, does it still make a sound?" Sound needs no ear to hear it. It occurs whether one hears it or not.

Sound waves can bounce off objects and appear to come from different directions. If you have been in a noisy public place, surrounded by hard, bare surfaces, you may remember how difficult it is to converse with people near you. Sounds from other conversations and other noise bounce off these surfaces and literally fill the room with their presence. If you have experienced an echo, the same principle applies except that the bouncing sound wave is more focused and not mixed with other sounds.

Sound waves can be amplified by electronic means or by acoustic devices such as megaphones. Guitars, violins, and other stringed instruments make use of an acoustic amplifier by designing a way for the vibrating string to set up vibrations in an attached or surrounding structure. This changes the volume of the sound you hear. In the TCT, the can or cup into which the child speaks vibrates according to the sound waves made by the speaker. These sound waves are transferred to the string or wire and transmitted through the medium to the other cup, which in turn vibrates in the same way and also amplifies the sound transmitted down the string to the listener. It may be an important clue for you to know that amplifiers usually have cones made of paper in them.

Different materials vibrate according to their structure. You will find that metal cans are not the best amplifiers since the construction of the can will cause different frequencies to travel at different speeds in the metal and produce garbled sounds. Plastic cups may be used to see how they act as amplifiers.

An object can produce sounds of varying pitches, giving a higher or lower sound. This usually is accomplished by changing the speed of the vibrating object. If you are plucking a rubber band or a guitar string, you may make the pitch higher or lower by either stretching (higher) the vibrating strand or relaxing it (lowering). You may also use a thinner string (higher) or a thicker string (lower), which, respectively, makes the plucked string vibrate faster or slower.

There are other things that vibrate, which are not so easy to see. Let's say someone drops keys on a tabletop. You hear the sound and from experience recognize the sound as keys hitting a tabletop. This is a combination of your brain's memory of past experiences and your ear's ability to capture the resulting sound wave and send the vibration to the brain through the auditory nerve. But I just said that all sound was caused by vibrations so what caused the sound wave and vibration? I didn't mention any strings or drum skins, just keys and a table. Here is the problem that escapes most adults and children. Both the table and the keys vibrate as the keys hit the table and set the sound wave energy in motion and straight to our ears and ultimately our brains. We live in a world of sound and most of us hearing folks have learned to identify the sound vibrations that enter our ears. It is a good thing too, since screeching tires, auto horns, and other alarms help us to avoid nasty confrontations with moving objects larger than we are.

Technology is an important aspect of science and technology education. In this story, there is an opportunity for children to see the aspects of problem solving and its relationship to design. The use of the term *technology* in the Standards is often confused with "instructional technology," which includes computers, digital microscopes, and other devices that help science teachers conduct their lessons. The difference is in goals. In the Standards, technology aims at giving children the opportunity to modify the environment to meet human needs. There are a series of five stages, which provide a framework for teachers to use in planning and assessing outcomes in technology. These five stages are:

- Stating the problem
- Designing an approach
- Implementing a solution
- Evaluating the solution
- Communicating the problem, design, and solution (NRC 1996, p. 137)

These stages are not to be construed as steps but as guidelines. Sometimes the objective will be to evaluate, for example, the relative properties of paper towels or shampoos. Other times they are guidelines to improving the mousetrap or in this case, the TCT. And at other times, the development of a specific invention or a device needed to solve a problem or challenge will be necessary.

reLaTeD IDeas From THe NaTIONaL SCIeNCe eDUCaTION STaNDarDS (NrC 1996)

K–4: Position and Motion of Objects

- Sound is produced by vibrating objects. Changing the rate of vibration can vary the pitch of the sound.

5–8: Transfer of Energy

- Energy is a property of many substances and is associated with heat, light, electricity, mechanical motion, sound, nuclei, and the nature of a chemical. Energy is transferred in many ways.

K–4: Abilities of Technological Design

- Identify a simple problem.
- In problem identification, children should develop the ability to explain a problem in their own words and identify a specific task and solution related to the problem.
- Propose a solution.
- Students should make proposals to build something or get something to work better; they should be able to describe and communicate their ideas. Students should recognize that designing a solution might have constraints, such as cost, materials, time, space, or safety.

5–8: Abilities of Technological Design

- Design a solution or product.
- Students should make and compare different proposals in the light of the criteria they have selected. They must consider constraints—such as time, trade-offs, and materials needed—and communicate ideas with drawings and simple models.
- Implement a proposed design.
- Students should organize materials and other resources, plan their work, make good use of group collaboration where appropriate, choose suitable tools and techniques, and work with appropriate measurement methods to ensure adequate accuracy.
- Evaluate completed technological designs or products.
- Students should use criteria relevant to the original purpose or need, consider a variety of factors that might affect acceptability and suitability for intended users and beneficiaries and develop measures of quality with respect to such criteria and factors; they should also suggest improvement and, for their own products, try proposal modification.

reLaTeD ideas From BencHmarks For science LiteraCy (aaas 1993)

K–2: Motion
- Things that make sound vibrate.

6–8: Motion
- Something can be "seen" when light waves emitted or reflected by it enter the eye—just as something can be "heard" when waves from it enter the ear.
- Vibrations in materials set up wavelike disturbances that spread away from the source. Sound and earthquake waves are examples. These and other waves move at different speeds in different materials.

K–2: The Nature of Technology
- Tools are used to do things better or more easily and to do some things that could not otherwise be done at all. In technology, tools are used to observe, measure, and make things.
- When trying to build something or to get something to work better, it usually helps to follow directions if there are any or to ask someone who has done it before for suggestions.
- People alone or in groups are always inventing new ways to solve problems and get work done. The tools and ways of doing things that people have invented affect all aspects of life.

K–2: Design and Systems
- People can use objects and ways of doing things to solve problems.

3-5 Design and Systems
- Even a good design may fail. Sometimes steps can be taken ahead of time to reduce the likelihood of failure, but it cannot be entirely eliminated.

6–8: Design and Systems
- Design usually requires taking constraints into account. Some constraints, such as gravity or the properties of the materials to be used, are unavoidable.
- Technology cannot always provide successful solutions for problems or fulfill every human need.

3–5: The Nature of Technology
- Throughout all of history, people everywhere have invented and used tools. Most tools of today are different from those of the past but many are modifications of very ancient tools.
- Any invention is likely to lead to other inventions. Once an invention exists, people are likely to think up ways of using it that were never imagined at first.

NATIONAL SCIENCE TEACHERS ASSOCIATION

USING THE STORY WITH GRADES K–4

After reading the story, students should be asked to list their statements explaining why the TCT works. You will get a great many ideas of how sound gets from one person to another. It is really necessary that children have an idea of how sound travels from the vibrations set up in the cup, through the line, and is amplified in the receiving cup. List these on a "Best Thinking" chart for future referral. Next, try to elicit from the children their ideas about what kinds of things can be changed in the TCT in order to test what changes might get it to work better. You may also help them to realize that they need to decide what "better" means. Does louder make it better? Does hearing words more clearly make it better? Since the purpose in the story was to allow the girls to talk to each other, perhaps the latter is more important but the former can be a responding variable too, if the children so desire. They must be clear on what they are measuring and should keep notes and drawings in their science notebooks. Obviously, the activity will require working in pairs at a minimum since the TCTs must be far enough apart to test their efficiency.

Making the phones is a simple process but may need the help of an adult for safety's sake. First, make sure that the cans are the same size, are open on one end, and that any jagged edges are either eliminated or covered over with heavy tape. A small hole should be made in the center of the intact end so that a string, wire, thread, or other medium can be pushed through the hole, knotted on the inside (so that it will not slip back out) and tested by pulling. Now that the cans are ready, the children can test them and see if they are able to understand each other. They will certainly hear some sounds although the exact words may not be clear. Thus comes the need to try different materials to see if the system can be improved. You are now into the technology standards as well as the science standards.

You may want to have on hand, larger cans, paper cups of varying sizes, plastic cups of varying sizes, wire, cotton twine, plastic cord, and so on. The cord's length may also be a variable the children want to test, but for starters you may want to suggest that four to five meters be standard for all trials. If the children forget to keep the strings taut, reread the part of the story that makes this point. With younger children it will probably be necessary to allow them to experiment with vibrating objects and make sounds so that they can see that the string must be free to vibrate. If they use rubber bands, help them to see that the bands must be tight in order to produce a sound. If they stretch balloons over cans like a drum skin, they can also see the amplification caused by the sound box. Many of the tried-and-true sound activities will be more meaningful once they are attached to the story. Finally the children will probably come to the conclusion that the larger paper cups and cotton twine will work the best but their results may vary. The most important thing is that they have a better understanding of how sound travels through various media and will have experienced the technology techniques involved in improving a device.

USING THE STORY WITH GRADES 5–8

Once again I recommend that you read the suggestions given for grades K–4 before moving on to this section. Many of your students will own cell phones and will already have caused a problem in your classroom. They may have difficulty in understanding the relevance for improving this "low tech" toy. It helps to turn this story into a technology-oriented task by asking them to become a toy company R & D (Research and Development) department given the task by the president or CEO of the company to produce the best product for sale to the public. In this case, you may want to develop with the help of the class a rubric with minimum standards set up that must be met. In other words, each group of students must develop a telephone that performs to standards set up by the entire class. Meeting these standards becomes the goal for those wishing to receive the highest grade and since they have been involved in setting the standards, they are involved in the evaluation of their product and their group's effort.

I have used a letter "written" by the company president giving the R & D group the challenge for producing a good toy. The letter should state that including the principles of how the toy works is important because written material describing these principles will be distributed along with the toy. They might also consider cost and suggest a price with a profit margin if you would like to integrate your math, science, and technology. You may want to use this material as an additional embedded assessment tool. Another way of testing their understanding and ability to explain the principles involved is to invite a class of younger students to your class so that your students can help them go through the process of developing the best toy. Regardless, I think your students will end with a better understanding of the transmission of sound energy as well as a more realistic view of the technology of improving a product.

RELATED BOOKS AND NSTA JOURNAL ARTICLES

Brown, R., and K. Boehringer. 2007. Breaking the sound barrier. *Science Scope* 30 (5): 35–39.

Cottam, M. 2006. Waves on the fly. *Science Scope* 29 (5): 22–25.

Farenga, S., and J. Ness. 2002. Sound science of the symphony: Sound intensity. *Science Scope* 25 (5): 50–53.

Palmer, D. H. 2003. Modeling the transmission of sound. *Science Scope* 26 (7): 32.

Tolman, M., and G. Hardy. 2001. Sound fun with noisy cups. *Science and Children* 38 (7): 6.

Wise, K., and M. Haake. 2007. Coffee can speakers: Amazing energy transference. *Science and Children* 44 (7): 36–40.

references

American Association for the Advancement of Science (AAAS). 1993. *Benchmarks for science literacy*. New York: Oxford University Press.

National Research Council (NRC). 1996. *National science education standards*. Washington, DC: National Academies Press.

CHAPTER 25

INDEX

NATIONAL SCIENCE TEACHERS ASSOCIATION

NATIONAL SCIENCE TEACHERS ASSOCIATION

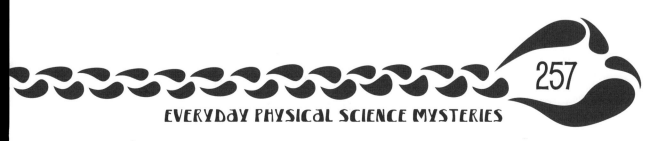

NATIONAL SCIENCE TEACHERS ASSOCIATION

NATIONAL SCIENCE TEACHERS ASSOCIATION

INDEX